GADFLY

GADFLY

The Life and Times of
LES KINSOLVING

☆ *Foreword by* ☆
SAM DONALDSON

Kathleen Kinsolving

WND Books

GADFLY
WND Books

Published by WorldNetDaily
Washington, D.C.

Copyright © 2010
By WND Books

WRITTEN BY KATHLEEN KINSOLVING
JACKET DESIGN BY MARK KARIS
INTERIOR DESIGN BY NEUWIRTH & ASSOCIATES, INC.

WND Books are distributed to the trade by:
Midpoint Trade Books
27 West 20th Street, Suite 1102
New York, NY 10011

WND Books are available at special discounts for bulk purchases. WND Books, Inc. also publishes books in electronic formats. For more information, call (541) 474-1776 or visit www.wndbooks.com.

FIRST EDITION

ISBN: 978-1-935071-80-8

Library of Congress information available

Printed in the United States of America

10 9 8 7 6 5 4 3 2 1

For Martin Scorsese, *Honorary Worker Priest*

Lester, you are the gadfly that this great and wonderful old
Episcopal Church needs.

—Rev. Kenneth Waldron,
Grace Church, Middletown, NY, 1971

Gadfly: n. (gād'flī') 1.One that acts as a provocative stimulus; a goad.
2. Any of various flies, especially of the family Tabanidae, that bite or
annoy livestock and other animals. **Synonyms:** annoyance, energizer,
excitant, irritant, motivator, mover, pest, prod, spur, stimulator.

*"If you kill a man like me, you will injure yourselves more than you will
injure me,"* because his role was that of a gadfly, *"to sting people and whip
them into a fury, all in the service of truth."*

—Socrates, during his defense when on trial for his life

Humilis humilibus inflectens arrogantibus.
[Humble to the humble, inflexible to the arrogant.]

—Kinsolving family motto

Contents

Foreword

by Sam Donaldson

Lester Kinsolving is a big man with a big voice and a big appetite for rocking the boat and for the publicity that goes with doing that. As longtime members of the Washington press corps, he and I often found ourselves at the same press briefings and the same news conferences.

So, what do I think of him? Not an easy question, for Kinsolving is anything but easy to pigeonhole.

The great former executive editor of the *Washington Post* Ben Bradlee has called him a "monstrosity," an "embarrassment," and a "great pain in the ass"—to the applause of many, many other members of the press corps. However, against all the vitriol hurled his way, he can count some notable people as his fans. Years ago when he was writing a column on religion, a letter arrived that said, "I read you every week in the *Ashville Times*; if I'm out of town, I have you clipped," signed Billy Graham.

Kinsolving has always been the vigorous, relentless, irritating, and controversial, but forever interesting, gadfly that his loving daughter has chronicled in this book. And as for me, long ago I concluded that

Foreword

life is too short to associate with dull people, and Lester Kinsolving has been *anything but dull.* Moreover, I like someone who marches to a different drummer, even though I must say at times the Kinsolving drum beat is incomprehensible.

Consider:

He was once an Episcopal priest. But for assorted heresies, he was suspended from the priesthood in 1978 and removed in 1979. Shortly after his ordination he preached a sermon questioning whether there was really a Hell as described in the Bible, and he further postulated there had been no such thing as a "virgin birth." He said a man must have aided in the usual way in Jesus' conception. For this, and other heresies, one of his early parish halls was burned to the ground by true-believer vandals. Is it any wonder that many wanted him defrocked? He is now a minister in the Anglican Church.

He has been a fervent supporter of civil rights for African Americans; he was on hand to hear the Reverend Martin Luther King, Jr., at the end of King's march from Selma in 1965. However, he is selective in his civil rights heroes. Once on a radio program a caller asked how he felt about Reverend Jesse Jackson.

KINSOLVING: I think he's a horse's ass.

CALLER: Oh, yeah? Well, what about Minister Louis Farrakhan?

KINSOLVING: He's a horse's ass as well.

And though he has been a liberal on such matters as abortion (a woman has a right to choose) and the death penalty (it should be abolished), he has been a conservative on most other matters, such as in his vigorous denunciation of homosexuality. But it is his work as a member of the press that has made him famous . . . writing nationally syndicated columns on religion, hosting radio and TV programs, and working as a reporter in Washington.

In his early days of covering the White House, the Congress, and other Washington beats, he would wear his Episcopal priest's collar while asking questions often considered by us mainstream reporters to be both irrelevant and "wacky."

This from a White House Briefing in July of 2005 conducted by press secretary Scott McClellan:

LES KINSOLVING: Scott, when the Rev. Jesse Jackson admitted that he fathered a child out of wedlock, the president, as you remember, telephoned him after this admission. And since Karin Stanford, the mother in this case, has just stated, "I was attacked by friends, strangers in the black press, without mercy, and labeled by them a political stalker, gold digger, and opportunist," will the president now telephone Jesse's victim, as he did Jesse?

And this from a Reagan press conference in March of 1981:

KINSOLVING: [Mr. President,] you said during the campaign you noticed that all the advocates of abortion are already born. And since this also applies to all the advocates of contraception, are you opposed to contraception which also denies the right to life?

However, as a member of the press in California, Kinsolving was one of the first to report on the unsavory activities of cult figure Jim Jones. Few listened . . . until, of course, Jones moved his flock to Guyana, where he ordered the murder and suicide of his followers.

And in Washington, he was one of the first reporters to enquire at the White House during a press briefing what the administration was doing about HIV-AIDS.

"What's AIDS?" asked deputy press secretary Larry Speakes, who then proceeded to ridicule him for his question. Does the old phrase "He who laughs last, laughs best" come to mind?

Foreword

Kinsolving is aware of his mixed reputation. He once said he knew some people consider him a "leper" in the press corps, but he would continue to ask the questions he thought were important, and if anyone didn't like it they could "take a long walk off a short pier."

There is a more blunt way to say that, but I have never heard Kinsolving use vulgarity.

There's another old saying, "Love me or hate me, but don't ignore me." Readers of this book can make up their mind as to which of the two first camps they fall in to . . . but ignore Lester Kinsolving? Not a chance, Lester old friend, not a chance!

—SAM DONALDSON

Acknowledgements

First and foremost, I'd like to give thanks to Joseph Farah, who was so gracious in giving *Gadfly* an opportunity to be published, and to his stellar staff at WND Books who honed this book from a creaky first draft into a polished, marketable read: Editors Ami Naramor, Jim Fletcher, and Megan Byrd; Creative Director Mark Karis; Marketing Director Ike Crumpler, and Copyeditor Jay Boggis.

To all of Dad's fans, who continually encouraged him to have his biography written. I'm glad that I stepped up to the task, and I certainly hope I haven't let you down.

To Sam Donaldson, who wrote *Gadfly's* superb and moving forward. I will never be able to thank you enough for that. I'm also very grateful to your assistant, Jennifer Bost, who was so friendly and helpful.

To Tom Swiss, whose brilliant insight into meticulous details made the business side so much easier to understand for this befuddled writer.

To my mother Sylvia, who was very amenable during my constant visits to the house for questions and to conduct further research in Dad's two home offices. You were very cooperative and very loving throughout this long process. Thanks also to my sister, Laura, for her continual interest and positive input.

Gadfly

To my brother Tom, who, twelve years ago, really taught me the craft of writing. Thank you for passing on the preliminary taped interviews with Dad, which were extremely valuable in helping to shape his biography.

To my cousin Elinor Rose, who sent a packet of early newspaper and magazine clippings she kept over the years which I might never have tracked down, even with the extensive research I conducted. I'm also very grateful for your love, enthusiasm, and support.

To my other beloved cousin Charlie Kinsolving, who was so helpful with facts about early Kinsolving family history, and for his recollections of Dad when they were both young college students in Philadelphia; for accompanying us to Fort Delaware to learn more about Ovid Americus Kinsolving's time as a prisoner there, and for his wise comments and suggestions about *Gadfly's* first draft. You are my favorite Kinsolving, and I'm completely devoted to you.

To Helen Thomas (and her agent Diane Nine), the Grand Lady of the White House Press Corps, thank you for being so generous in offering a splendid endorsement of Dad.

To Marvin Kalb, the most respectable and dignified journalist in our nation's capitol – I'm so grateful for your tremendous display of courage in standing-up for the truth. Thank you so much for your wonderful endorsement and for being a friend to Dad.

To Ron Maxwell, a magnificently talented filmmaker, who admires Dad for exactly who he is; thank you for expressing that in your great endorsement. Your friendship and generosity in allowing us to contribute to your great productions has meant so much to our family. Thanks, too, to dear Karen.

To *San Francisco Chronicle's* Rick Romagosa, who did his best in trying to track down a needed photograph, and to Jerry Telfer, who took the infamous photo of Dad's walk with the naked hippie, Terry Lee Kinley.

To Luisa DiPietro, who gave me a break and winning author's photo – you are a true and cherished friend.

To Bryan Borah and the English Department at Centrevile High School – your support and enthusiasm is a great gift. Thank you!

To Chip Brown, writer extraordinaire, who clarified a remark Ben Bradlee made, after he wrote his feature on Dad for the *Washington Post*.

To Clinton Macsherry, who graciously sent a copy of his interview with Dad for the *Baltimore City Paper*, and to David Dudley, who led me in the right direction in locating Clinton.

To R. Hugh Simmons of *Fort Delaware Notes*, for providing more specific details on Ovid Americus Kinsolving.

To the following librarians, researchers, and archivists: Marsha Bates of the Kennewick Branch of the Mid-Columbia Libraries for mailing the newspaper clipping of the Church of Our Savior fire; Mother Pam of Holy Trinity Episcopal Church for e-mailing info on Rev. Ridgeway's tenure; Stephan Novak of Columbia University Medical Center for searching for Dad's birth record; Laura Vetter of Episcopal High School for e-mailing valuable excerpts of EHS yearbooks; Christine Forest of the *Christian Century* for sending the article on Valerian Trifa, and Adam Daniels of the Rodeo, CA Public Library for identifying the correct name of the movie theater where Dad conducted church services. Thank you all, so very much!

Most importantly, I am filled with boundless gratitude to my husband Kevin Willmann, who has walked this incredible journey of writing a biography with me every step of the way. His tremendously wise comments and suggestions were more than helpful; they were completely necessary. Thank you, Sweetheart, for reading every night after I finished writing, and for laughing and crying at all the right spots.

To my darling son Spencer, who graced me with the most important role I'll ever play: being his mother. I love you and Daddy more than I can ever say.

And lastly, I'd like to thank my father, Les Kinsolving, for providing me with what I've always called his own Library of Congress. Dad, because you saved so much invaluable research material over the years, both in your many file cabinets and dozens of scrapbooks, you helped make my job as your biographer so much easier. In addition, you were extremely patient in answering the countless number of questions when I phoned or visited you so many times.

Thank you, Dad, for your amazing life, your courage, your wisdom, your humor, your faith, and your confidence in me as a writer.

Introduction

PASCO, WASHINGTON. ASH Wednesday, 1961. The young Episcopalian rector stood looking at the sign on the side of his church, where words of comfort were now covered with egg-stains: "Come unto me, all that travail and are heavy-laden, and I will refresh you." He stepped inside, and noticed how the fire had gutted the ceiling of Church of Our Savior. In a large, blackened hole, there was the cross outside, still standing.

Four years earlier, Rev. Lester Kinsolving had preached a sermon on "The Damnable Doctrine of Damnation," in which he told his congregation what he firmly believed to be a hypocritical ideology, responsible for a large measure of the world's hatred: God commands us to love our enemies and yet damns his own. The next day a headline appeared in the *Columbia Basin-News*: "Rectors Clash on Hell: Kinsolving Says There Is No Hell, May Says the Hell There Isn't."

Time magazine also reported the controversy, in which Rev. Charles May, rector of St. Paul's Episcopal Church in nearby Kennewick, stated, "The pulpit should not be used to express personal views when they are contrary to the doctrines of the church." Rev.

Gadfly

Kinsolving retaliated with, "I came into the priesthood to preach the truth as I see it . . . and I'll keep preaching it if I have to preach on the sidewalk."

He continued with his mission, and Church of Our Savior became the victim of vandalism: twenty-eight acts were committed, before it was set ablaze, four years later. His six-year-old daughter Laura saw the wreckage, and was very worried. She walked up to her father and asked, "Daddy, did God die in the fire?"

A Difficult Birth

FOR ARTHUR BARKSDALE Kinsolving II, driving his pregnant wife on a cold December evening proved to be a daunting task, especially in 1927. Edith Lester Kinsolving was advised to deliver their first-born son in New York City, rather than West Point, where Arthur was finishing up his first year as chaplain to the Corps of Cadets. The Sloane Hospital for Women, located in midtown Manhattan, was well-equipped for more difficult births. Sloane was known for upscale sanitary conditions and lower rates of mortality. Here, Charles Lester Kinsolving, a ten-pound baby, spent the first week of his life. He would make it home just in time for Christmas Day.

"Charles," a name he never used, paid tribute to his paternal uncle, a former American pilot who flew with the Lafayette Flying Corps in World War I. "Lester" was in honor of his maternal grandfather, Wharton E. Lester, a renowned attorney in the nation's capital. As a young boy, he preferred his nickname "Les," which he would later use in professional life. Lester rhymed with "pester," as in "Lester De Pester." Somehow, this was a label he resented.

Lester's first memory was hearing the sound of vigorous music while lying in his crib. It was graduation, and the cadets were marching in full regalia in their final salute to the United States Military Academy at West Point. This was most thrilling for a very young boy, and it continued to be throughout his life. He later collected Mitch Miller records, and, always, whenever a rousing march was broadcast over the car radio, he would declare to anyone within earshot, "Doesn't that just lift your spirits?!"

As a three-year-old, Lester loved exploring the West Point chapel, where his father officiated. During one Sunday service, he and his younger brother Arthur "Putch" Barksdale were being supervised by nursemaid Dorothy Johnson in the upstairs play area. While "Dotta" was checking on Arthur in an adjoining room, Les climbed up on a chair and unlocked the latch on a wooden panel. When it opened, he was offered a full view of his father pronouncing the Benediction. He shouted down to him with absolute delight, "Hi Pop—HI POP!!" The mortified chaplain froze, amidst ripples of laughter from the congregation.

His mother had already suspected that her "Boodie," as she called him, was a bit different. For one, Lester's favorite story was Beatrix Potter's *Peter Rabbit*. He was especially fond of Peter, since he was "the naughty one." Edith assumed she'd married a rather genteel man in Arthur, only to find out later what type of genes her oldest son had inherited from the Kinsolving family.

Lucien Lee Kinsolving, Lester's paternal grandfather, had been appointed Bishop of Southern Brazil in 1898 after bringing the Episcopal Church to that country in 1889. It was riddled with disease, squalor, threats of revolution, and, above all, Catholic priests who deeply resented Protestant missionaries. One in particular came to Lucien's service in an inebriated state, causing quite a commotion. He later wrote to Lucien in a feeble attempt to apologize: "Your sermon was swell—so sorry I was too drunk to sit through it."

Lucien's sons, Charlie and Arthur, "were famous for their naughtiness," according to younger sister Lucie. "They knew all Rio Grande do Sul was watching as they chased the poor fat cook Manuella around the Shakra garden with carving knives . . . they teased me dramatically, always drawing attention to themselves . . . the slogan for the little Kinsolvings was 'For heaven's sake—if this is what the Protestant clergy produce, let's go back to celibacy!'"

Uncle Charlie, who later received the French Croix de Guerre as a pilot in World War I, detested boredom. In order to make life more amusing, he informed his younger siblings that he was "the favorite child," and was therefore "the only one invited to their parents' wedding." Horrified, Lucie and Arthur "didn't speak to mother and father except in monosyllables, then sobbed out evidence of lovelessness"; Charlie was spanked, "but it didn't do one bit of good!!!"

During one of Lucie's return trips home to the U.S. with her parents, sixteen-year-old Charlie's "love of mischief continued even after attending boarding school." Left alone to tend to his younger sister, Charlie "couldn't go out to flirt with Lillie Christfield until later, so he took out a paddle, and said, 'Now Lucie, would you rather be spanked or killed?' He flourished it in the air menacingly, never touching me, so I screamed: 'No, Charlie, please kill me! I bare my chest and kneel much in the manner of Helen of Troy before Menelaeus . . . !'"

Arthur, however, was "not as violent as Charlie, but he loved to make fun of me when I was trying to be like mother, and would mimic me, causing tears . . . he ended every lost argument with, 'I hope you have hangnails.'" Lucie's conclusion to all this hell-raising behavior was due to the "congenital Kinsolving egotistical need to show off, hold the stage, be a sensation, if not from the pulpit, then in evil!"

FOR A TIME, their behavior sobered when they were shipped off, on the SS *Byron*, to Episcopal High School, at ages ten and twelve. Alexandria, Virginia, was several thousand miles away, but the two boys waved bravely to the family they were leaving behind. It was 1906, and the journey would take twenty-one days. At one point Arthur stopped waving, and put his head down on the ship's rail. Charlie promptly swatted his younger brother's head, and the two continued their earnest attempt at courage, until they finally disappeared from view.

Gadfly

Although Charlie kept a stiff upper lip and resumed his mischievous ways at school, the little boy known as "Tui" (a nickname for the Portuguese "Artui") was, as Lucie recalls it, "bewildered, lost, awkward, and lonely without any of Charlie's bravado." Arthur's decision to persist, however, eventually paid off, and in the eight years he attended Episcopal High School, he became captain of the baseball and the All-State football teams, was head monitor, coach, chaplain, editor of the *Chronicle*, and won a Reader's Medal for reciting "Mistress Sherwood's Victory." The 1913–1914 *Whispers* Yearbook included the following statistics:

> The most popular man is A.B. Kinsolving. . . . A.B. Kinsolving, the wearer of four "E's," is the best all-around athlete. . . . Wimberly is the funniest man, with A.B. Kinsolving second. . . . Cronly received the vote for the hardest worker in studies, with Phil Sheild (A.B. Kinsolving voted for himself).

After graduation, Arthur accompanied his brother to France during the "War to End all Wars" but didn't fly; he drove an ambulance instead. While Charlie led his unit on many dangerous missions as commanding officer of the 163rd Aero Bombardment Squadron, Arthur's contribution to the war effort was equally dramatic. Driving his ambulance under heavy shellfire, he went far into a battlefield and rescued two badly wounded French soldiers. At one point he tried to outrace a German bomber, but his attempt was futile. Pulling to the side of the road, Arthur watched the plane continue on, much to his relief.

Arthur was also awarded the Croix de Guerre for bravery and the American Victory Medal with five clasps. No doubt the incredible bravery of these two men was instilled in them as little boys, when they were separated from their mother on the SS *Byron*, so long ago.

Arthur's son Lester would also experience similar separations throughout his life. At age five he bid good-bye to West Point, when his father was appointed Dean of the Cathedral of the Incarnation in Garden City, Long Island. He was saddened, being so inspired by the cadets, and for many years ached to join the ranks. As tribute to these cherished boyhood memories, Les would later play the graduating march, which he first heard in his crib, as theme music on his nightly radio talk-show.

"My dear Bishop Perry," wrote West Point's Superintendent Major General Wm. D. Connor to the Episcopal Church's presiding bishop in 1933. "I would like to make it a matter of record in your office that Chaplain Kinsolving's services have been eminently satisfactory . . . not only has he at all times maintained the high standard that is expected of a minister of the gospel, but he has always shown an exceedingly human side that allowed him to have a close contact with the members of his congregation . . . I feel that he will go far in his chosen work if health and long life are given to him."

Like his father, Arthur would be promoted through the ranks of the church. There were many expectations to meet, for the Kinsolving family was busily contributing more Episcopal clergymen than any other. Arthur's grandfather, Ovid Americus Kinsolving, was the first in line. He also served as a Confederate spy during the Civil War.

George Washington Kinsolving, a staunch Virginian, was determined to eradicate any trace of inherent restlessness in his son Ovid. Although a devout layman, George once interrupted a long-winded sermon with the following inquiry: "Parson, isn't it grog time?" From the very start, there was a tendency for Kinsolvings to be completely devoted to decorum but eager to rebel at any opportune moment.

George had inherited an estate called Temple Hill from his father James, a Piedmont Planter, in 1829. It was located near Charlottesville, and the University of Virginia. This was an institution George wanted to avoid, for its Jeffersonian near-Unitarian ideal might steer Ovid off the path toward priesthood. George chose Kenyon, an Episcopal college, in Gambier, Ohio. While attending Kenyon, Ovid became great friends with fellow student Rutherford B. Hayes. At one point the two friends participated in a schoolwide debate, which Ovid won. Although he was defeated, Rutherford went on to Harvard Law School, and then joined the Union army during the

Civil War. Later, he would serve as the nineteenth president of the United States.

Ovid also did well, and graduated at the top of his class at Kenyon. Although filled with religious skepticism in the beginning, Ovid eventually felt a deep calling to the priesthood, and entered the Virginia Theological Seminary in Alexandria, near Washington, D.C., in 1842.

Seven years later, a future bishop would be born to Ovid and first wife Julia. He was George Herbert, younger brother of Charles James, who was named after the original Charles Kinsolving, one of the first Kinsolvings on American soil, after ancestors had migrated from the Isle of Man and settled in Tidewater, Virginia. He fought in the Revolutionary War, and was killed in the Battle of Cowpens. Julia would bear a third son, William Leigh, born 1852, when Ovid took charge of three churches in the Piedmont section of Virginia: Middleburg, Upperville, and Aldie.

After Julia died in 1858, Ovid married an exceptional woman named Lucy Lee Rogers a year later. She was more than willing to take the three young motherless boys under her loving wing. She also ministered to the downtrodden, always conveying an enduring spirituality that became legendary in the surrounding vicinity. After giving Ovid two more sons, Arthur Barksdale and Lucien Lee respectively, Lucy passed on in May of 1862, during the bloody battles of the Civil War. Her death was due to lack of sanitary conditions after giving birth. Lucien was a mere thirteen days old, and Arthur, only a year. Before dying, she dedicated each of her two sons to her Lord for service in His ministry. She wouldn't be disappointed, for this is exactly what was granted.

During Lucy's burial service at Sharon Cemetery in Middleburg, a skirmish broke out between Union and Confederate soldiers. Everyone fell to the ground, except the officiating minister, Dr. Joseph Packard. He knew the duty he had to perform, and held fast to his faith. Fortunately, he would serve as future teacher to Lucien and Arthur Barksdale I as they followed in their father's footsteps at the Virginia Theological Seminary.

In July of 1864, a year after Lucy's death, Ovid Americus was arrested by Union soldiers at his home in Middleburg, after word spread that Ovid had recited prayers for the president of the Confederate States. He was then sent off to Fort Delaware, a prison for Southern insurgents. Although the Union army didn't realize he was also a spy for Robert E. Lee's army, Ovid had served his commander well. Using his Bible as a cover, he'd ride into the hills and spot where the Yankees were heading next. George Herbert, now fourteen, would deliver the message from his father to Colonel John S. Mosby. If caught, Ovid most likely would've been hanged.

The Union soldiers marched Ovid and his group of fellow Southerners in sweltering heat from Middleburg to Washington, D.C., where they were loaded on a ship to Philadelphia. Upon arrival, amid hoots and catcalls from the Northerners, Ovid was hurried past the Church of the Epiphany on Chestnut Street toward the pier, where a vessel would take them to a fort on the Delaware River. This church was the exact spot where George Herbert would be consecrated Bishop of Texas in 1892, after serving as its rector for eleven years.

On September 10, 1864, Ovid arrived at Fort Delaware, where he would be imprisoned until March 3, 1865. His father-in-law, sixty-year-old General Asa Rogers, was with him, since he too had been rounded up in Middleburg. While Ovid still served time in this deplorable place, General Rogers, upon his release, went to President Lincoln and implored that his son-in-law be returned home. So did Ovid's great friend and former Kenyon College classmate, General Rutherford B. Hayes. The request was granted, although President Lincoln hesitated at first, stating, "I may have some trouble with Secretary Stanton in getting him out."

After the war, in which 600,000 American lives were lost, Ovid made his way back to Middleburg, where his five sons, ages two to fifteen, welcomed him with open arms, along with their Aunt Silla. Ovid was bitter after his experience at Fort Delaware, and vowed never to cross the Potomac River again. However, after his school chum Rutherford was elected President in 1877, a military courier was sent to Ovid's home, with an invitation to spend a weekend at the White

House. After breaking his vow by crossing the Potomac, Ovid met with Rutherford and his wife, "Lemonade" Lucy, where they, according to Lester, "had a marvelous time."

To this day, whenever Charles Lester Kinsolving crosses the Delaware Bridge, he never fails to recite a quiet prayer as a tribute to his great-grandfather, the Reverend Ovid Americus Kinsolving.

We pray that, having opened unto him
The gate of a larger life
He may go from strength to strength
In the life of the world to come.

A Challenging Childhood

ALTHOUGH *PETER RABBIT* was Lester's favorite story, the one he feared most was *The Scissors Man.* "The door would fly open, and there he stood, tall, thick, and tailored; if The Scissors Man caught you sucking your thumb he would chop it off." With Peter Rabbit, there was victorious revelry when this naughty four-legged rebel outran Mr. McGregor within an inch of his life—a true hero in Lester's eyes. The thought of being helplessly cornered and having your thumb cut off by such an ominous authority as the Scissors Man was terrifying. Lester, like Peter, was determined to outsmart any enemy and get away with his mischief; never, for one second, did he consider the cost.

As a first-grade student at the Stratford Avenue School in Garden City, Long Island, Lester spotted a classmate wearing a matching outfit of white shirt and shorts. Outraged by this ridiculous attire, Lester went up and slugged him. This was perfectly justified—he never expected retaliation for setting the record straight. As a result, Les was knocked down.

When he was nine years old, Lester longed for a particular toy, an air-rifle BB gun. He engaged in fifteen different types of arguments with his parents, in a year-long battle to win them over. Finally, he succeeded. Holding the beloved rifle firmly in his hands, Lester marched to the roof and began shooting. Mom and Pop weren't at home, so the coast was clear. Inevitably, one of the pellets shot itself into the closed window of a passing car, and Lester ducked for cover, convinced he'd outwit the driver.

Fifteen minutes later, a policeman appeared at the front door of the Deanery, and confiscated the gun. It was gut-wrenching, losing something so quickly that he had fought so long to acquire. Inevitably, Lester realized that shooting randomly at anything was a terrible thing to do. He didn't have the guts to tell his parents, but they found out nonetheless.

While Arthur served as Dean of the Cathedral, Edith gave birth to a third and final son, William Lee, in 1936. He played kid brother to Lester and Arthur III, who were less than two years apart and very close. Lester would always refer to his younger brothers with their mother's nicknames, "Putch" and "Wink"; however, Arthur and William always called their elder brother "Les." Any reference to "Boodie" might get them in a bit of trouble.

In 1937, with two young boys and a new baby on their hands, the Kinsolvings felt it was time for Lester to spend time away during the summer. Their friends the Caswell Stoddards recommended Camp Pasquaney, located in Bridgewater, New Hampshire. It was hundreds of miles away, but a very fine camp for boys. And it might teach Lester the kind of fortitude and discipline they desired in their oldest son.

Lester was only nine, and was sent away for two months. He was afforded one two-day visit from his parents at the end of July, but wouldn't see them again until the end of summer. After his first week, the director of Pasquaney sent Lester's first progress report home: "Bright, lots of imagination . . . has his own ideas about camp and seems to feel self-sufficient; not needing advice from other boys . . . is rather slow in catching on to dormitory routine; takes his time in following suggestions . . . has a very interesting personality and should make definite progress this summer."

Three weeks later, another report was sent: "Lester has been making very definite progress. He is an interesting boy, with an independent mind. We have discovered that he responds much better to quiet suggestions and requests than to commands . . . emotionally, Lester has an intense desire to do the right thing and to make a good record. Our work with him has in general consisted of attempting to help him transfer this desire into effective action. Since Lester acts impulsively, and since he sometimes tries to gain attention by boyish mischievousness, I cannot report that we have yet been entirely successful." However, they were impressed with his athletic prowess and avid interest in history.

Les wrote a brave letter to his parents:

Dear Mother and Father, How are you? I am having a swell time. I swam my triangle which is a quarter of a mile. I expect to swim my half-mile soon. I received father's letter. Please tell me about everything. I belong to the Hawks, one of the clubs of camp. I won an obstacle race which counted for my club. I am doing fine. I wish you were here. Love to all, Lester.

Lester would return to Camp Pasquaney every summer for the next three years. The long summer months away from his parents probably helped to buffer a deeper bout of separation, similar to what his father had suffered when he left Brazil. At twelve years old, Lester too was sent off to Episcopal High School, and remained enrolled for five years.

At the same time, his father resigned his post as Dean of the Cathedral in Garden City, Long Island, in 1940, and accepted the position as rector of Calvary Episcopal Church in Pittsburgh, Pennsylvania. Calvary was one of the largest parishes in America, and was graced with a magnificent nave. After the press conference to welcome their new pastor, Arthur stepped into the pulpit and tested the acoustics, wondering if his voice would stand up to the task of preaching in a such an awe-inspiring place. According to Pittsburgh's *Bulletin Index,* Arthur began to intone richly from the *Book of Common Prayer* . . . *"Direct us, O Lord,"* chanted the bass voice . . . *"with Thy most gracious favor, and favor us with Thy continual help;* (Is that loud enough?) *that in all our work begun, continued, and ended in Thee, we may glorify Thy holy Name;* (Can you hear me behind those pillars?) *and finally by Thy mercy obtain everlasting life, through Jesus Christ Our Lord, Amen . . . "*

When he saw his dorm room for the first time, Lester was terribly disappointed. Episcopal High School wasn't like camp, where there were plenty of fun activities and swimming in the sun. This was a strict boarding school, and longer periods of time were spent away from family. Les was one of the youngest freshmen that year at EHS, since he'd skipped eighth grade. His father expected him to be a courageous young boy, just as he had been when his parents sent him off from Brazil. It was part of the family tradition, to be stoic in the face of insurmountable obstacles.

Instead of following his father's shimmering legacy, Lester rebelled, and with a vengeance. One of Episcopal High's methods of doling out punishment was in the form of demerits. If you were late to class or a meal, you'd receive two. For each demerit, you'd have to walk four times around the school's quarter-mile track. On an average week, Lester would receive up to fifteen. One of the few at EHS who ever received more demerits was his Uncle Charlie.

Although Arthur and Charlie were known as hell-raisers in their early schooling, Arthur began to conform and achieve. Charlie never gave up the mission; his behavior was perfectly outlandish, which meant walking the track over and over. He decided at one point that for each demerit he received, he'd break a window of the school. With each broken window, he received ten more demerits. As a result, he was required to walk the track all summer long.

Aware of his father's early reputation, Lester was impelled to impress him with various antics. Although he was considered by his classmates to be an unpopular loud-mouth, Lester also carried the title of "ingenious planner of disruption." Two of his greatest acts of rebellion involved study hall and a night out on the town.

There was nothing worse than being forced to sit in a quiet room and expected to study, especially at such a dreadful time: 7:20–9:45 P.M. What added to the mirth was a teacher named Graham Rodwell, who sat hunched over a book at the front of the study hall. Barely containing his glee, Lester scribbled a note and passed it around the hall: "At approximately 8:10 P.M., everyone drop a book. *Don't be chicken*." He'd also placed four baby Big Ben alarm clocks in wastepaper baskets, situated in four corners, which were each set at two minutes apart.

Mr. Rodwell nearly flew out of his seat when he heard the thunderous pounding of dictionaries and encyclopedias dropped onto the floor. Suddenly, at 8:11 P.M., an alarm clock went off in one of the corner wastebaskets. Then, another clock went off, and another, and another. After study hall was over, Les placed a filthy mop against Rodwell's door, which, when he opened it, fell right into his face. The enraged teacher charged into the culprit's room, where Les was promptly "cuffed."

The United States was in the middle of World War II, and food rationing had begun. Lester wrote in his diary how he detested the artificial food at breakfast: "Had powdered eggs for the 37th time . . . they tasted putrid!" Other repugnant dishes like scrapple were also served, which left Lester pining for some genuine cuisine.

One night, five minutes after bed check at 11 P.M., Lester and a few of his cronies slipped out of the dormitory and into the woods, having arranged for a cab to O'Donnell's Sea Grill in downtown Washington, D.C.. This was a popular restaurant that offered delicious seafood fare. What a relief for Lester, to chomp on a succulent shrimp cocktail after having to force those disgusting eggs down his throat every morning. He was even taught how to eat oysters in the correct fashion by Jack Jenkins, a classmate from Charleston, South Carolina. When Les first spied the strange creatures in the shell, he refused to indulge, in spite of Jack's prodding: "They look like something you'd hock up!" Although that reduced Jack to hysterics, he still managed to convince Les to partake in an exciting taste sensation. He's been eating oysters ever since.

Gadfly

Sneaking back at 4 A.M., an exhausted Lester quietly crawled back into bed. Being obliged to go to breakfast at 8 A.M., Les slipped out of study hall and into a cubicle on "New Dorm," only to be awakened by teacher R.E. "Laughing" Latham, who chortled, "You've got ten demerits!" At this, Lester said under his breath, "You missed it by ninety!" The policy for going off school grounds was 100 demerits—apparently Latham thought Les only left his room for a short while.

Headmaster Archibald Robinson "Flick" Hoxton finally had enough of Lester's continual misbehaving. He gave the recalcitrant youth an ultimatum: either Flick would call his parents, or Les could volunteer to take a paddling. Lester chose the latter, too ashamed to have his parents know he'd gone too far.

Five senior monitors had set up a bookcase on the floor, with an opening lined with pillows on which Lester could lean. With Lester in position, they began to paddle him, but with brute force. It really began to hurt very badly after the tenth swing, and Lester hoped they would finish soon, but it went on and on, until he was screaming for them to stop. Without a teacher present, they took the liberty of beating him twenty-eight times.

Lester wasn't able to sit comfortably for weeks, and had recurrent boils for twelve years. These senior monitors informed him that he had to adhere to the code of silence, and that he was forbidden, until the end of the school year, to tell his parents about the paddling, but he did. They were very concerned, although his father, as head monitor, had paddled a president's son, Quentin Roosevelt, who was later killed in action during World War I. Lester wanted to go back, since he didn't want to let his father down, nor ruin the legacy of being the twelfth Kinsolving to attend. A year later the paddling was abolished, and later a new head master, Richard Thompson, was brought in. Lester was very devoted to him.

History and football made up for some of the blows that Lester suffered at EHS. He had a wonderful teacher, John Daniel, who taught American History, a subject that Lester mastered throughout his life. At fourteen years of age, his writing was already showing a potential for dramatic narrative. In "The Hero of the Oak Tree Guards," Les described the story of a young drummer boy, Cary Randolph, who died heroically at the Battle of Fredericksburg:

> In a flash it was revealed to Cary what this serious threat to the greatest military genius in the Confederate army meant. Was not the life of one Confederate drummer boy worth the life of this great leader? . . . Slipping the bayonet from his unloaded gun, Cary went quietly but quickly after the Yankee. Just as the soldier had taken a bead on General Jackson, he heard a noise behind him. He wheeled, he fired!—And Cary Randolph fell mortally wounded . . . .When Cary regained consciousness, he was in his room, a small group around him . . . he knew his days were over. And as his mother sobbed, as many other mothers had done, Cary repeated the 21st psalm: ". . . and I will dwell in the house of the Lord forever . . ." and the Hero of the Oak Tree Guards passed away.

Lester dedicated his essay to his cousin, General William Barksdale of Mississippi, who fought at the Battle of Fredericksburg, and was later killed in action at Gettysburg. Fifty years later, Les would be given the honor of portraying Barksdale in the film *Gettysburg*, where he, like Cary Randolph, bravely died in the line of duty.

At fifteen years of age, Lester was too big to join the junior varsity football team, so he tried out for varsity and made it. He'd already played last string on the smallest team when he was twelve, so he had some experience to contribute. As a senior, he won a letter "E," which he treasured, knowing that his father had ten of them. One of the most unforgettable experiences at EHS was traveling with the varsity team to Lynchburg, Virginia, where they played against Virginia Episcopal School.

Head football coach "Bus" Male looked over three of his players, one of whom he'd choose to travel with the team to Lynchburg. He realized that Lester hit harder and got through the line two out of three times, while the others didn't at all. He asked them, "Now, who's going to make the trip?" As the three stood there sweating,

Gadfly

Coach Male made the announcement: "Kinsolving is." It was pure euphoria: Les was assigned a jersey and traveled in a train with older students whom he respected very much. The most exciting part of all was playing in a stadium, something he'd never done before. And the greatest reward was beating V.E.S., 37–6.

Besides these two passions, Lester won a prize for declamation when he recited "Horatius at the Bridge," all about the man who defended Rome against raiders:

> . . . Then out spake Brave Horatius,
> the Captain of the Gate:
> "To every man upon this earth
> Death cometh soon or late.
> And how can man die better
> Than facing fearful odds,
> For the ashes of his fathers,
> And the temples of his Gods?"

Undoubtedly Les's winning oration was attributed to a growing faith that God was always there to comfort and protect him, even in life's darkest hour.

Instead of dropping books or setting off alarm clocks in study hall, Lester became gossip editor for the *Monthly Chronicle* during his final year at EHS. This is where he learned to channel all the mischief, which meant avoiding further demerits. Most importantly, he had a "marvelous time needling people." Unbeknownst to him, a savage thirst for controversy was in its first stage of fruition.

Triumph and Tragedy

A FTER SERVING HIS parish at Calvary in Pittsburgh for over four years, Arthur Barksdale Kinsolving II was elected Bishop of the Missionary District of Arizona in 1945. It was around the same time that Lester, along with twelve other classmates, had contracted a debilitating case of scarlet fever and was quarantined in the medical ward at EHS.

Lester lay in a sleepless delirium, barely able to swallow as the red rash spread over his entire body. His tongue resembled a strawberry, and his skin scratched like sandpaper. The nurse who checked on him that night contributed tenfold to this agony. Miss Annie was a stocky apparition in white who rarely smiled. She glowered as she examined Lester and turned away without a word. For a moment she hesitated, and then said, in a monotone, "By the way, your parents were almost killed in an auto accident."

Luckily their recuperation, as well as Lester's, was swift, and Arthur was consecrated bishop in Pittsburgh on May 29, 1945. By September, the Kinsolvings had moved to Phoenix where the new bishop was installed in Trinity Cathedral. Although Lester had been at Episcopal

Gadfly

High for five years, he still had credits to make up, and did so at Phoenix Union High School. After that, he made a second attempt to enlist in the military, during the last summer of World War II.

The first time was in 1941. After the bombing of Pearl Harbor, Lester tried desperately to enter the Marine Corps by forging his hand-written birth certificate. He altered the year from 1927 to 1924. Unfortunately, it was impossible to get a release from the school board physician, so Les was forced to admit that he lied: "I'm sorry, but I felt called . . . I'm really only fourteen years old." At seventeen, he enlisted in the army in July 1945.

Even though the war ended in August, Lester remained with the army and was sent off to basic training and then to the Armored Medical Research Laboratory in Fort Knox, Kentucky. His job was to test shoes by marching seven miles a day. They wanted to make sure the shoes didn't damage the feet, and to select which socks were suitable. There was a chance of being shipped out to Korea, but instead, Les was honorably discharged in October 1946. He never faced combat, but felt he had helped soldiers who would be equipped with comfortable, well-fitting shoes.

Returning to his parents in Arizona, Les worked as a salesman for Southwest Pest Control, offering free termite examinations door-to-door. At times, he was given the opportunity to crawl underneath a house and inspect for any termites feasting on wood. After a year, it was nearing the time to enter college. He applied to the University of Pennsylvania and was accepted for the fall semester of 1947.

Facing another summer, Les needed to earn some extra money for school. He was offered a job as a camp counselor at Saranac Lake, New York. It was La Jeunesse, A Camp for Boys, run by Henry Blagden. Les wrote to his parents, when Mary Blagden Kinsolving, Henry's sister, was visiting:

> Mary Blagden is the coldest, meanest, nosiest woman I've almost
> ever met. . . . I asked why the Crows (an honorary organization)
> were called crows when in most places they're shot on sight—
> Hank Blagden in his usual impulsive bull-like manner replied

he'd told us (in other words I didn't listen or was dumb) where-upon 5 boys replied they didn't hear him either. . . . Mary made all the boys tell me one by one what a crow was. . . . When I replied that that wasn't my question (and one of the boys pointed out this fact too) she saw she was obviously dead wrong so she said, "I've never seen a boy so open to ridicule in my life so you just keep quiet for the rest of the meal!"

Because he was outspoken and free-spirited, Les was considered the "black sheep" by this snobbish side of the Kinsolving family. Other patricians included Anne Kinsolving, who married Rhode Island's John Nicholas Brown. Anne once remarked of Lester, "That boy should've been strangled in his crib!" Disgusted by additional mistreatment from his relatives, Lester staged a walk-out, along with five other counselors, when Henry Blagden refused to pay them, while he was paying a number of other counselors.

Since he'd spent early summers with his family in nearby Lake George, Les hitched a ride, which took less than two hours. Over-joyed and nostalgic, Les searched for more work and found a job at the Orchard House, where actor Kirk Douglas had been a previous employee. He was desperate for anything, and was put on garbage detail. Every morning, Les gathered up all the garbage, drove to the dump, and emptied all the cans, dodging the flies as they swarmed in. He had to adhere to a state law that required the smashing of each bottle he loaded onto the truck.

As he performed this duty, a filthy, mangy-bearded fellow who resided at the dump would rustle from his bed of newspapers, and sit on his haunches. He'd stare at Lester, and begin shouting instructions on the fine art of bottle-smashing. Lester gritted his teeth through this morning ritual, only to be assigned toilet cleaning and dig-ging a new septic tank in the afternoon. After three weeks, he'd had enough, and hitchhiked his way down south to Matunuck, Rhode Island, where he participated in summer stock theater.

It was a relief from garbage and cesspools, but exploitive just the same. Since Lester wasn't a principal player, he'd be expected to work eighteen-hour shifts, the only compensation being room and board. He'd arise at 9 A.M. and work hard until 3 the next morning, as working crew, and then acting in bit parts.

One of the stars was Will Geer, who later performed in the 1970s as Grandpa on the highly successful television show *The Waltons*. On a night off, Will invited Lester to go swimming, and later offered him a rub-down. Surprised and shaken, Lester refused his advances. He was fired shortly afterward by the manager, who yapped, "Kinsolving, you eat too much, you talk too much, get out!"

Lester made his last hitchhiking trip to Philadelphia, just before school began at Penn. For the fall semester, he enrolled in English Composition and wrote about working for Southwest Pest Control, in "My Most Interesting Experience":

. . . You must have nerve and gall (it does take nerve when the door is opened by a gorilla like man whom you have, at no invitation of his, awakened from a deep sleep). . . . When I was inspecting the State Insane Asylum I noticed a long wide wooden box. Since this could well be a haven for termites, I opened the box when to my sudden horror an aged hag leaped up at me screaming "I've found you!!" Needless to say I was in no mood to act Prince Charming to this personification of a bad dream, so I retreated swiftly . . .

His professor, Dr. Conklin, gave him the "Quite satisfactory" grade of C+.

LESTER ALSO WENT out for freshman football; Penn's biggest rival was the Princeton team, who had come down the previous year, and painted Penn founder Benjamin Franklin's statue orange. In retaliation, Penn organized a "revenge party" before that year's Penn–Princeton game. At 2 A.M., the Princeton tiger statues were painted the Penn colors of red and blue, the words "PENN" were found on several pillars, and a huge tiger skin was taken from one Princeton student's dormitory room.

As the vandals drove off, a suspicious clicking sound was heard in their Oldsmobile. At the very minute the car conked out, the red light of a police car appeared behind them. The officer ordered them to open the trunk, and was greeted by a huge tiger's head. He knew that the thieves would be amply punished at Penn, so he collected the tiger skin and let them head back to Philadelphia. Les was later informed that if the Princeton team had caught them, they would've shaved every hair off their bodies and painted their heads orange.

The next morning, the dean of Student Affairs suspended the Penn raiders for two weeks. Les was also put on probation, which meant he couldn't play football anymore. But page one of the *New York Times* carried the story with the headline, "Penn Pranksters Bedaub Princeton." Lester's name was printed among the guilty. At a church convention in Arizona, fellow clergymen gleefully passed the article on to Bishop Kinsolving and asked him, "Are you related to this person?" The Bishop studied the article and then nodded with a smile.

The following January, Lester was inducted into the Delta Kappa Epsilon fraternity, known as the Deke House. During Pledge Week, he made fast friends with a fellow who was related to one of the big five families in Hawaii. Everyone referred to him as "King Kamehameha." Lester had never indulged in drinking alcohol, but Kamehameha surely did.

One night, Lester noticed his buddy from the Pacific Islands was weaving a bit more than usual. As he plunked down next to Les during one of the more severe initiation rites, he smiled obliviously while bowls, spoons, pitchers of milk, and tall stacks of bread were passed down the tables where all pledges sat.

"All right!" yelled the pledge master, "Grab a bowl and three pieces of bread!" Everyone scrambled while the master barked, "Tear the bread up, and pour the milk on!" It was ice-cold as it splattered, making all the victims grimace. The master then doled out the objective: "Be one of the first three to finish and you can leave—now GO!!"

Lester dove into the plate of freezing mush, gulping it down furiously. For a split-second he looked over to his left, and there sat King Kamehameha, paralyzed with drunken horror. Lester practically choked with laughter as he gobbled down the last of the milky remnants, only to notice that he had finished too late. The three winners ran out as fast as they could, while the others awaited their fate. The pledge master began slowly, "All right . . . START OVER!!" It would be his second try when Lester was released from this revulsion, only to leave King Kamehameha in a state of misery, barely having touched the first round of the nauseating concoction.

A month earlier, during the Christmas season, Lester's brother Putch had written a heartfelt letter:

> My dearest Mother, I'm afraid that this letter is all I can offer to you for this Christmas, but what I shall attempt to put into writing will, I hope, partially make up for the missing box with all the wrappings . . . the home you have made for me and all of us has far overshadowed any gloom I possess . . . it is with deep love and affection, that I, as one of three very lucky, foolish boys, give you this humble letter . . . and may God bless you for what a great deal you have done for me in return for so little. With all my love, Putch.

In January 1948, Putch attended a church youth group picnic in Phoenix, and participated in a game of roof-jumping. As he stepped forward to leap across to the other building, part of the roof gave way, and he fell to his death, at the age of eighteen. Uncle Charlie immediately went to Penn, and informed Lester of the terrible accident.

There was no describing the unbearable devastation to Lester when he heard the news. Unable to sleep on the overnight plane to Phoenix, he met his parents and younger brother Wink, who were stoic in their grief. Les visited the sight of the accident at South Mountain Park, and saw traces of his brother's blood. This confirmed to him that Putch was truly gone.

At Trinity Cathedral, Bishop Kinsolving demonstrated the bravery of a hero: he delivered the Order of Holy Burial for his son's funeral. His parishioner, future U.S. Senator Barry Goldwater, considered this the most magnificent act of courage he'd ever witnessed. In a private family ceremony, as Putch's casket was lowered into the ground, Arthur finally broke down.

That night, Lester wondered how he might continue to live without his dear brother, his closest friend. He knew he'd never be the same again. Awakening after a twelve-hour sleep, he still felt the agonizing mourning, but it was somehow different—perhaps almost bearable to live with.

Les would grieve this excruciating loss throughout his life, and for many years after, he sent Putch telegrams to his parents in Phoenix, one dated on his twenty-fourth birthday, November 20, 1953: "Our beloved Putchie, you shall not grow old as we who are left grow old, age shall not weary you nor the glass condemn at the going down of the sun and in the morning we shall remember you. We'll always be together, God bless you as you go from strength to strength."

Returning to Penn from Phoenix, Lester went to his room and saw a basket of flowers on his bed. A note read, "Dearest Sympathy—Penn Fraternity Brothers."

Wanderings before
the Calling

D R. REICH, LESTER'S new professor for English Composition, insisted that his students pronounce his name "Dr. Rich." Les disagreed; it should be pronounced the way it was spelled. "Dr. R-R-R-e-i-c-h!!" he'd call as he raised his hand to ask a question. In revenge, the professor planted "Fs" on his essays, no matter how well-written they were.

In "The Immortal Charge," Les provided a startling scene from a soldier's point of view as he died during a Civil War battle:

Come on! Yaaahhhoooo! We'll show you blue bellied bastards! There it is! They've got that flag up, they're breaking through! Here we come—Oh, Oh Christ—— please stop that burning—it's killing me! Oh, God, just take me—please for sweet Christ's sake kill me! . . . If I was only dead and then something would ease this Christ awful burning in my stomach . . . I can't even reach my canteen and that stinking water . . . Water, for God's sake water! Oh Lord, they're falling back—those stinking Yankees have got our flag and we're breaking . . . I can't see them well, everything's getting dark . . . Oh don't take me God! I don't want to die . . . it hurts so much—it's much darker—I guess I'm pretty weak . . . I guess I'm going—I'm going home . . . The Lord is my Shepherd, I shall not want, he maketh me to lie down . . . The End.

Although Professor Reich had to admit that "some of this is very good—particularly so in achieving realism of action and thought," he wrote another "F" since it was "still very careless—several individual sentences not clearly formed, four spelling errors, and almost no attention to punctuation."

Lester didn't fare any better in Spanish I, finding it completely dull, along with Psychology, Ethics, and even Geography. With a dwindling GPA, he was put on strict probation in June 1948, and by the following May, Bishop Kinsolving received a letter from Miles Murphy of Penn's Personnel Office:

> Your son, Charles Lester Kinsolving, suggested that I might write you concerning his withdrawal from the University of Pennsylvania . . . no one has questioned his capacity to do college work, but only his interest in it. . . . I believe it is Charles' intention to go to work. He has many personal qualities which should be decided assets. . . . He has energy and enthusiasm and a great deal of persistence in following out those intentions which he has really made his own. We all trust that he will be successful and will have on occasion to regret his failure to complete his college education.

And off to work Les went. His fraternity brothers gladly let him stay on until the end of the year at the Deke House, and he became a trainee for management with the Slater System, in their industrial feeding department. This involved distribution to cafeterias and the like, and it lasted only six months. He became a salesman again, this time with Filter Queen Vacuum Cleaners.

The pitch was simple: "Ma'am, were you aware that the human body has seven layers of skin, and that you shed a layer every year?

Did you realize, then, that after seven years, you're sleeping with a dead body? Filter Queen will get rid of those discarded layers of skin from your mattress, so you can sleep like new again!"

He stomached this absurdity for a month, and then was off to selling advertising space for a more credible business, Goodwin and Company. One of his clients included the Philadelphia Shooters' and Mummers' Association, who were featured in the 1950 New Year's Day parade. Their brochure displayed several photos, one showing men playing accordions, in gigantic feathered headdresses and sweeping gold lamé capes. The caption proudly read, "Mummers in Action as Thousands Roar!"

To ease the 9-to-5 grind, Lester volunteered politically, helping the Philadelphia Democrats win the 1949 election. He worked street corner rallies, and drove a sound truck, where he posed as speaker. Les was so impressive that Richardson Dilworth, Chairman of Committee for Philadelphia, wrote to thank him:

There is no doubt about it, without the courage, imagination and enthusiasm of people like you, we would never have been able to achieve such an overwhelming victory . . . p.s. You were mighty effective on that sound truck. No side show barker ever had a more persuasive line.

After moving out of the Deke House and into a rented room with a kind family through the duration of these various jobs, Lester decided that it was time to go home to Arizona. Around May 1950, he traveled cross-country in a used car that was wrecked, as sixth in a seven-car collision. Although Les escaped physical injury, he had little money left, and traded his damaged car for a dilapidated panel truck with a defective steering wheel, which led it to run off the road. Stranded and broke in Fort Smith, Arkansas, Les sought help from a very kind Episcopal clergyman, who contacted his parents in Phoenix to arrange a flight home.

It was humbling to return to his parents and to realize that he was restlessly searching, while many young men were settled in their

lifelong goals. Les decided to continue working in advertising and public relations, and created the Phoenix Welcoming Committee, modeled
on the Welcome Wagon. He worked with about twenty-five clients,
who would provide gift baskets with samples and coupons to new residents. One of his clients, Chevrolet, even provided him with a car.

Lester went all-out in the 1950 Phoenix Rodeo Parade, where his
employee, Fifi Baldwin, dressed in an Arabian Nights costume, rode
on an elephant with a large sign which read, "Welcomed by Phoenix
Welcoming Committee—Headin' for Bank of Douglas." That bank
put up $500 to bring the elephant from California, along with his
burly trainer. A local newspaper gave Lester's parade entry a special
caption under its photo: "Proving you can see anything in a Phoenix
rodeo parade, at the right comes the elephant entered by the Bank of
Douglas. Putting a horse saddle on his broad back was some job."

It was 1951, and the Korean War was on. Les felt a duty to re-
enlist, and was sent off, first to Leadership Training at Fort Ord, then
to Officer Candidate School in Georgia. Half way through the training, the Kaesong Peace Talks began, and the fighting stopped. It was
then that Lester felt a special call, and decided to leave the army for
another mission.

After receiving his second honorable discharge, Lester paid a visit
to Bishop Noble C. Powell of Maryland, who agreed to accept him
as a postulant for the theological seminary. "Uncle Noble" was considered a trusted friend of the Kinsolving family; he was rector at St.
Paul's Memorial Church in Charlottesville, where Arthur had served
as student chaplain before being appointed to West Point.

Les needed to make up college credits and achieve better grades
for seminary, so he attended Johns Hopkins University's night school
in Baltimore, where he studied history and sociology. During the day
he taught drama and public speaking at St. Paul's Episcopal School.
He also coached football and supervised study hall.

Working at St. Paul's was challenging; for one thing, Les didn't
get along with Ace Adams, the coach of the football team. Because
of that, he was moved from coaching varsity to junior varsity. To add
insult to injury, Episcopal High School beat St. Paul's, 86 to 0.

In addition, Lester thought the headmaster, Atherton "Appie" Middleton, was "awful." When eighteen dollars was stolen from his wallet in the dormitory, Les decided to plant another with a few dollars in it, and nabbed the thief, who was a janitor. He reported it to Middleton's office, and incredibly enough, no follow-up took place.

Finally, Les dealt with a royal hell-raiser named Fuller. This delinquent had already been thrown out of three schools, but managed to get into St. Paul's with the help of his father, a wealthy attorney. During one afternoon, a teacher called Les and complained that he couldn't control Fuller and that he was sending him down to study hall.

Fuller had no intention of studying; instead, he created a noisy havoc. He was ordered by Les to do ten push-ups. Fuller complied, but laughed as he sprang to his feet, quickly saluting Les with his middle finger. Lester ordered him to do ten more push-ups, but was greeted with clenched teeth and a swinging fist. While the other students cheered, Les grabbed Fuller by the neck, took him to the gymnasium, and sat on him.

Headmaster Middleton heard the screaming Fuller, and ran into the gym shouting, "WHAT are you DOING?!" He then ordered Lester to release him, and demanded that he return Fuller to study hall. Fuller paid his respects to Mr. Middleton and the rest of St. Paul's, when he spat out a "FUCK YOU!!!" stormed out, and was never seen again. During Christmas, Lester received a holiday card which read, "Friend and Countrymen, *Season's Greetings and Best Wishes for the New Year*—your's truley, Ben H. Fuller, The Juvenile Delinquent."

During this time, the U.S. Army contacted Les and offered him a job of posing as a Soviet agent at Fort Holabird, the Intelligence school in suburban Baltimore. He didn't accept, for he knew he was destined for the priesthood. After finishing up at Johns Hopkins and leaving St. Paul's, Lester worked temporarily as an office manager for a right-wing group (the National Education Foundation), in hopes that he'd be accepted into the seminary. Although Les was a postulant in the Diocese of Maryland, there were no Maryland Episcopal seminaries, so he applied in Virginia, Ohio, and Tennessee. All of them turned him down. It was anguish, working at a desk and thinking his dream was gone.

Karl Morgan Block, Episcopal Bishop of California, responded to Les's mother's phone call on behalf of her son. Karl and Arthur were great friends since their chaplain days, although Karl served at Woodberry, Episcopal High School's great rival. He was more than happy to do a favor for them and found a place for Lester at the Church Divinity School of the Pacific, located in Berkeley near the University of California. Elated, Les contacted the Maryland diocese to get permission to transfer as a postulant to California. To his astonishment, he discovered Bishop Powell had never even registered him as a postulant.

Before leaving for California in 1952, Lester paid a final call to the bishop's office in Baltimore. He was hoping it would be the last time he'd have to pass by Powell's "poisonous, nasty" secretary. "Uncle Noble," Les announced, as he walked up to the Bishop's desk, "I've been given a chance to go to the seminary in California by Bishop Block." "Well," the Bishop quipped, "that's interesting news, I'll have to consider letting you go." "Oh, you don't have to; because you never registered me . . . I just wanted to say good-bye." "Well," Uncle Noble snapped back, "I'm sorry you feel that way." It was Lester's first taste at exposing deceit in the clergy. His truth-fighting mission was well underway.

Les Meets the
Berkeley Democrat

L ESTER'S LOVE LIFE began at age fourteen, when he went on a chaperoned date with Patsy Schoen in Pittsburgh. A year later, he kissed Peggy Heard. For several years after, there was a series of long- and short-term relationships with young ladies, but nothing that was very promising. Finally, at twenty-one years of age, his first serious romance began, with Caroline Tiers.

Lester met Caroline on the eastern shore of New Jersey, at a summer resort. They had a date set up on the beach, and he was immediately smitten. Les always preferred brunettes, which she was, along with being "gorgeous and adorable" and possessing "an irresistible personality." They both lived in the Philadelphia area, she near Germantown. Caroline was a teacher at the Academy of the Assumption, which actress Grace Kelly once attended.

It was frustrating that Lester couldn't kiss Caroline until the fifth date, since she was such a devout Catholic. These were very rigid times, before more liberal mores were put into effect under Vatican II. Although he was deeply in love, Les worried about his job insecurity and that he wasn't settled enough to support a wife and family.

The biggest problem was their religious differences—she was very committed to her church, and he to his.

Lester regularly attended St. Michael's and All Angels Church in Germantown, after seeing their ad in the church directory section of the newspaper: "Joy, Joy, Joy! It's Great to Be Alive!" The Rev. W. Hamilton Aulenbach was rector of this parish, and exuded an extraordinary love of life and warmth toward people. He took Lester under his wing, and whenever he'd send a letter, he addressed it to "'My Son' Lester Kinsolving!"

Agonizing over his one-year relationship with Caroline and allegiance to remaining an Episcopalian, Les met with Aulenbach early one Sunday morning, before the church service. The wise rector was very sympathetic with his ordeal, but suggested he be loyal to his faith. It was then that Les realized he had to break up with Caroline.

The same dilemma was true for Sylvia Alice Crockett, who was also seriously involved with a Roman Catholic. She sang in the choir at All Soul's Episcopal Church in Berkeley, California, while he attended Mass every Sunday. They had dated for four years, until she realized that their relationship had to move forward. They discussed marriage, but Sylvia didn't want to give up her denomination. Sadly, they would part ways. A week later, she would meet her future husband for the first time.

In late March 1953, when Les was in his first year in seminary, classmate Spencer Rice was concerned about the various women Lester was dating, especially one whom he considered "vivid" and "too wild." Spence was a seminary assistant at All Soul's Episcopal Church in Berkeley, and had become acquainted with a young woman in the choir "who'd stop traffic." She was a senior at the university, and her name was Sylvia Crockett. Lester agreed to go to next Sunday's service and was "enthralled" when she walked in with the rest of the choir.

After church, Les stood at a distance and watched Sylvia, noticing how "absolutely beautiful" she was. Spence spoke very highly of her: she was sweet and kind, and very devoted to the Episcopal Church. Les considered this to be a very suitable match, and a date was arranged by Crockett friend Marge Goddard.

Gadfly

Marge had spoken previously with Les during coffee hour at All Soul's, when he would visit the church on occasion. She was taken by this fellow from the East Coast and would convey this to the Crocketts during coffee hour, telling them more than once how "interesting Lester Kinsolving was." Sylvia, who was torn between her Catholic boyfriend and her own faith, thought, "I sure would like to meet him and go out with a good Episcopalian!"

Sylvia was bewildered when she walked downstairs at her sorority house and saw Lester for the first time: "He looked so different; his hair was slicked back, and he was wearing a navy blue suit *with a vest!*" The many boys she dated wore cashmere sweaters, white T-shirts, and had crew cuts. "If they did wear suits, they never included a vest—of all things to wear on a date!" As a rule, Sylvia always studied a man's hands—she was impressed, in that Lester's were "very strong." And even more importantly, his blue eyes were "very beautiful."

Although Les felt they had a wonderful time dining at an Italian restaurant and dancing to fast music, Sylvia wasn't that interested; if she didn't go out with him again, she wouldn't have minded. But they did and then made plans for a third date. Sylvia would accompany Spencer Rice and his wife Biz to hear Lester preach at Grace Cathedral in San Francisco, where he had charge of the Sunday evening services.

After hearing Les's sermon, Spence noticed that Sylvia was looking at church pamphlets on the subject of marriage. He mentioned this to Lester, which gave him the incentive to give her a passionate kiss in the backseat. In addition, he was the perfect gentlemen, having honored Sylvia's third-date rule.

It wasn't until a church supper in Crockett, California, that Sylvia felt deeply intrigued with Les and, during a dull speech after dinner, almost told him that she loved him. Later, they rode on a romantic ferry ride, and Sylvia considered being a minister's wife would be a wonderful thing.

In late April, after three weeks of dating, Les and Sylvia were alone in a car up in Berkeley's Tilden Park, overlooking a beautiful view of San Francisco Bay at Inspiration Point. He told her he loved her terribly, but then engaged in one of his "most flagrant falsehoods" in informing Sylvia that he couldn't allow her to distract him from his studies any longer. She had to say yes, or else he had to let her go. Luckily, Sylvia "fell for it."

Les wanted to get married in September, after Sylvia visited him during the summer, when he was on assignment as seminarian at Trinity Church in Gooding, Idaho. He went to Suffragan Assistant Bishop Shires, who decided they needed to wait until the end of the year. Les wanted to argue, but complied. A date was set for his twenty-sixth birthday, December 18, 1953.

In December, Edith and Arthur Kinsolving traveled to Berkeley to meet the Crocketts. After raising three sons, it would be a joy to welcome a daughter into the family. Meeting future parents is never easy, especially when it involves having a bishop for a father-in-law. Arthur could sense Sylvia's slight consternation, and, upon introducing her to Edith, remarked, "There's a very nervous young lady who wants to meet you!"

When Louise Crockett asked how many wedding invitations he'd need, Les replied, "About six-hundred." Luckily only half of the invited guests showed up at All Soul's, where Arthur solemnized the marriage with his beautiful, booming voice that resembled Franklin D. Roosevelt's. The guests were delighted when seventeen-year-old brother and best man Wink conveyed theatrical shock as Sylvia cut an oversized piece of wedding cake and shoved it successfully into Lester's mouth.

During the reception at Hillside Club, an annoying photographer continually harangued the happy couple, going so far as to follow Lester into the bathroom. As the newlyweds attempted to escape on their honeymoon, the same shutterbug leaped onto the hood of their car for one last photo op. Sylvia beamed a beautiful smile, while Les, eager for retaliation, bulged his eyes and snarled. First cousin Charlie Kinsolving, who was unable to attend the wedding, sent this telegram of congratulations from New York:

There was a young lad named Kinsolving
Who from caveman was slow in evolving

Gadfly

Now at last his ontogeny
Has recapitulated phylogeny
And round Sylvia his world is revolving.
God rest ye gentle Sylvia
Let K. not ye dismay
Make sure he keeps on laboring
And makes a bish some day
I'm sure your sense and beauty
Will stop him going astray . . .

And it never has. In December, 2009, they'll have celebrated fifty-six years of marriage.

Seminary Rumblings and Missionary Challenges

B EFORE LES ENTERED the Church Divinity School of the Pacific, he took courses at the University of California during the summer of 1952. One of them was a huge sociology class with an anonymous sea of student faces. Everyone, including future wife Sylvia, could hear Les asking questions to the professor. As one Episcopal colleague remarked, "If you were talking to Les on the phone, and you put the receiver down on your desk, you could still hear him." The built-in boom box in his throat has served him well as a radio talk-show host.

At seminary, Lester was confronted with the problem of students and professors who were committed to a "high church" ideology, in that they catered to the sacraments of Catholicism. This was displayed in the Episcopal services where they'd don birettas and chasubles, and genuflect whenever necessary. Incense and the ringing of chimes would also be used.

Militantly "low church," Les was among the minority. He was a firm Protestant who did not believe in the virgin birth, nor in a place known as purgatory. Hell was an emotional separation from God, not a horror show of suffering and torture for the damned. He also abhorred the Anglican Missal, which the high church used in place of the *Book of Common Prayer*.

In an act of protest, Les would walk down the hall of the second floor, where high church seniors and professors congregated at class time. To the tune of "Jesus Loves Me," Lester would belt out the following parody:

> Mary loves me this I know
> 'Cause my missal told me so
> Little ones to her belong
> 'Cause the prayer book's weak
> And the missal's strong . . .

He even rebelled against "broad church," which was a combination of high and low church. As his mother would state, "High and crazy, low and lazy, broad and hazy."

Fed up with these antics, members of the seminary were bent on ousting Lester De Pester. Among those who led the movement were Rev. Greer Taylor, a "young smart-ass from Harvard." After reading Lester's "Hell and the Mercy of God," Taylor scrawled a confrontation on the front of it:

> What does Paul mean by eternal damnation? Even the most loving father can't live his child's life for him . . . the point in the doctrine of damnation simply describes what you don't have when you won't accept what's given you. It makes sense!!!

Luckily for Les, there was Rev. Charles Whiston, former missionary in China and fellow low church advocate. Whiston was a kindly man who thought highly of Les's writing, and gave a favorable response to "The Person and Work of Jesus Christ: "A good, honest paper; shows personal faith—I commend you." As a result, Lester remained, until he was ordained into the priesthood in 1955.

Returning from Idaho in September 1953, Les was assigned to found

St. Thomas Episcopal Church, a new mission in Rodeo, California, north of Berkeley. New missions are churches that are in the process of being built, so parishioners meet for services in a temporary facility. For Lester's small congregation, it would be in a movie theater.

Photographer Barry Evans caught the young vicar greeting his flock on Sunday, under the marquee which displayed a typical 1950s double-feature of a top-billing film and the less-publicized, lower-budgeted "B" movie: *Act of Love*, an overseas war drama starring Kirk Douglas, contained such dialogue as, "The River Seine. All my life I wanted to see it. Finally, I saw it, with a gun in my hand." This was followed by seventy-one minutes of *The Marshal's Daughter*, starring Hoot Gibson and Laurie Anders. The poster displayed outside of St. Thomas exclaimed, "She's a Rootin' Tootin' Straight Shootin' Bundle of Curves!" Parishioners who didn't look away either blushed or cringed on their way into the church service.

At times, after his ordination to the priesthood, serving communion at his new mission had its challenges. Offering the chalice to a young woman, he noticed her eyes widening into saucers. Immediately distracted by her terrified look, Lester proceeded to spill the wine all over his vestments, while the frightened lady explained that she'd seen a rat run right behind him. On another occasion, as Les was passing out wafers, a huge fan was suddenly turned on by an electric timer. The wafers were flung everywhere, while Les frantically picked up as many as possible, snapping the clean ones in two in order to serve everyone.

The second mission he would serve, St. Philip's, began in the fall of 1954. Sylvia was pregnant with their first child, Laura Louise, who would be born the following December, two days before Les's birthday. The small Berkeley apartment they lived in didn't allow children, so after Laura was born they moved to El Sobrante, where St. Philip's was located. Again, it was another movie house, where embarrassed church members walked by a poster of scantily clad Mamie Van Doren gyrating to the swingin' beat in *Ain't Misbehavin'*. The main feature was World War II hero Audie Murphy's bio, *To Hell and Back*.

Les made a diligent effort to call on all parishioners and interested Episcopalians at their homes. As he greeted a new couple, he recognized the husband as being his first sergeant at Fort Benning, where he attended Officers Candidate School. The former sergeant laughed, and told Les, "You were a particular character!"

They reminisced on how Les achieved high grades by organizing soldiers to form different groups in his barracks—one to shine shoes, others to mop the floor, wipe the lockers, and so on. However, Lester's mischievous side soon took over. He couldn't resist slipping out of the barracks to make afternoon visits in nearby Columbus, Georgia. As the sergeant shouted out, "Kinsolving!" during roll call, three friends yelled out, "Here! . . . here!. . . here!!" in Lester's absence. As punishment, Les was delegated to garbage duty once again, scrubbing out large, filthy cans.

During one particularly dull class on the history of the Browning Automatic Rifle, Les began drawing a seal of the Officers Candidate School. It turned out to be a very nice illustration, so he snuck off to Columbus once more and had a printer make up about 5,000 sheets, which he started selling to each barracks. He was making a small fortune, so it was well worth the risk. Sneaking through the grass to the next building, he heard the sound of footsteps and then a loud, "Halt!!" Lester froze, and then another "Halt!" He still didn't identify himself, until he heard the *click, click* of a rifle. Les immediately sprung to his feet with his hands in the air, yelling, "I'm here!" As a result, he was put on report and turned in the rest of the copies. He did get to keep the money.

While serving at the two missions from 1954 to 1955, Lester became an Intern Chaplain at San Quentin, the oldest prison in California. His task was to interview new prisoners in an "office" cell, where he worked for four hours a week. He served during the time of Caryl Chessman, a rape offender who never committed murder, but was sent to death row in 1948 and executed in 1960. For eleven years, Caryl studied law and helped fellow prisoners with their court cases. Convicted murderess Barbara Graham, another infamous inmate, died in the gas chamber in 1955. Hollywood painted a sympathetic portrayal of her in *I Want to Live!* starring Susan Hayward.

Lester found the murderers he talked to "not unpleasant." One convict, sentenced to life for killing his wife because she had cheated on him, was "appealing" and "very bright." San Quentin's warden, Harley Teets, explained that these individuals were con artists and that he had to be very careful not to be taken in, in case any of them were plotting to escape. That very thing had happened to a previous chaplain, who took a letter from an inmate and sent it out illegally. As a result, he was fired. After hearing this story, Lester was extremely careful. Leaving San Quentin after each shift always gave Les a sense of gratitude, in that he wasn't one of those individuals behind bars.

Being a Protestant, Lester never prayed to any saint, but was most inspired by Thomas, since he was "the doubter." Les himself grappled with questions of faith—if God did exist, why was there so much suffering? Would there be an afterlife, or would it all be over at death? As he stated in a seminary term paper, "I still in all my strivings despair occasionally of ever reaching a systematic analysis of Christology—I cry out with my patron saint, Thomas, 'Lord we know not whither thou goest and how can we know the way?'"

Shortly before he became a priest, Lester had what can only be described as a transcendent, spiritual experience. Standing alone up on a hill, he was suddenly overcome with a great sense of the Lord. Any previous doubt immediately vanished, because he felt Jesus' spirit was right beside him. Like Thomas, he now had a firm belief in the Resurrection. With deep gratitude, Les whispered the words his patron saint said so long ago: "My Lord and my God."

It was Christmas Eve, 1955, when Charles Lester Kinsolving was ordained into the priesthood. The ceremony took place at Holy Trinity Episcopal Church in Richmond, California. A year later, at St. Philip's in El Sobrante, members of the Holy Trinity congregation began attending Lester's services, since his sermons, being controversial right off the bat, were very interesting to listen to.

This made Holy Trinity rector George Ridgway furious. He complained to Bishop Block, who had ordained Lester at his own church.

Gadfly

The bishop was also to blame for having brought this new trouble-maker into the ministry in the first place.

In January 1956, Les was asked to return to San Quentin as teacher of apologetics in their School of Religion. Here he could support and defend the Christian faith, and refute any claims that God didn't exist. It was also during this time that Les began his political work in the ministry. There was one cause that he had thought about for several years, ever since he argued with an attorney in a Phoenix nightclub in 1950.

While Les waited for a Phoenix Welcoming Committee client, he struck up a conversation with an affable-looking man at the bar. It turned out he was defense counsel for two killers and was fighting to keep them from being executed. Since Les was in favor of the death penalty, he jumped at the chance of winning yet another hot debate. "Never was I so beautifully demolished in my life!" Les later exclaimed. The attorney's brilliant analysis made him think twice, and he began studying the subject, for six years before pursuing it politically.

Les perused the Royal Commission on Capital Punishment Report, which discussed the case of a British man named Timothy Evans who was hanged in March 1950, for the murder of his daughter and wife in London. Three years later, six bodies were found buried at the home of John Christie, Evans' neighbor. This serial killer would later confess to murdering Evans' family. The wrongful hanging of Timothy Evans resulted in one of the worst cases of injustice in British history.

Since he wasn't a full-time staff chaplain, Les wasn't allowed to counsel those prisoners on San Quentin's death row. However, he became one of California's strongest advocates to abolish the death penalty. He went on countless speaking engagements, debated district attorneys, and testified before the California State Legislature. Needless to say, San Quentin didn't go along with this campaign. Les's one-year teaching assignment would be over in a few weeks, so he promised Warden Teets he'd keep quiet.

If the warden's office had known earlier of his political leanings, they would've never invited Les to witness an execution, which instigated further belief that the death penalty was wrong. The condemned man's name was Byrd, an Episcopalian who had formerly resided in Ventura, California. One night, as he had attempted to reunite with his wife at her home, they ended up in a heated argument, and he went berserk and killed her. Later, Byrd was found wandering up in the hills. The District Attorney, who was running for reelection, prosecuted him for first-degree murder, thus sending him to the gas chamber. Les understood this case to be second-degree, since he believed Byrd went temporarily insane, meaning the crime was not premeditated.

Before execution, Les gathered with a group in the viewing area, and watched as Byrd was ushered into the chamber. Strapping his arms and hands down, they also applied wires to his heart, in order to make sure death would occur. As the poisonous gas filled the room, Byrd quietly took three deep breaths as instructed, and put his head down.

Five minutes later, his head suddenly jerked up, and there was a loud howling, as his lungs expended what breath he had left. After several minutes, a voice announced, "All right, gentlemen, it's over." There was one moment that Les would never forget, having dreams about it for years afterward. Just before the gas filled the chamber in which he sat, Byrd looked over at Les, and, with hands strapped, did his very best to wave good-bye.

IN MAY 1957, a son was born to an elated Les and Sylvia. To continue the Kinsolving legacy, he was enrolled as a candidate for admission to Episcopal High School, for September 1972. He was named after the two missions, Thomas Philip. St. Thomas had extricated itself from the theater in 1956 and was now a fully built church. It would take more time to build St. Philip's, after Lester was called to serve another congregation, in Pasco, Washington.

Controversy Ignites the Flames

IN JANUARY, THE Rev. Andrew Daughters, rector of the Church of Our Savior, had driven almost four hours from Pasco, Washington, to Camp Cross, an Episcopal youth retreat located on Lake Coeur d'Alene, Idaho. He was traveling to the camp to attend a conference for youth, along with other clergymen. He didn't return as expected, so a search was conducted. They found his car parked on the edge of the lake, near a boat that had capsized. They concluded that Daughters had drowned, and a memorial service was held that spring in Pasco by the Bishop of Spokane, Russell Sturgis Hubbard.

Rectors of local parishes came to the aid of the traumatized flock while they grappled in finding a new rector. Finally, they decided that Kinsolving would be the perfect choice. He was a young, fresh new face who had built two churches and served well at San Quentin in California.

Les felt called to take Daughters' place, knowing that the Church of Our Savior was in a desperate situation. However, it was terribly difficult to announce his resignation on the morning of June 30, 1957. He was very devoted to the parishioners he had served since September 1953.

As he returned home that afternoon, he received a call from the Associated Press who asked him, "Are you still going to Pasco?" When Les replied that he was, they broke the news to him that Rev. Daughters had walked into San Francisco's Grace Cathedral that very morning, with a case of amnesia. Ironically, this was where Lester delivered his first sermon.

Completely astounded, Les consulted his father on how to handle this inexplicable situation. "You've got to resign, it's his church," Bishop Kinsolving said. Les did, only to find out later that Daughters' doctor required he take two months rest. With much regret, the rector resigned from Church of Our Savior, and Lester was elected a second time.

Before they left for Pasco, the Kinsolving family attended the Bishop's Ranch in Healdsburg, California, for a brief vacation. Dick Byfield, seminary friend and assistant to Bishop Block at Grace Cathedral, told Les, "We're going to miss you, and for good reason— you've got guts."

When Les arrived at Church of Our Savior in September, he was presented with yet another building campaign. The old church couldn't accommodate the growing number of members, so there were plans for a ground-breaking on Christmas Eve. In October, the *Tri-City Herald*'s front page read, "BEAUTIFUL STRUCTURE: PASCO EPISCOPALIANS PLAN NEW CHURCH," which discussed a completion in May. Along with this announcement, several promotional ads, all written by Les, would appear in the paper throughout the month:

HYPOCRITES IN THE CHURCH? YOU BET!!

Plenty of them! And there is always room for more! If you happen to be one of the few that is free from all hypocrisy then come over and help us!

WHY DID THEY CALL JESUS A "WINEBIBBER?"

The Episcopal Church is one of the very few churches where you can have a glass of beer without feeling like a hypocrite.

"Judas . . . Went and Hanged Himself . . . Go and Do Thou Likewise"!

The scripture captioned above illustrates that if you take from context the Bible can say almost anything you want it to say . . . apparently some people believe that every word in the Bible was dictated by God himself, or that the Bible authors were all momentarily infallible while writing!

Like to Find Out More About It?

Send the coupon below. NO ONE WILL CALL ON YOU— unless you request it by visiting the Episcopal Church in this area—which is noted for its friendliness.

Besides his many responsibilities, Les also inherited the monthly bulletin entitled *The Crucifer*, with its motto, "Carrying the Cross into Your Home." Typical of church bulletins, he considered it "one of the dullest things I ever read." He tried to make *The Crucifer* of some interest by including his own editorials, along with inviting contributing writers. And, instead of monthly, he'd make it a weekly bulletin.

On January 5, 1958, parishioners read the following from their new rector:

Your welcome when we arrived, your willingness to thrive, the congeniality of this grand community and congregation, your loyalty in time of a controversy that became nationwide, and your tolerance and understanding in view of my many mistakes—these are things that touch my heart. All I can offer you is a certainty that I will make more and perhaps bigger mistakes, I will not cease to speak the truth as I see it, I will not cease to ask your help in this noble cause. . . .

The controversy mentioned was the now-infamous sermon he preached, just two months after his first service at Church of Our Savior. Lester was inspired to write it based on an experience he had when he was seven years old. Visiting the library one day, he opened a large volume of Dante's *Inferno* and looked at several illustrations depicting the horrors of Hell. Terrified by these ghastly images, Les returned home and asked his father about it, wondering if he might be sent there someday. Arthur looked into Lester's worried eyes and tried to reassure him: "Son, you know that I love you very deeply . . . never, ever think that I have more love and mercy for you than God does."

In November 1957, the Rev. Lester Kinsolving spoke these words in the pulpit, from "The Damnable Doctrine of Damnation":

The repugnant theory that disgusts so many of the intelligent, terrifies the gullible and portrays God as a sadistic hypocrite . . . Jesus tells us not to call anyone a fool and yet he seems to be doing this very thing in berating the Pharisees . . . that God is merciless seems to be the only possible reaction to the repugnant idea that he damns . . . although it is the belief of this writer that there is no Hell in the next life, it is clearly obvious that there is an overabundance of hell in this world . . . it is only reasonable to proceed under the clear conclusion that God does not wish to damn . . . Der Führer [Adolf Hitler] might well have answered Fundamentalist Christian critics with, "Well at least my torture was quick in comparison with the eternal punishment by the God you preach."

The outcry was so strong that word quickly spread across the country and around the world, with news reports in *The Living Church, Arizona Republic,* and *Columbia-Basin News.* Under the title, "Is Hell Necessary?" *Time* magazine's December 30 issue discussed how the Rev. Charles May, rector across the river in Kennewick, publicly denounced Kinsolving, along with May's supporters who, proclaimed, "Kinsolving's theology is sensationalism . . . he preaches on sex and questions the virgin birth. He's completely different from the rest of us in every way—he gets up at 11 in the morning and goes to bed at 4 A.M."

Before he preached his sermon on sex, Lester reassured his flock that the subject would be "handled by a gifted layman, a priest and an M.D . . . with all of the tact possible to avoid dissimulation. I would, if necessary, rather have our young people shocked than ignorant and in some future trouble—because their church was afraid of controversy."

Les later reiterated his stance on the virgin birth after being denounced:

> I simply, in all honesty, doubt that our Lord was born to a woman without the intervention of a man. . . . If God worked through the human woman, Mary, why not Joseph? How can I honestly say "Born of the Virgin Mary" in the Apostles Creed? How can anyone say "Sitteth on the right *hand* of God"?!! Do we take *that* one literally?

There were those who defended the controversial rector, such as School Principal Woodrow Epp: "What Kinsolving said is, in my opinion, completely compatible with what I thought was the Episcopal Church. He's shaken up a lot of people's beliefs since he came here, and by the holy gods of war, this congregation needed a shaking."

Although a fellow clergyman who was familiar with the Kinsolving Episcopal legacy stated, "*Who's Who* is on his side—even if the Episcopal doctrine is not," Bishop Hubbard had the final word: "Kinsolving's preaching had been 'within the allowable latitude of the church.'" An outraged Anglican priest from British Columbia accused Hubbard of violating his consecration vows by not putting Lester on trial for heresy.

Frightened of this possibility, Les wrote to his friend Joseph Fletcher, who taught Christian Ethics at Episcopal Divinity School in Cambridge, Massachusetts. Fletcher referred him to the Very Rev. James A. Pike, a former attorney who was now serving as the Dean of the Cathedral Church of St. John the Divine. Dean Pike told Les:

> I somewhat doubt if the District convention will take such an action and I doubt if any move will be made against you for "heresy." However, if I am wrong on this and you are brought up for heresy, I will certainly do all that I can for you . . . let

me assure you of my deepest sympathy as to what you are going through; I have been going through a good deal myself.

Much to his relief, no trial ever took place. Shortly after the *Time* article appeared worldwide, Les received an avalanche of letters, the majority of them very supportive, with most requesting copies of "The Damnable Doctrine of Damnation."

Several envelopes containing fundamentalist literature were sent anonymously, warning him against the flames of hell licking at his feet. One letter signed by "A friend" included a small Pilgrim Tract Society pamphlet, entitled "Is There a Hell?" with the subtitle, "Ungodly men say, 'No, there isn't any.' But is that a safe bet?"

An illustration showed blindfolded individuals (some carrying bags of money and others wearing college graduation caps) holding banners marked "Atheists" and "Infidels," and falling into the crevice of Hell, screaming, "Oh if we only had . . . !" The long-winded, proselytizing message then began with, "On They Go, Down, Down . . ." The friend ranted a righteous vitriol at Les:

If you do not believe what the Bible teaches about Hell, just how do you believe anything it teaches? Do you believe you can take out only what you want, and disregard the rest?. . . It seems to me that you a bit mixed-up . . . read your Bible again. EVERY WORD IS TRUE, even the subject of hell."

Most were overjoyed at Lester's outspokenness in the pulpit. Comments ranged from the inspired to the amused: "Don't get defrocked till you have succeeded in shaking up the whole Church" . . . "Congratulations on giving Hell the devil" . . . "How we need many thousands who will expose the satanic hypnotism of the God-dishonoring yarn of eternal torture" . . . "You are to be commended for your outright stand against a doctrine that is not to be found in God's word" . . . "We compliment you and bless you for your courageous and noble stand. May you live forever" . . . "Maybe you better put a few gargoyles on the roof of your new church" . . . "I wasn't the least bit surprised to find that Kinsolving was raising hell somewhere" . . . "All I can say is 'Hurray!'" . . . "Remember Les, you're only 30—they didn't crucify Christ until he was 33!" . . . "I had no idea that you went to bed at 4 AM and got up at 11 AM—my, what a horrible man you must be. Honest, Les—I haven't been able to stop laughing all morning!"

In the midst of this whirlpool, Church of Our Savior celebrated the good news: in 1957, all attendance records were broken, a new church was being built, the three choirs welcomed more members, and pledges were doubled from $7,000 to $16,000. Rev. Kinsolving was reputed to have made more house calls than any other local clergyman, and his weekly bulletin would start bringing in paid subscribers, eventually covering a circulation in twenty states, the District of Columbia, and England.

As one fan letter gushed, "I would rather give up *Time* or *The Post* than *The Crucifer*." To its detractors, it would come to be known as *The Crucifer*. In response to those riled individuals who insisted that the church remain out of controversy, Les wrote a short editorial:

> . . . a congregation of Christian people dedicated to living in Christ-like love should be the one place where controversial subjects can be presented without fear and without acrimony. It is the very nature of a fellowship of Christians to be able to speak and hear the truth in love, which frequently means to disagree sharply and yet love one another.

On Saturday, February 22, 1958, a large, three-quarter-page ad was run in the *Tri-City Herald*: "Murphy Motors Presents the Rev. Lester Kinsolving in 'Cross and Crisis,' Every Sunday—10 P.M. to 10:30 P.M., exclusively on . . . KTRX-TV, Channel 31." The ad featured a television camera zeroing in on the impassioned preacher raising his right arm dramatically as he delivered yet another provocative sermon. His piercing eyes were enough to convince any reader to tune in to the weekly program. *Cross and Crisis* would also feature the Church of Our Savior Senior Choir, and would run for thirteen weeks.

"The Rector is going to prison," claimed the February 23rd edition of *The Crucifer*:

> (Hurrah! Say some who feel he should be there permanently!), but only as guest preacher this Sunday at Washington State Penitentiary. This is an exchange with The Reverend James Thompson, Protestant Chaplain at Walla Walla . . . we count it a privilege to have him with us in remembering that he is engaged in following our Lord's admonition, "I was in Prison and Ye Visited Me."

After his sermon, Les was given a tour of the penitentiary. Although he was familiar with the state's method of capital punishment, he was still appalled to see the long noose hanging over a trap door. Photographs were taken, which Les would later use in presentations during his statewide campaign to abolish the death penalty. He preached on the issue on "Cross and Crisis," where a similar noose dangled over his pulpit.

According to *Tri-City Herald*'s story on the religious show, "[Rev. Kinsolving] termed [hanging] the most brutal of the four forms of executions in the United States. He compared this 'relic of barbarism' with crucifixion, and while admitting crucifixion [is] more agonizing physically, capital punishment is more brutal considering the confinement in death row which may last for two years and be coupled with frequent last minute reprieves."

> "It is now 4 A.M.," Les wrote in the March 9th edition of *The Crucifer*, "and I am writing from the Beta Theta Pi House at Whitman college where I am one of four guest speakers at the annual 'C.C.O.R.' or Campus Conference on Religion . . . last night I must have gotten about three hours' sleep, interspersed with snores, alarm clocks, and somnambulistic conversation. This lack of sleep is certainly worth the sacrifice because the interest these people have in religion, as well as their questions, is simply amazing."

Gadfly

After two days of "addressing classes, bull sessions and individual counseling," Les was invited on a panel with the Rev. James Grant, a Catholic priest from Walla Walla. Speaking before a jammed-packed auditorium, the two clergymen were invited to discuss "Birth Control: Is It Justified in a Christian Society?"

FATHER GRANT (reading from a typewritten statement): I consider birth control immoral, unnatural, and am against all dispensers of this indecent material. . . .

{During Grant's introductory comments, Kinsolving quickly scribbled notes in preparation for a counterattack.}

REV. KINSOLVING: Our two churches agree that birth control is permissible; the Roman Church demands birth control from its clergy and encourages it for the laity by means of the "Rhythm Method." This is sometimes referred to as "Roman Roulette"; but it isn't even reliable as Russian Roulette and the people who use it are called "Parents."

FATHER GRANT (with righteous indignation): I did not intend this to be a debate! If this sort of thing continues, I'm going to leave the platform!

REV. KINSOLVING (after a short pause): It's obvious that our two positions, if expressed together, would automatically constitute a debate, and that if I could continue . . . without being interrupted.

After a bit of contemplation, Father Grant returned to his seat, allowing Rev. Kinsolving to continue. The audience then directed most of the questions to the position held by Father Grant.

The next month Les received a letter from Bishop Hubbard, who expressed concern about his "public statements" and that they might "bother the clergy who are under the general impression that they are not really forwarding esteem and respect for the Episcopal Church . . .

you just seem to find it impossible to live peaceably with your brethren." The bishop, however, took note of the "splendid parish program and the way the parish is growing under you."

To prove that was so, a twenty-page program was offered to those attending the dedication of the Church of Our Savior and the Sacrament of Confirmation. It was held in the evening of the first Sunday after the Ascension, on May 18. The program featured "A Short History of the Church of Our Savior," where attendance ranged from 0 ("Dust storm prevented service") in 1911 to 27 ("Mrs. Marshall said, 'Your sermon was much better this morning'") in 1929.

It was now 1958, and there was much cause for celebration:

Perhaps the most significant achievement on the part of this congregation is its growth in numbers. . . . Easter of 1958 saw 497 people jammed into every nook and cranny of the sacristy, chancel, nave, and crypt. Tens of thousands were reached by the parish's commercially sponsored program Cross and Crisis over KTRX-TV. In comparing this with the nine people who attended Easter services in 1912, the congregation has come a long way. May God guide us as we face the future in His service which can turn obstacles into achievements.

Among photographs of the Laymen's Sick Calling Committee, Cherub Choir, and Men's Club Breakfast, the Episcopal Youth Fellowship's play was featured. "Slowboat," a "Musical Massacrepiece in 3 Acts," was Lester's spoof of the classic *Showboat.* "Penned" by Alonzo K. Stunk, the cast of characters included "Gaydog Wattaswell," "Mint Julep Schtunk," "Ellie Mae Yummy," and "Schotzi."

Sung to the tune of "Cotton Blossom," the chorus belted out the following:

Rotten Blossom, Rotten Blossom, hate to smell you when it's hot
When they load you with your cargo you're an awful stinking yacht
Rotten Blossom, Rotten Blossom, love to see you sink someday
With your cargo you would poison San Francisco Bay

"Slowboat" donated $108 to Calvary Mission in Roslyn, and received a Western Union telegram from Bishop Hubbard, who stated, "The Entire National Council of the Protestant Episcopal Church joins me in hailing the launching of 'Slowboat.'" Another was sent from Washington, D.C.: "Youth are the future of America. Heartiest Congratulations and Best Wishes—The President."

On the night of Sunday, May 24, Les regrettably informed his television audience that *Cross and Crisis* was leaving the air until further notice. He thanked his sponsor and station, but then remarked, "There have been poor sports . . . since my first telecast a minority has tried to get me off the air." Melvin B. Voorhees of *Columbia-Basin News* wrote about it in "CB Notebook," ending his column with, "So, friend Kinsolving, fret not too much. Good or bad, holy or horrid, acceptable or not, you have company and comrades in the long, soul-searching, life-taking, undone struggle for simple kindly tolerance."

Letters and postcards poured into KTRX-TV, demanding that *Cross and Crisis* return to the airwaves: "I believe Rev. Kinsolving is a great preacher of religion and I wish he could continue through the summer" . . . "The program is dramatic, inspirational, and controversial. It makes one feel it's good to be alive" . . . "Please do everything in your power to bring Rev. Kinsolving back in November" . . . "For many weeks now all other programs take a back seat at 10 P.M. on Sundays" . . . "Getting my husband to church has been an impossible task for me so thank you for bringing the church sermon to us. Hope it will continue in the fall."

Although *Cross and Crisis* was discontinued permanently, Les responded to each supporter who wrote in: ". . . One letter like the one that you wrote is worth five denunciations or threats and you have no idea how much my sponsor, the station, and I, myself, appreciate your kindness."

The summer of 1958 turned out to be one of Pasco's hottest, especially for Church of Our Savior. Washington, at that time, was the nation's most unionized state. Nevertheless, in the June 15 issue of *The Crucifer*, Lester announced his next sermon would be "Christianity and the Right to Work—An Examination of Initiative 202." He forewarned his flock of the looming controversy, explaining that "If God's people care about this controversial question, then so must God. We have heard discussion from practically every direction, and yet almost no direction from the pulpit."

Like Easter Sunday, the church exceeded its capacity on June 22, forcing the ushers to borrow folding chairs from Sunday School classes. The heavily unionized congregation listened intently to its pastor, who favored Initiative 202:

> The only ones who have to fear the right to work are those who ought to: the few dishonest labor leaders who have mutilated labor's good name and who need compulsion rather than merit to ensure membership. . . . I favor majority rule, if that rule is just. . . . Christianity's darkest hours came during the era of enforced membership. Labor unions must not deprive members of the right to quit—which seems the only effective protest against union officials before whom constitutions and ethical practices committees have been demonstrated helpless.

To Lester's surprise, only three letters of protest appeared in the local media, while four others were sent directly to the church, including one sent anonymously:

> mister kinsolving:
> The Columbia Basin News of June 15th (Father's Day) published a story on your sermon to the Church of Our Savior congregation where you urged with pious pleading that they sign Initiative 202 petitions.
> Your explanation that it took months to prepare your sermon is a fabrication and you know it. In a "Charlie McCarthy" fashion you fed your congregation the lies of big business prepared by pseudo crusaders for workers freedom.
> Ordained parrots like you are a disgrace to the cloth. Does Allen of Boeing's and Johnston of General Electric donate a few coppers for your blasphemus remarks in The Church of Our

Gadfly

Savior? Sanctimonius hypocrites like you are a disgrace to fundamental christianity.

There were two church members who swore they'd never return, but one did by the following week. "No matter what may come," Les wrote in *The Crucifer*, "I reiterate that no consequence could be as terrible as trying to face my Lord knowing that I had disfigured his pulpit with cowardice."

He braved these storms with a sort of oblivious joviality, implementing humor among the polemics:

> On showing the movie "Little Women"—The rector thinks it was the longest picture he ever endured . . . it was hot to start with, and with the hall packed with little folks, it was hotter'n ever . . . the parson sat beside two 1,000 watt movie projectors . . . a few small boys stayed through the cartoon comedy, but walked out in disgust after 10 minutes of "Little Women" . . . here are some statistics of the movie:
>
>> times very small children asked "how much longer?"—50
>> times extension cords knocked from socket by kids' feet, completely stopping show—5
>> times children bobbed in front of projectors en route to drinking fountain—350
>> times small children asked direction to wash room—700
>> number of assorted dogs attending—7
>> number of popsicles dropped after show—43
>> number of times the parson will show a 2-hour feature in summer—0

Later, Les was delighted with a call from Hollywood by legendary director Cecil B. DeMille, who invited him to Paramount Studios. DeMille was filming a short on the Right to Work, and planned to distribute 35,000 copies of the rector's sermon. During their conversation over lunch, Les broached the subject of fundamentalism in

The Ten Commandments. DeMille shot back with, "I didn't write the original script!"

Rev. Desmond O'Connell, Vicar of St. John's Episcopal Church in Ephrata, Washington, joined in fellow clergy denunciations of Les by accusing him of "pontificating as though he were an oracle of God" and insisted that he should stick to the good news of the Gospel of Jesus Christ. Lester responded with, "How can the Gospel be good news if when preached it ignores the subjects of deepest concern to God's people? How can Mr. O'Connell say anything in his pulpit without running the risk of being accused of 'pontificating as though he were an oracle of God'?"

Shortly afterward, the first wave of vandalism struck. Lights that lit up the back of Church of Our Savior were smashed, and several windows were broken. Eggs stains and spray from a fire extinguisher were splattered everywhere. Les wondered if disgruntled parishioners were involved, or perhaps residents who'd read the denouncements in the local press committed the crime. He considered it a minor act, and reminded himself of what his Lord endured in telling the truth.

Now pregnant with their third child, wife Sylvia drove through the snow one February evening to attend an audition at a local high school, for the Richland Light Opera Company. It was for the musical *Li'l Abner*, inspired by the Al Capp cartoon series. She landed the leading role of Daisy Mae, playing opposite a seventeen-year-old boy whose young wife was also pregnant. Sylvia considered this theatrical adventure one of the happiest times of her life; it was a badly needed departure from the sobering duties of a minister's wife.

Onstage, Sylvia would appear barefoot in a hillbilly-inspired costume, consisting of nothing more than a polka-dot blouse and miniskirt. Her brunette hair was covered in a shiny blond wig with a long braid. During production stills, Sylvia smiled proudly with the rest of the characters, including Moonbeam McSwine, Hairless Joe, and Lonesome Polecat. In one song, "Put 'Em Back," the racy lyrics included:

Put 'em back, the way they was,
Put 'em back, the way they was,

Gadfly

They were logy and lanky but
They loved hanky panky, put 'em
Back the way they was
Put 'em back the way they was!

Sylvia's joy was soon squelched by a letter she read one morning in *Dear Abby*. It complained about the wife of a minister who scandalized the community by appearing in a scantily clad outfit while onstage in a local theater production. They also remarked that she wore shorts in the summertime, and was dressed in a strapless gown at the Bishop's Ball. Sylvia, a native from the Bay Area, wasn't used to the stifling mores of a small town. She simply, but not deliberately, added to the fodder of the ever-brewing Kinsolving controversy. Les also received the following letter of protest:

How is it that you, as head of your home, could allow your wife to perform in the play "LI'L ABNER"? Paul said "In like manner also, that women adorn themselves in modest apparel, with shamefacedness and sobriety; not with braided hair, or gold, or pearls, or costly array. . . . A godly woman, who loves her husband loves her children, keeps herself in the home, and is chaste, will not be found as an actress, and especially not in the role which you permitted your wife to portray, Titus 2:3-5 . . .

In *The Crucifer*, Lester printed the letter along with his response:

I confess that I have never been able to agree with this particular admonition of St. Paul's—that a long face and drab clothing are the real marks of a woman's Christian character . . . as a matter of fact I didn't allow her—or forbid her . . . I urged her because I know she enjoyed it, and a great many people have been kind enough to say that they did too. . . . Your impression that the role was lust-provoking was apparently generated by one of the most unprincipled newspaper headlines I have experienced since coming into the Tri-City area: "Minister's Wife

Plays Sexy Role." Readers of this particular journal have become accustomed to such tactics used in an attempt to outdo a more successful competitor. . . .

Besides continuous media coverage ("DAY, KINSOLVING DIFFER ON GUIDO DEGRASSI HANGING," "MINISTER, FIGHT PROMOTER SPAR BETWEEN SERVICES," "KINSOLVING RAPS FACILITIES IN JAIL"), Lester too met outcry when he accepted the role of Lt. Barney Greenwald in *The Caine Mutiny Court-Martial*. Produced by the Kiwanis as a benefit for the Pasco Boys Club, it proved to be a big success, even at Washington State Penitentiary in Walla Walla. According to columnist T.V. Blues, "20 guys broke into the prison just to see it."

On a sweltering July evening in 1960, twenty-six actors took their places on a small stage at the prison and performed the almost three-hour courtroom drama in front of 350 inmates. Fifty of them left during the beginning of Act One, after realizing that no females, nor comedy, would be included in that evening's entertainment. The remaining 300 sat transfixed, so much that when prosecuting attorney Stuart Mullen rose and shouted "Objection!" a disgruntled audience member bellowed, "AW, SIT DOWN!!"

Shortly after the curtain fell, thunderous applause was heard throughout the prison walls. A guard declared, "It was the greatest show I ever saw—amateur or professional," while one prisoner exclaimed, "Man, did you hear that preacher cuss?!" Although Lester received rave reviews for his performance as Defense Attorney Greenwald, another letter appeared in the *Tri-City Herald*:

I . . . abhor profanity and obscenity! . . . If the Caine Mutiny was produced merely for the money . . . then it definitely should not have been produced . . . I . . . wish the producers of . . . Caine Mutiny would have used more discretion and cut a few nasty lines. . . .

This anonymous author appealed to *Dear Abby*, who wholeheartedly agreed. Abigail Van Buren denounced the reckless rector in her December 5th column, and took him to task for uttering three lines

Gadfly

of profanity while in a "drunken stupor" on stage. Although Sylvia chose to ignore previous wrath directed at her from the columnist, Lester couldn't resist temptation and retaliated:

> "Withhold My Name" and you seem to have the same sterile pedestal concept of the ministry that keeps many good men out of it. Then again, your attitude is not new. There was one minister who was called a winebibber and a glutton because of the indignity of providing drinks (alcoholic) to prolong a wedding party—in a town called Cana. Unwitholdingly yours,
> (Rev.) Lester Kinsolving

Sixty letters from all over the country were sent to Church of Our Savior. Many contained periodicals such as "Who Will Rule Space?", "A Lost Preacher Saved" (two copies), "Awake," and "Two Deacons Met in a Beer Parlor." Responses, both for and against, included the following: "Your critics can all go to 'hell'" . . . "Why don't you go to Hollywood where you can curse all you want to?" . . . "How we need to have ministers who are human in their piety . . . stay off the pedestal—you are way ahead" . . . "No earthly worm could persuade me to sink so low as to use such words. I am saved. Wish you were too."

That previous February, the twenty-fifth attack of vandalism had taken place. *Tri-City Herald* displayed photos of young altar boys holding twisted candle holders, and Les bending down on the acid-stained red carpet to pick up smashed candles and a Bible which had been shredded to pieces. The beleaguered pastor expressed "consolation in the fact that we have not been bombed like certain southern churches or synagogues," and that "our church will remain open at all hours, for public prayer, despite the fact that in two years we have suffered more than $2,000 in damages due to vandalism."

It was 6:30 P.M., February 15, 1961, when the first fire started. The altar and chancel area were damaged, but it would be possible, after a meeting with church officials, that Church of Our Savior would be repaired in time for Easter. At 10:30 P.M. Lester went back to his office in the old church building and resumed work.

As he was getting ready to leave at 5 A.M., Les heard a sound, like metal falling. He opened his study door and was hit by billows of black smoke. He rushed to his phone to call the police, but the line was dead. Slamming fireproof cabinets shut which contained over 200 sermons, Lester jumped in his car and raced to the fire department. By the time they made it back to the church, flames were surging through one side of the roof. As the firemen connected hoses, another flame was engulfing the other end of the building.

By daybreak, a photographer from the *Tri-City Herald* caught Lester in front of his destroyed parish, still wearing a fireman's coat he had borrowed when he joined in the fight to save Church of Our Savior.

One young parishioner tried his best to comfort his pastor with, "Don't you worry, Reverend. God will revenge Himself on the person who did it." Lester related his response in the February 23 issue of *The Crucifer*:

> We don't want revenge and neither, can I believe, does the God of Love. What we want is to be left alone—to live and worship in this community in peace—to be protected by those whom we invest with the authority of government.

Although he received countless calls of sympathy and offers for help, there were those who thought otherwise. Ken Anderson, a former vestryman, told Les that someone had remarked to him, "Well, Kinsolving asks for it—he had it coming—always getting into controversies."

Although slightly damaged from the intensity of the fire's heat, Lester was able to retrieve the sermons and files in the fireproof file cabinet. Among them was a paper he had written in seminary on January 15, 1953. It was a mock-up of the *New York Times* front page, with the following headline: "SHEEPHERDER'S SPEECH INCITES RIOT IN MEXICO: ATTACK ON CHURCH AND NATION BRANDED COMMUNISTIC BY CARDINAL ANAZIA."

Darkness
before the Dawn

"IN ALL OF our adversity we are provided with a magnificent symbol," Les wrote in the February 26th issue of *The Crucifer*, ". . . there, silhouetted against a clear sky, through the broken ramparts of our ruined church, stood the giant cross—which has provided Christians with unconquerable hope . . . to those whose churches are bombed instead of burned, to those whose churches are forcibly closed instead of merely vandalized. . . ."

Sunday services, now held in the old church building, were jammed-packed; the Episcopal Youth Fellowship worked feverishly to scrub, paint, and put Lester's smoke-infested office back into order; and pews, chairs, and equipment were donated from several churches, including St. Paul's, whose pastor had denounced Lester four years ago.

With the exception of one acolyte robe and the bishop's processional cross, all music, robes, and the church organ were lost. A benefit concert, proposed by the First Methodist Church, was held on April 23rd in the Pasco High School auditorium. "We hope," wrote choir president G.K. Epley, "every church choir in Pasco will join together to help our friends of the Episcopal Church replace their loss in the tragic fire."

Lester was grateful that Church of Our Savior would be fully covered by insurance, since damages from the fire were estimated at $85,000. Bishop Hubbard, in a cruelly corrupt gesture, attempted to seize it from the vestry. Scrambling for help, Lester called upon Ted Peterson, a brilliant attorney who had given a masterful performance as Captain Queeg in *The Caine Mutiny Court-Martial*. He explained the situation to Peterson, who nodded and said, "Let me at 'em." With Peterson's consummate skills at work, no lawsuit was filed, and the fire insurance was collected in full.

LESTER REMEMBERS THE day, when he was a three-year-old at West Point Military Academy and a beloved soldier retired. Although General Smith was a "strict disciplinarian," he always made a point to be kind to Lester, and they became good friends. On the day of his departure from West Point, in the midst of the "entire Corps of Cadets, officers, regiments of infantry, cavalry and Academy band," a crushed little boy wailed, "Oh, General Smith, don't leave us!"

"This is the way I look on you, my beloved people," said Lester from the pulpit, and this is the way I will feel when I say good-bye on Sunday, June 18, in order to begin a new ministry in the Diocese of New Hampshire. You have been my comrades in arms in one of the most extraordinary sets of circumstances and battles ever seen in any church in this state." These words of farewell would be included in the June 11th issue of *The Crucifer*, the last issue to which Lester would ever contribute.

Letters and cards poured in, some heartbroken that their pastor was leaving: ". . . We all feel that we are losing not only our very able Priest but also a dear friend, who has been there whenever we have been in trouble . . . you have touched our lives in such a way that none of us shall ever forget you" . . . "I feel that since listening to you I have a much better conception of The Church, and a better understanding of myself". . . "I have never met or known anyone who fought so hard for what he believed . . . I have always been proud to say, 'Rev. Kinsolving was my minister.'"

Two letters, in particular, seemed especially prophetic: "You are, in my estimation, destined for great things. The tragic element is prominent in the life of one who has not been one with his destiny" . . . "I always felt you were working and due for bigger and better things . . . you are going to have a great opportunity to use your talents to the fullest. This is good."

Senior Warden Harold Muzatko, stepping in as provisional rector, held the books of parish records as the Kinsolving family sped off in a cloud of dust, after Lester's final service at Church of Our Savior. It would be too agonizing to say good-bye to each parishioner, and they had a long drive to the East Coast, where Les would serve as the new vicar of St. Andrew's Episcopal Church in New London, New Hampshire.

New Hampshire's Bishop Charles "Tod" Hall was impressed with Les's record of building new churches and wrote him in May of the "exciting vacancy." For over thirty years he had struggled to raise funds for a new and larger church building, since the present sanctuary was made of logs and situated in the woods. Although the pews were filled in the summer, hardly anyone attended during the winter months.

As soon as Lester heeded the call to this new parish, Sylvia knew it was a mistake. She felt that her husband was far too progressive for a congregation of New Englanders, who were very set in their ways. Les was forewarned by vestry member Phil Cates of the impending struggle: "We are a much more conservative set of people in New England . . . your conservative businessman does not like to be high pressured."

As early as July, problems began to surface. When Les suggested a large sign be placed in front of the rectory, Mr. Cates reminded him that "this is a conservative town, quite different from many of the growing western communities and, perhaps, such a sign as you suggest might well be out of place." He also gave him a slight reprimand when Les appeared shirtless during preparations for a summer fundraiser: "Mr. Kinsolving, remember yourself, there are ladies present!" to which Les replied, "Well, I go swimming without a top and there are ladies present!"

During a particularly lengthy meeting, vestry members haggled with such calamities as the three-cent postage stamp, and exactly where the bathrooms should be located in the new church. This latter debate went on for hours, so Lester opted for some comic relief: "Why don't we just rename the church 'St. John's'?" He was met with a few guffaws, while the majority of his flock glowered.

Although Mrs. Harry Cook sent a formal welcoming card to the Kinsolvings, she later took Sylvia to task and insisted that she should attend all of the Guild meetings. There was much unkind gossip among the church ladies about their new rector's wife, making matters worse for Sylvia, who was very homesick for the West Coast.

After a groundbreaking ceremony on Christmas Eve, 1961, where a blowtorch was needed to break up the snow, Lester went to the woods and conducted services at Old St. Andrew's in sopping shoes. Anticipating a warm bath at home, he was greeted by freezing water, since the plumber, who'd made an earlier promise, hadn't yet fixed the pipes. His winter vacation to warm Arizona would be a welcome one.

Returning to the East Coast after visiting his parents in Phoenix, Les phoned his senior warden, physician John Ohler, from Boston. Ohler reluctantly informed him of a vestry meeting that had just taken place, at which they had decided to postpone the building of the new church. When John asked Les if he had any kind of reaction, the disgruntled rector responded with, "You'll learn about it on Sunday."

For Lester, conducting a vestry meeting without him was the ultimate betrayal.

His sermon that Sunday would touch on the subject of "leaving the Lord's house in ruins," and include an announcement of his resignation, effective in sixty days. Before his leave in March, Les was invited to the Midwest by Arnold Lewis, bishop of Salina, in West Kansas. He was looking for a pastor for one of their local churches in Salina, and after a very cordial meeting and tour of the parish, Bishop Lewis made a verbal offer to Lester. He said he would contact him again within two weeks.

The Rt. Rev. Lauriston Sciafe, successor to Arthur Barksdale II at Calvary, was now serving as bishop of Western New York. During an informal clergy get-together, Lewis informed Sciafe of how impressed he was with Lester Kinsolving, and how he'd be serving as a pastor in his diocese. Bishop Sciafe warned him, "You'd better watch out." It was apparent that, after the national scandal of "Damnable Doctrine of Damnation," 95 percent of the bishops had put Kinsolving on their black list. Only one would come to his aid, several months later in California.

Two weeks went by, without a word from Kansas. Finally, a telegram came, signed by A. Lewis, stating that the offer had been withdrawn. With much distress, Les told Sylvia, who burst into tears. "That was," Les recalls, "one of the lowest points in my creation." The Rev. David A. Works wrote Les, Bishop Hall, and Rev. Sam Taylor a letter, after finding out about the resignation from St. Andrew's: "Les is a good guy who needs some type of discipline . . . if he gets this, I can see him having a useful life. If not, he won't amount to much."

Shortly after, Les received a call from Bishop Appie Lawrence of Western Massachusetts, who learned they needed help at Grace Church in Providence, Rhode Island. Their rector had recently passed away, and they wondered if he could fulfill an interim position after another clergy member retired. Since his resignation from St. Andrew's "stipulated on or before April 1," Les jumped at this offer, which would begin on February 5, 1962. His duties would include assisting Assistant Pastor Fred Kirby.

Moving to another town was very tough on Laura, now seven years old. She was scared of the "huge house in 'ugly' Providence," and had to adjust to another first-grade classroom after leaving New London very abruptly. She remembers "running home from school one day, desperate to know from Mom what a sentence was." Tommy, four, and Kathleen, who'd just turned two, were still young enough not to suffer such hardships.

Sylvia began to realize that she might not play the role of the parish priest's wife for the rest of her life, and wondered how long Lester's assignment might last, after she attempted some inquisitive cordiality with Rev. Kirby during a church social. His response was, "You ask a lot of questions!" It was a warning of the trouble that lay ahead.

Les began calling on Episcopalians in Providence who hadn't gone to church in years. They were most grateful for the visits, and when they returned to Grace Church on Sundays, they expressed to Rev. Kirby how kind and attentive the new priest was. After the services, they raved to Rev. Kirby how much they loved Kinsolving's sermons. Kirby, whom Les considered to be "a rotten preacher," always printed his entire sermon in the church bulletin. With a burgeoning grudge, he refused to print any of Lester's sermons. Unwilling to tolerate this abuse any longer, Les preached a sermon on May 6, which later got him fired. It was entitled "Who Spake by the Prophets," a quote from the Nicene Creed:

> . . . In today's ministry there are just too many men who volunteer for the priesthood while leaving the mantel of prophecy gathering dust in some neglected back closet. This is done because it is (1) much safer, (2) much easier. . . . What is wanted in too many churches is an amiable, dignified, machine-oiling, King-of-clichés who will keep the Holy Ghost ghostly, the preaching platitudinous and the spirit of the living Christ locked safely in the sacristy. What too many churches demand today is by no means a moral leader—but a round-collared, or plain-tied, country club manager. . . .

Ironically, Les also preached on the following: "Part of today's tragedy in the Christian religion is that most of the prophets are not in pulpits. Many of them are in editorial rooms, making the news rather than merely quoting it when it is safe and acceptable."

The following Thursday, Lester was called into Kirby's office, where he was greeted by the fuming pastor and senior warden. "We're bringing in a seminary student," Kirby growled at him, "so we won't need your services any longer." It was a blessed relief to leave, although terrible uncertainty lay ahead for the Kinsolving family.

By the end of May 1962, Les, Sylvia, and their three young children packed up the car and a small trailer, and headed toward Marshall, Texas, where Lester's younger brother, William, was celebrating a June wedding. William, now a professional actor with Ashland Shakespeare Festival in Oregon, had met and fallen in love with a brilliant young actress named Anne, who played most of the leading roles at Ashland. They were quite a fetching couple at their wedding—William dressed in gloves and tails, and Anne adorned in a stylish 1960s gown and veil. Laura was thrilled to be the flower girl, throwing daisies as she walked down the aisle, while Tommy held the coveted pillow bearing the ring.

Lester was delighted to officiate his kid brother's wedding, although his heart was sinking. He wasn't certain as to exactly what his future role would be in the Episcopal Church. Leaving Sylvia and the children in Phoenix at the vacant Bishop's House, Les made his return to California in July, where James A. Pike was now serving as Bishop at San Francisco's Grace Cathedral. Like the Rev. Hamilton Aulenbach in Philadelphia, who considered Les his "son," Pike would prove to be another mentor. He was a heroic, powerful man who possessed the guts of a saint.

Bishop Pike took Lester under his wing, and gave him the assignment of one new and one old mission, starting in the fall. St. David's and St. John's were located in Pittsburg and Clayton Valley in the East Bay. Les made a temporary home in Russian River at Nid Amor, the cabin his father-in-law had built, and where he and Sylvia stayed on their honeymoon. He became reacquainted with old friend Ernie Joiner, editor for the *Sebastopol Times*, and worked during the summer writing general assignments and selling ads for the paper.

Back in Phoenix, Edith Kinsolving assured neighbors that the three children were safe in the Bishop's House without their father: "Don't worry; those children will make enough noise to scare any burglar away!" She decided her daughter-in-law deserved a little treat, after all she'd endured since the burning of the church in Pasco. She was aware that legendary film star John Wayne would be appearing in Phoenix, for a zoo benefit to promote his new film, *Hatari!* It was all about men hunting wild animals in Africa and selling them to zoos.

After Edith pulled a few strings, Sylvia was given the honor of greeting Mr. Wayne at the airport. Surprised that his family didn't come along for the trip, Sylvia politely asked him about it. "Oh, the kids have chicken pox!" he exclaimed. Sylvia was shocked to learn that a movie star of his caliber would have to cope with such realities, like any average Joe.

In September 1962, Lester sent for his family, settling them in Pittsburg, and began his work with the two mission churches. Times were rough at St. David's, where, as Les recalls, "two terrible 'Lay Popes' tried to run everything." When Les resisted their compulsion to control, they walked out. It was equally difficult at St. John's, where a nearby rector believed the mission was taking members of his congregation. In a retaliatory gesture, parishioners of this parish heckled Lester at the Bishop's Committee Meeting.

In the midst of this backbiting, Les had much success with another of his fund-raising parodies, *Schmoklahoma!* Produced by the Episcopal Youth Union of St. John's and the Young People of St. David's, its proceeds went to Henry Ohlhoff House, an alcoholic rehabilitation center in San Francisco. *Schmoklahoma!* contained such characters as Sweet Mother McCreep, Olive Pitts, Lucifer "Lucky" Pieceapizza, and Lodestone Squat.

Sung to the tune of "Oh, What a Beautiful Morning," the opening song went as follows:

There's a bright golden haze on the meadow
We don't care about things in the meadow
The corn may be high as an elephant's eye
But the elephant's eye ain't as high as am I

Oh what a potent martini
Oh what a glorious drink
That elephant's color is changing
It's growing progressively pink.

The show ran through February 1963, and toured up and down the California coast. In a photo of the cast and proud director, a large

Gadfly

Schmoklahoma! banner was draped over the tour bus, with the words "Los Angeles!!" written on top. It would be a welcome escape from the difficulties of running the two missions.

By 1964, Les consulted with Bishop Pike about the many troubles he'd experienced with St. David's and St. John's. Pike decided to relocate him to Salinas where Church of the Holy Spirit, another mission, needed a new vicar. He also gave him the opportunity to work with the *Pacific Churchman* as assistant editor.

Shortly after, Les attended a diocesan convention and was confronted by the "holy terror" who ran St. Paul's, a large, established Episcopal church located in downtown Salinas. This bullying rector barked orders at Lester and attacked his political work and his controversial sermons. He even told Les, "If you speak like that in Salinas, I'll fix your wagon." An outraged Kinsolving fired back: "If you put your foot in Northern Salinas, I'll chop it off!!"

Concerned with these kinds of conflicts, which he'd suffered throughout his ministry, Lester decided to seek counseling. He wanted to figure out how much a part he played in them and resolve the matter entirely. The diocese provided such medical services to clergy, and so Les made an appointment with a psychiatrist. Her name was Freidi Heisler.

By the third visit, Lester rejoiced that he'd come to the right person. He was very comfortable with Freidi, and they had wonderful conversations. However, he was getting restless, wondering when they were going to get to the heart of the matter. Finally, he gathered enough courage to ask, "When do we actually start the psychoanalysis?" Hearing this, Freidi threw back her head and let forth peals of laughter. Les was surprised, but reassured when she asked him, "Do you know how many notes that I've taken so far?"

It was during the sixth visit that Les was confronted with a searing question, which would change the direction of his life forever. In a previous session, he'd described to Freidi that while giving communion in the church in Pasco several years ago, a thought struck him: "Is this what I'm really meant to do?" It was terrifying, and he resisted it. However, the thought was beginning to scratch at him during services once again. It was then that Lester related to Freidi how guilty he felt about it.

Like a skilled surgeon with a knife, the psychiatrist quietly asked him, "Why do you feel guilty?" Lester fell silent. It was an even more terrifying question than the one he grappled with at the altar years ago. He went away from the session quite shaken, realizing that he wouldn't betray his family if he left the Episcopal Church and searched for his true calling. Freidi had unlocked a wonderful truth and an incredible freedom, and he would be forever indebted to her. Lester's days as a parish priest would soon be dwindling.

At Church of the Holy Spirit, Lester continued the controversy, preaching on migrant workers' rights during the grape boycott in California. He displayed his unwavering support for César Chávez, although it rattled some members of his congregation. He also played the role of First Gangster in the Salinas Performing Art production of *Kiss Me, Kate*. Kathleen, now four, watched in bewilderment as her father, the vicar of Church of the Holy Spirit, entered from the wings in a foot-tall headdress and cracked a thunderously loud whip, scaring the daylights out of audience and cast members alike.

In the play program, his theatrical bio read as follows:

Among his previous roles, a bloodthirsty grandfather in *The Petrified Forest*, a murderous lech in *Billy the Kid*, an atheist (Clarence Darrow in *Inherit the Wind*), an agnostic (Greenwald in *The Caine Mutiny*), and . . . a perfectly amoral neer-do-well: Alfred P. Doolittle in *My Fair Lady*. He wonders if he's becoming type cast!

In March 1965, Les volunteered with twenty other clergy members to join Martin Luther King, Jr., in the Selma to Montgomery march. He caught an all-night train to Montgomery for the final day, where he met up with 25,000 marchers in a Catholic school stadium. Les would walk side by side with Assemblyman John Knox of Richmond, and carry the state flag which was donated to the California delegation by Congressmen Phil Burton and Jeffery Cohelan.

Gadfly

Before Lester left for the trip, he made an addition to his will, in case anything happened to him. His fears were confirmed when train conductors told the marchers to close the window shutters, so they wouldn't be shot at. The Alabama state guard was there to protect them when they joined the march, but they couldn't help them avoid the shouting and screaming from the white southern mob at the train station in Montgomery.

During the overnight trip, Les became quite amicable with a fellow marcher, disagreeing agreeably with him on the subject of damnation. He was a Lutheran professor who didn't share Lester's viewpoint, at least on this particular subject. They were, however, united in the fight for civil rights.

As they walked from the train to the stadium, the professor was pulled away by the violent faction of the mob, and beaten so severely that he was rushed to the hospital. They were also informed of the murder of Viola Liuzzo, a mother of five and fellow activist, by the Ku Klux Klan.

As all marchers gathered at the state capital with Martin Luther King, Jr., Lester heard many powerful and inspiring speeches. However, there were those who delivered hateful words, lashing out at the entire white race. This was awkward, considering there were so many whites present who had risked their lives that day. It gave Les a terrible feeling, knowing that the eloquent and spiritual message of Dr. King might be overshadowed by such destructive and irrational rage.

Returning home safely to his family, Les continued as vicar with the mission and began research on an article he was writing for the *Pacific Churchman*. To his chagrin, he discovered that rectors were getting three to four times the salary as assistant rectors, along with bigger car allowances. He felt a duty to expose this injustice and submitted the article for publication. The editor, and a number of rectors who were receiving these large salaries, read Lester's article, and, knowing that Bishop Pike was safely overseas in Israel for six months, terminated Les's employment with the *Pacific Churchman*.

On November 5, 1965, Lester wrote the following letter to Scott Newhall, executive editor of the *San Francisco Chronicle*:

I am interested in working part-time for The Chronicle . . . I would like to continue in the parochial ministry in this mission church, which is small enough to allow me time for what I would conceive to be a part time, worker-priest function in the field of communications. . . .

Although tentative at first, Lester was well on his way to fulfilling a dream. This time, it would be his own.

9

From Pulpit to Press Room

TWO WEEKS LATER, Managing Editor Gordon Pates responded to Les, after he received his inquiry from Newhall:

> I may be able to able to use you on a one-day-a-week basis to cover religious news . . . the publisher will want to know just what type of thing you intend to do and will be most concerned that you will be fair to all denominations in your reporting. . . .

Pates requested a sample article of 750 words, which Les submitted with a cover letter, on November 25:

> I have tried assiduously to avoid any editorializing, and confine myself to reporting news. . . . I do wish to tell you . . . how profoundly grateful I am for all the time you have devoted . . . as well as to consideration to the possibility of my working for you at the *Chronicle*.

The article covered three topics, including "The New Morality," "Pope Paul VI Contemplates Contraceptives," and "Resurrection through Refrigeration." The next month, Pates wrote back, saying, "Just as Pope Paul is pondering the subject of birth control with glacial speed before making a pronouncement for the laity, so is your column being pondered on the more rarified executive levels of *The Chronicle*."

In January 1966, another letter from Pates came, much to Lester's relief:

> If you still have the will to, write me about 500 words on each of these [three] subjects so that we have separate columns. I will then introduce them at the curial level in some diplomatic fashion and maybe we can get the show on the road again. However, if you have lost all interest due to the passage of time and become a Trappist Monk out of sheer despair, I will understand. . . .

Although Pates informed Les that "our version of the Vatican is still wrestling with the problem of a religious column by Kinsolving" in February, by March he sent along the good news: "I will hire you as a part-time reporter on a temporary basis until we see whether the project is working out to everyone's satisfaction."

An elated Lester saw his first "News in Religion" column published in the *Chronicle* on March 19, 1966—its headline, "Catholicism and Birth Control."

> Pope Paul removed discussion of the subject from the Vatican Council to this commission. He also expressed to the United Nations his opposition to "artificial birth control, which would be irrational." In contrast to the widespread enthusiasm evoked by his visit to the United States, this statement on birth control was received with regret by non-Catholics. . . .

A week later, "The Jazz Mass Movement" reported how "some church members" regarded this new musical phenomenon as a "sincere and deliberately contrived stunt, designed for the sole purpose of attracting crowds" by including "guitar playing, drum beating and rock singing in church services." This prompted a lively letter to the editor from Lester's friend and cohort, the Rev. Robert W. Cromey of San Francisco:

> I have told him to his face so I can tell you that I regard his writing style as that of an "ecclesiastical Lucius Beebe." His funny but inappropriate illustration about [stripper] Carol Doda playing Salome Dancing the Seven Veils is a case in point. . . .

Father Cromey ended his epistle with a blessing: "I do hope we will hear more from Mr. Kinsolving. He has much to say that is creative, and that is grist for dialogue and wild disagreement." The colorful Cromey, whom Les nicknamed "Barnum Bob," was a fellow vicar and, according to Lester, "a kindred spirit, since he was always making news." They also shared an insatiable desire to outwit each other's pranks. During one summer's retreat at the Bishop's Ranch, the incorrigible Cromey lit a small fire underneath Lester's chaise lounge.

After his third weekly column, "Refrigeration—and Resurrection" appeared on April 9, several others were published through June, including: "The Parish Church May Be Dying," "Right Wingers in Episcopal Church," and "Film about Christ by a Communist." By July 1966, *Chronicle* editors felt they had a sure thing in this fiery worker-priest and offered him a permanent position on their staff.

While Laura, Tommy, and Kathleen played in the park during a summer family outing, Les pleaded with a hesitant Sylvia to move back to the Bay Area. He was ready to resign from Church of the Holy Spirit and begin his new career as a full-time journalist. Sylvia gave her consent, as long as they relocated to her native Berkeley, where she could be near her parents. She prayed that Les would settle down and that this would be their final move.

Beginning his early morning commute to the San Francisco–Oakland Bay Bridge in August 1966, Lester made his way to the *Chronicle* offices at 5th and Mission Streets, located near the Tenderloin section of San Francisco. According to a local tour guide, the

Tenderloin got its nickname from the police officers who could afford better cuts of meat, since they were paid a bonus for patrolling this crime-ridden area.

The *Chronicle* newsroom, a large gallery filled with steel desks and manual typewriters, was a real "cesspool" in Lester's eyes. It was cluttered with messy, dirty piles, and the walls were adorned with old, dilapidated posters. In spite of the dreary work environment, Les was surrounded by such featured columnists as Herb Caen, Arthur Hoppe, Charles McCabe, and Terence O'Flaherty. One, in particular, was filled with "elfin mischief." He was John L. Wasserman, an entertainment critic who was fairly new to the *Chronicle,* having written his first film review for the paper in 1964.

Since Kinsolving and Wasserman's desks were located in close proximity, they began a long exchange of nonstop needling. At one point, John L. cleaned out Lester's desk, leaving the phone unplugged. As soon as John walked away from his desk, Les launched a counterattack and hid everything in Wasserman's desk. The antics continued over the airwaves, when the two were simultaneously offered their own talk shows on San Francisco's KCBS Radio.

Driving his family to a party one evening in the city, Lester tuned in to John's show, where they heard the host gossiping about his collar-wearing colleague. He even went so far as to perform an impersonation of Kinsolving, making him sound like an overbearing buffoon. As the board lit up, a caller was put through, exclaiming how "wonderful and marvelous the Rev. Lester Kinsolving truly is," and that "I listen to his radio program and read his column every week—I wouldn't miss him for the world!!" That left Wasserman speechless—and a gleeful Lester giggling in triumph.

Besides his fight to abolish the death penalty, Les's other passionate cause involved a woman's right to choose. In his April 2 column, "Therapeutic Abortion . . . Past and Current Views," Les reported how Catholics who adhered to Pope Pius XI's *Casti Connubi* regarded "any kind of abortion as a form of infanticide. They consider their duty to oppose any change in the present law as being the equivalent of saving the life of any child—regardless of denomination."

By July, 1966, Les was appointed vice president of the California Committee on Therapeutic Abortion, and joined with Bishop Pike to change the "archaic and evil law" that had prohibited state-wide legal abortions in 1873. He would preach these words in a televised weekday service at Grace Cathedral in September, where Pike read prayers "for the nine physicians under investigation by the State Board of Medical Examiners for performing therapeutic abortions on victims of German measles," according to *San Francisco Examiner* reporter Clint Mosher.

When interviewed on Radio KMJ's "Direct Answer" in Fresno, Les responded to those who alleged that abortion was murder: "Of course the embryo has life . . . so has the sperm, and so has the placenta . . . by what possible stratagem can you say this (unborn child) is a human being, a citizen of California, when it's something you have to have a microscope to find?"

With the help of a petition containing 3,000 signatures from clergymen, lawyers, and doctors, the 1966 California legislature passed the first law to allow abortions to victims of rape, incest, or if their pregnancies threatened their lives. It was a landmark victory that Lester celebrated, having done his part in delivering speeches, collecting signatures, and participating in debates with six different Jesuits. Seven years later, the cause achieved national success, in the 1973 Supreme Court decision of *Roe v. Wade*.

In October 1966, a meeting was held in Wheeling, West Virginia, by the Episcopal House of Bishops. Led by Southern Florida's Bishop Henry Louttit, an archconservative, the bishops made a motion to censure one of their brethren, James A. Pike. Pike's theology was becoming far too "radical" for the doctrines of the Episcopal Church; he questioned the Virgin Birth, the Trinity, and the existence of Hell. Furthermore, he was known to advocate "fewer beliefs, more belief."

Pike wasn't alone. As reported by United Press International (UPI) on October 25, "Bishop Henry Louttit . . . sought unsuccessfully today to get the Episcopal House of Bishops to revoke the press credentials of a priest covering the bishops' meeting for the

San Francisco Chronicle." Louttit focused on Kinsolving's report that a potential heresy trial for Pike was a "drumhead court," since the accused had a mere ten minutes to tell his side.

Thankfully, the motion to oust Lester was tabled, and Pike was never tried for heresy, although he was censured. A promo for *Ramparts,* a Catholic literary quarterly, highlighted Lester's story, "The Bishop's Not for Burning," for its January 1967 issue:

> A penetrating investigation into the methodologies utilized in attaining a censure of Bishop James Pike. . . . Was the conduct of the censure proceeding an example of due process, or even minimal fairness? Was the conduct of Bishop Henry Louttit and his priest, the Reverend Frank Brunton of the John Birch Society, conduct that becomes a clergyman? Read the entire behind-the-scenes story in January *Ramparts.* . . .

Shortly afterward, James Pike resigned as Bishop of California and began work at the Center for the Study of Democratic Institutions in Santa Barbara. In 1969, while visiting the Holy Land, he and his new wife Diane went hiking through the Israeli desert. They became lost and decided to separate in search of help. Pike's body was discovered days later, after he had fallen from a steep ascent. He was found in a kneeling position, as if in prayer.

Lester would carry on the work of his beloved mentor, a man who was censured, but who was courageous enough to speak words that needed to be heard:

The poor may inherit the earth, but it would appear that the rich, or at least the rigid, respectable, and safe—will inherit the church.

We Cover Eternity

"THE REV. LESTER Kinsolving has little patience with what he calls injustices and pettiness in his church and has organized a clergy's union to change things," reported the *Santa Barbara News-Press* on December 31, 1966. After discovering that the $200 million pension fund was sending clergymens' widows only $153 a month, Les incorporated the Association of Episcopal Clergy. Other issues to tackle were the scant starting salary of $4,000 annually for priests, and a demand for unemployment insurance, "because if an Episcopal priest is without a church or a job in the church administration, he is on his own." Undoubtedly, Les could speak from his own troubling experiences in the parish priesthood.

Once again, an outspoken Lester received national media coverage, when the following was reported in Michigan's *Macomb Daily* in early 1967: "An Episcopal clergyman who is leading the battle against what he terms 'injustice behind the purple curtain' stopped briefly in Macomb County Tuesday, seeking help for clergyman in trouble in the stained-glass jungle." *Look* magazine was also interested and included Les's story in their February feature, "The Restless

Clergy." A photo of the Kinsolving family was included, along with the following caption: "Since we [the association] organized, he says, 'we have had a stabilizing effect. No one is in terror anymore. Vicars know they can't be shoved out,' although 'Bishop Clarence R. Haden of Northern California has advised that the priests' association is not welcome.' [Kinsolving] says, 'I do not worry that we are welcome. We are already there.'"

Even though the association garnered many members and news stories, its attempt to stage a picket line against C. Kilmer Myers, the new Episcopal Bishop of California, was unsuccessful. "We couldn't get enough people to organize against Myers, who was going after the Rev. Jim Kirchoffer, a vicar in Moraga." Regretfully, the association eventually folded.

In May 1967, Les was taken off his post in the Department of Social Relations for the California Episcopal Diocese. Although Bishop Myers retracted a statement that Lester's role "as a reporter for a daily newspaper" had interfered with his priestly duties, it was stated in one newspaper report that "several of Kinsolving's newspaper articles distressed church dignitaries." In truth, Lester's service with the diocese was no longer needed, after he helped with the passage of the Beilenson Therapeutic Abortion Act. As time progressed, Kinsolving and Myers would come to serious blows.

The summer of 1967, more popularly known as "The Summer of Love," became a worldwide, hippie-celebrating phenomenon after making its debut in San Francisco's Haight-Ashbury street scene. At downtown's Glide Memorial Church, the Rev. Cecil Williams held a special service in June, "protesting San Francisco officialdom's rejection of hippie visitors." The pastor invited such personalities as poet Lenora Kandel, author of *The Love Book*, to recite excerpts from her poem, "Circus":

EXPOSE YOURSELF!
ACCEPT THE CREATURE
AND BEGIN THE DANCE
CATCH ME!

Gadfly

I love you, I trust you
I love you . . .
CATCH ME!
Here I come, flying without wings
. . . WITHOUT A
SAFETY NET . . .

Les covered the spectacle for the *Chronicle*, reporting such high-lights as a nightclub singer's performance of "'Born Free,' scripture readings, passages quoted from Arthur Miller's *Death of a Salesman*," and, finally, a rendition of "The Battle Hymn of the Republic." The Rev. Mr. Williams proudly asserted, "The most important thing in the world has to be human beings . . . . Jesus had no hang-ups on whether a man smells or not, or whether he has lots of hair or is bald . . . . The meaning of being a free man is that we no longer have to worry about how men look."

Aside from the antics at Glide Memorial, Les reported on a "New Version of [The] Lord's Prayer" that was being implemented by the United Church of Christ:

One denomination has taken the bold step of an official rewrit-ing (or retranslation) of the classic prayer. "Keep us clear of temptation," says the new version. . . "Forgive us our debts" substitutes "sins" for "debts" (debts by no means being intrin-sically sinful—but the means by which most Californians are housed) . . . .

Another story, "Jesus—Pacifist or Revolutionary?" concerned *Jesus and the Zealots* by Professor S.G.F. Brandon, who taught Comparative Religion at England's University of Manchester:

Brandon's most striking contention . . . that Jesus' image as a pacifist . . . was manufactured by the authors of the Gospels according to St. Matthew and St. Mark. They were written, he contends, after the Zealots had brought about the disastrous slaughter and fall of Jerusalem. . . . [Brandon] regards Jesus' admonition "Take up thy cross and follow me" as being directly related to the fact that the Cross was a symbol of Zealot sacrifice before it was transformed into the sign of Christian Salvation.

Since Lester was now firmly ensconced as a full-time worker-priest, he displayed a large sign at his desk at the *Chronicle* which made the following pronouncement: "WE COVER ETERNITY." It paid tribute to all reporters of religion, although he took them to task, in an interview: "there should be more hard-hitting religion writers; after all, our beat is the best—we cover eternity."

As the Summer of Love's escapades drew to a close and winter descended upon the Bay Area, the Kinsolvings sent their annual Christmas greeting to friends and family, which included the following news:

> One night this month, Sylvia found posted on the refrigerator the following theses:
>
> ### THE FIGHT OATH
> "I, Tommy Kinsolving, solemnly swer to not butt in to Laura's and Kathleen's fights. Sighned, Tommy Kinsolving."
> "I, Kathleen Kinsolving, promise not to butt into Laura's or Tommy's fights. Sighed. Kathleen Kinsolving." "I, Laura Kinsolving, solemnly swear not to butt into fights between my brother and sister—unless a terrible violence is going on."
>
> And so, as Christmas approaches, there appears to be a remote possibility of relative Peace on Earth and Good Will among the young men and women in the Kinsolving home in the hills of Berkeley. And may it be with you also.

On Saturday, April 6, 1968, the *San Francisco Chronicle* reported tragic news: "Grieving Catholic, Protestant, Jewish, and Orthodox leaders will conduct an extraordinary memorial service tomorrow for

Dr. Martin Luther King. . . . This 'Interfaith Memorial Service of Penance' was devised . . . after the news from Memphis."

Immediately following the Sunday service at Grace Cathedral, a procession of 4,000 mourners marched silently through the streets of the city, after hearing the sermon preached by Bishop Myers: "Whites, because of their vicious racism . . . have brought death to a sainted follower of the Prince of Peace. . . . " Myers, along with Episcopal Bishop Richard Millard and Archbishop Joseph T. McGucken, followed behind Lester, who held the California flag he had carried in the 1964 Selma–Montgomery March.

A few weeks later, Les exposed clergy who were not willing to practice Dr. King's message of nonviolence, most notably Rev. Albert B. Cleage, Jr., pastor of Central United Church of Christ in Detroit: "One thing I don't want you to forget today: Dr. King was killed by a white man . . . so don't go around and apologize . . . . He believed in the goodness of white folk and America. There he lies dead." There was also Bishop Angus Dun, who "presided over a committee that censured Bishop Pike for 'vulgarizations of great expressions of faith,'" but "preached a sermon in which he drew a comparison between Rap Brown and the prophet Isaiah."

Although the Rev. Ralph Abernathy stated that "Black power is not violence," Lester asserted that "certain aspects of the black power movement" were "being run by maniacs," such as "Rap Brown, Stokely Carmichael, Eldridge Cleaver and Ron Karenga. . . . One of the many problems with liberals today is that they don't recognize this fact and they take the attitude that—'if it's black it must be good.'"

Lester spoke these words to the press after delivering a guest sermon at his father's former post, Calvary Episcopal Church, in Pittsburgh, Pennsylvania. A few days later, he received a grateful letter: "In today's Post-Gazette, you said something that should have been said long ago, that Rap Brown, Stokely Carmichael, Eldridge Cleaver and Ron Karenga are 'maniacs.' This is exactly what they are and they should be treated as such."

Later that April, "The Free City," a hippie group formerly known as "The Diggers," made an appearance on the steps of San Francisco's

City Hall. They were there to recite poetry, in an attempt to expand their Haight-Ashbury mission into other vicinities of the city. Over at the *Chronicle*, Les received a tip "that a group of hippies was going to ask some Catholic nuns and priests out for a 'love feast.'" By the time Lester and photographer Jerry Telfer arrived at City Hall, a group of about forty nuns, who were visiting from Bakersfield and attending a Catholic convention nearby, had gathered and were listening to the poetic recitations.

One Free City member, in an effort to liberate his body of all worldly restrictions, suddenly stripped nude in front of the astonished sisters, who quickly ran down the street. As Kinsolving and Telfer stood by, the naked hippie, seventeen-year-old Terry Lee Kinley, walked down the steps of City Hall and began to march on Grove Street. Prompted by Telfer, who saw a juicy photo op, Lester quickly caught up with Kinley and reported the following:

> He got all the way to Fillmore Street and then doubled back to Gough Street before he was arrested. . . . During the 13 blocks of total exposure, reactions to Kinley by pedestrians and motorists were varied. Kinley walked resolutely, his hair flowing in the wind. Some witnesses stared straight ahead, angrily refusing to acknowledge him. Others grinned and shrugged their shoulders. And only one onlooker cried, "Only in San Francisco!"

As Lester walked alongside the threadbare young man, Jerry quickly snapped photos, one of which would later appear in *Time* magazine. While they waited for the light to change at Fillmore and Grove Street, Les asked Terry, "Why exactly are you doing this?" He was greeted with a philosophical response: "I'm making a point—I characterize myself as a 'man of nature.'"

After his arrest, Kinley proudly proclaimed, "I want the publicity. I want to be on national TV." During his booking at the Department of Justice, two Free City members, "Ana" and "Marty," wandered into the Catholic convention at the Civic Center, and announced at the speakers' platform that they had "apples and salami to share" with the 12,000 attendees. They were then referred to the convention office, but fled after the auditorium manager was called.

Word quickly spread through the newspaper channels about Lester's April 19 story, "A Startling Nude 'Walk-in.'" He soon received a call from Chronicle Features Syndicate, which informed him that there were editors interested in running his column. Being such an adept salesman at one time, Les decided to make appointments with papers all over the country, and go on the road to sell the column. An advertisement also appeared in *Editor and Publisher*, which featured the now-famous photo of Lester's long walk with the naked hippie. It included the heading, "A NEW DIMENSION IN RELIGIOUS REPORTING."

In the fall of 1968, another promo appeared, headlined with the question, "WHY IS REV. LESTER KINSOLVING NOW AMERICA'S NO. 1 RELIGION COLUMNIST?" with its answer, "BECAUSE HE GETS INSIDE 'THE STAINED GLASS JUNGLE,'" directly under a photo of Lester in between two guards. The caption read:

The Rev. Mr. Kinsolving, the man in the middle not trying to conceal his identity, is forcibly removed from Denver's St. John's Cathedral Parish Hall by guards employed by a court of nine Episcopal Bishops, after he broke the story of why they were holding a closed trial of the Bishop of Colorado.

Previously, Les exposed Bishop Joseph Minnis, who was "charged with repeated public drunkenness and sexual misconduct in six states and Juarez, Mexico." As Les covered the trial in Denver, the bishops holding the trial ordered that the court be cleared, an illegal act under canon law. Les refused to leave and was physically ousted from the parish hall. He then sought help from a lawyer, who contacted a judge, who then demanded the bishops open the trial.

When Les returned, the court had adjourned, since, they stated, Bishop Minnis had fled the state. "They let him go," Lester recalls, "and they never followed up on it." In his letter sent to the *Chronicle* on September 24, Rev. Richard Thrumston of Christ Episcopal Church in Canon City, CO, castigated Lester for his "aggressive reporting," which he claimed was not "consistent with the respect for authority. . . . I think you should give serious consideration to a renunciation of your orders."

The *Houston Post* would be the first syndicated paper to publish Lester's features. They ran the following promotional on June 16th, 1968:

THE WORLD OF RELIGION

Starting this Sunday, the controversial Reverend LESTER KIN-SOLVING will write a weekly column for The Houston Post . . . no subject is inviolable of his personal close scrutiny. He brings a unique point of view to society's most debatable topics. With the candor of a man who's seen many sides to many stories, he writes about religion for today's world. . . .

Les was able to meet with editors on the road while he covered religious events for the *Chronicle*. At one point, he sold his column to four papers in one day, including the *Virginian-Pilot* in Norfolk. With a photo of the worker-priest busily studying his latest copy, the ad ran with an enticing message: "Reverend Kinsolving writes a weekly column on the big moral and religious issues of our times. It appears in *The Virginian-Pilot*. Watch for it."

That July, the Kinsolvings made a trip to Hawaii, where Les covered the Western Jurisdictional Conference of the United Methodist Church. In the *Honolulu Advertiser*'s interview, "RELIGION BEAT DULL? NOT TO 'REV.'," Lester explained to reporter John Bilby how he'd broken the recent story of Bishop Myers demanding Grace Cathedral Dean Julian Bartlett's resignation "in an ecclesiastical power struggle. . . . The Bishop is trying to get control of Grace Cathedral properties worth $9 million to build a high-rise retirement home. . . . 'Of course, when I report things like that, they don't like it at all.'"

He also mentioned the time when State Senator (and future San Francisco Mayor) George Moscone "came in and tried to kill my story" that was to run on page 3 of the *San Francisco Chronicle*. It was all about "a couple of Catholic priests' testimony at an obscure obscenity trial."

Executive Editor Scott Newhall "called me in and asked me about it. After I told him the details, and showed him the proof, he phoned the city desk and ordered, 'Put Les Kinsolving's story on Page One—in a box.' Then he turned to me and said, 'Call up George, Les, and politely tell him to get lost!' Newhall was one of the truly great editors," Les remembers. "They don't make them like him anymore."

The *Houston Post* received a number of letters to the editor after Lester's column began appearing in June: "Rev. Lester Kinsolving's World of Religion article appears to belittle the importance of baptism when he refers to it as a 'public dunking' . . . such disrespect is shocking" . . . "Kinsolving's column suggesting moral liberality is totally offensive. A church is not a church if it would permit degeneracy, promiscuity, and homicide" . . . "I think I might sue you. I laughed so hard at Lester Kinsolving's satirical article about Southern Baptist's new president, W.A. Criswell that I hurt myself. The piece was well done and painfully honest. You are to be applauded for publishing it."

Despite a heavy schedule of traveling and selling the column across the country, Lester was still able to cover local stories, including the latest events in San Francisco:

Services at Grace Cathedral were brusquely interrupted yesterday when a group of 20 burlap-garbed, long-haired young people took over the sanctuary and called down the wrath of the Biblical prophet Jeremiah on the startled congregation . . . the cathedral echoed with the sharp cracking of the eight-foot-tall wooden shafts they rapped on the concrete floor. . . . One youth, his face covered with ghostly ashes like the others, angrily read a long scroll while another smashed an empty flower pot to the floor. . . . Bishop Myers said he had no idea who they were, nor what the purpose of the visit was—but they were colorful.

Later that year, an updated ad ran in *Editor and Publisher*: "A PHE-NOMENAL SUCCESS: Rev. Lester Kinsolving is now appearing in 103 newspapers in the United States and Canada with over 9 million actual circulation." The promotional then posed provocative questions to interested editors: "Is your church page a wasteland of free advertising for church notices? Is your coverage of the revolutionary world of religion incisive and hard-hitting, or is it vague and timid? Rev. Kinsolving knows the inside of the church like no layman possibly could." Because the *Chronicle* was so pleased, they nominated Les for the Pulitzer Prize, in the category of "Distinguished criticism or commentary."

The *Atlanta Journal, Tucson Daily Citizen,* and *Arlington Heights Herald* were added to the list of papers syndicating Lester's column, and ran their own testimonials: "The column is no ordinary religion column, as Rev. Kinsolving is no ordinary clergyman" . . . "He is not awed by the ecclesiastical 'brass.' He knows the questions to ask and is not afraid to ask them" . . . "Religion and morals are essential elements of American life and thought. Lester Kinsolving is a needed stimulant." By the close of 1969, over 200 papers had entered the fold.

On January 10, 1970, Lester's column, "An Unbelievable Day on a Campus," told all about his experience of being kicked off the campus of South Carolina's Bob Jones University. Promoting itself as an institution with an "intensely Christian atmosphere," it nevertheless "applied to the government of South Carolina for permission to equip its campus guards with submachine guns." Lester "had special cause to be grateful to South Carolina authorities for refusing this request."

Shortly after his arrival at the university, Les asked two students why other students were playing soccer in a football stadium:

"Years ago," explained the student, "a visiting football team left beer cans and cigarette butts in the dressing room. So now we play with ourselves—intramural club teams." Asking if I might look at a student handbook to see the campus rules, another of the invariably smiling, polite and well-dressed students replied, "Certainly, I'll arrange it immediately. Won't you have a seat?" Three minutes later the two squad cars arrived.

When placed in one of the cars, Lester asked exactly what offense he had committed. As they drove up to the front gate, the guards informed him that he was guilty of "interviewing students," and told him "to be gone." Two months later, Les received a certified letter from Mrs. Ward Andersen, who stated, "Someone has sent Bob Jones University a clipping from the February 28, 1970 *Casper Star Tribune* in which you were interviewed about Bob Jones University and made this statement, 'I'll be back, however; but next time I'll bring a large detective agency with me.'"

Mrs. Andersen enclosed a prepared statement, along with the warning, "so that you'll know what to expect should you decide to return":

> Mr. Kinsolving did not come to get the facts about Bob Jones University. He came just as all the other liberal newsmen come—wagging their liberal tails behind them . . . in addition to this, Kinsolving has an added disadvantage that most newsmen do not have—he is an unbelieving, Episcopalian, worker-priest, one of the many such clergymen who repeat a creed every week they do not believe . . . . Unholy men have unholy manners which they rudely display . . . we want it to be known if he comes again, he will not only be escorted from the campus but he will also be escorted to the city jail and booked on charges of trespassing.

This type of militant religious devotion could also be found in the world of Eastern spirituality, which Les featured in another column, "Those Chanting Krishna Monks." Describing the Krishnas as "groups of young men and women dressed in peach-colored sheets with their heads shaven, [they] are attracting considerable attention as they dance and endlessly chant: 'Hare Krishna, Hare Krishna, Krishna Krishna, Hare Hare. . . .'"

At the University of California at Berkeley, Babulazza Das, "current leader of the newly acquired house that is the Krishna Consciousness Temple . . . explained that he has been chanting for nearly two years—'We try to chant 24 hours a day. When you say Krishna's name anywhere, he actually becomes present in that sound vibration.'" Delighted by this assertion, Lester couldn't resist: "Whether Krishna is absent or displeased unless he is summoned and adored by the repetitious lung power of his devotees was not explained by Das. . . . "

Les also included some interesting facts of Krishna history:

> Southern California was well-perceived by another Krishna: a barefooted "Reincarnation of Adam" and "The Messiah" who, in 1949, established his own colony, "The Fountain of the World," in Los Angeles' San Fernando Valley. Krishna Venta's colony thrived—until 1958—when he made the mistake of issuing a Messianic order that all of the colony's wives were henceforth to "cleave only to him." Two of his male disciples strongly resented their spouses being so recruited—even to a Messianic harem. They manifested their displeasure with 20 sticks of dynamite, dispatching themselves and Krishna into an instant Nirvana. Only the Messiah's false teeth survived the explosion.

In addition, Les disclosed Krishna Venta's rap sheet, which "included seven convictions in five states: petty larceny, petty theft, vagrancy, burglary, sending threatening letters to the President of the United States, bad checks, non-payment of alimony and violation of the Mann Act."

On November 2, 1970, Lester's column, "Episcopal Decision Called Fateful," ran in the *World News* of Roanoke, Virginia. It caused quite a fury among two local clergymen, whose letter to the editor appeared on November 10. Rev. Charles Newberry and Rev. Frank Vest, both cardinal rectors in Roanoke, stated that they "[found] his column full of gross distortion and snide innuendo which has no justification either in his profession as a priest of the Episcopal Church or as a journalist."

Lester had recently attended the General Convention of the Episcopal Church in Houston, and reported in the column that "Since

1967, the GCSP [General Convention Special Program] has funded enough racially segregated organizations that the court and police records of officers and staffers of recipients of these funds would fill a good sized edition of the old police gazette." One particular group was the Black Economic Development Conference, which "demanded 'reparations' for black people from the nation's white churches and synagogues."

Printed alongside Newberry and Vest's letter was a rebuttal from Kinsolving, where he took the two rectors to task in that "they did not provide a single specific example to substantiate such grave charges" of "gross distortion" and "snide innuendo."

Lester challenged them to a debate on November 19th, when he would be traveling to Roanoke. Newberry and Vest (upon advice from Bishop William Marmion of the Diocese of Southwestern Virginia) refused, suggesting instead that they meet in private. Les felt that this matter "could not be resolved privately, since his honor and reputation as a priest and as a journalist were at stake." He went ahead and arranged a public forum at the Hotel Roanoke where he would discuss the General Convention and "answer criticism recently directed at his reporting."

As Lester delivered his comments at a podium, two empty chairs sat on top of the table he was speaking from. He addressed the audience of 200 Episcopalians, stating, "I don't see how Bishop Marmion can ever again be taken seriously as a moral leader, in view of the fact that he persisted in advising these two clergy to add cowardice to their ecclesiastical McCarthyism in remaining in hiding tonight. . . . Did they ask Bishop Marmion whether he approved of their public attack on me?"

In closing, Les urged his fellow Episcopalians not to cancel pledges because of the church's policies of supporting these groups, "since the people who are hurt by such withholding of funds are missionaries on small salaries."

At the end of 1970, Lester's column was now nationally syndicated in over 250 newspapers. In September, he had taken the opportunity to transfer from Chronicle Feature Syndicate to National Newspaper Syndicate, which would take effect the following January. Although his editors Scott Newhall and Gordon Pates were extremely pleased with Les's success, there was one who wasn't. City Editor Abe Melinkoff, a career journalist who had spent over thirty years at the *Chronicle* was, in Lester's words, "one of the dirtiest people I ever ran into; he ruled the roost of reporters, played favorites, and was jealous as hell of me." Melinkoff deeply resented that his own column, "City Notes," was syndicated in only five papers, as compared to Les's 200 plus.

"Melinkoff was constantly criticizing my column," Les recalls, "even going so far as to give another reporter the Myers story that I had originally broken. On at least two occasions he chewed me out, shouting at me in front of the whole news room . . . there was nothing I could do—I couldn't strike back at a city editor." Lester finally decided he'd had enough, and began searching for another paper to work for. He was acquainted with Executive Editor Tom Eastham at the *San Francisco Examiner*, the *Chronicle*'s competitor located around the corner on Mission Street. Since they were looking for an additional featured columnist, Eastham jumped at the chance to hire Les. He would begin his post at the *Examiner* in February 1971. Working for a bully, however, wasn't the only reason Les moved over to another paper. After the change in syndication took effect, the *Chronicle* cancelled his column.

Although Lester was relieved to be out of the clutches of the dreaded Melinkoff, he would often feel nostalgic for the familiar voice of fellow columnist Herb Caen, who would stroll by his desk with a broad grin, asking his usual morning question: "Hi Rev, how's the God business today?"

"I Think He Stinks!"

O N JANUARY 11, 1971, *Time* magazine ran a second article on
Les in their Religion section. Entitled "Irreverent Reverend,"
it featured the infamous walk-with-the-naked-man photo bearing
the caption, "Kinsolving Interviewing Hippie in San Francisco."
Describing his weekly columns "as much sermons as news," the
periodical discussed his present disgruntlement with the Episcopal Church's "funding of militant (and separatist) black groups,"
which "led Kinsolving, who once warned of a rightist takeover of
his church, into unlikely alliances with conservatives in attacks on
Episcopal leadership."

In reference to their earlier article, *Time* mentioned how Les "burst
into national news in 1957 by preaching "Hell is a damnable doctrine." Now employed as a worker-priest, "most of Kinsolving's colleagues accept, more or less, his role as ecclesiastical curmudgeon."
They included a compelling quote from George Cornell, religion editor for the Associated Press: "There's some solid work behind what he
does. He asks questions like a prosecuting attorney." The Kinsolving
update ended with another scintillating story from the press room:

Kinsolving's training in the *Chronicle* city room, where Managing Editor Gordon Pates calls him "the smart-ass reverend," has prepared him to handle critics. When five *Chronicle* newsmen received mail-order ordinations from Kirby Hensley, president of the Universal Life Church, Inc. (which claims some 700,000 members, including two cocker spaniels), they posted a note: "If anyone can ordain Kinsolving, why can't our leader ordain a cocker spaniel?" Replied Kinsolving coolly: "The old *Chron*'s department of religion has no more objection to Dr. Hensley's ordaining one son of a bitch than to his ordaining any others. Peace be with you."

Shortly after *Time*'s coverage, thirty-two more papers bought Les's column. He was also invited to appear on the *Phil Donahue Show*, which was broadcast January 25, 1971, on WLWD-TV in Dayton, Ohio. One irate viewer, Baptist Minister Paul Payne, shot a letter off to Donahue, who forwarded it onto Lester: "Someone who believes something needs to have a face to face confrontation with Lester Kinsolving. . . . I challenge him to a debate. I will personally pay my half on a hall anytime if he has the courage to face someone who has equal theological training. . . . I doubt if he is willing to back up what he doesn't believe with money."

Highly amused at Payne's assertion, Les sent the letter back with a note:

I accept this challenge with pleasure! Having just finished debating not one but two of Brother Payne's brother Baptist pastors for the *Casper Star-Tribune* in Wyoming . . . April 29, 30; May 1 [is] when I shall be returning from the Conference of Catholic Bishops in Detroit, so expenses should be minimal. Pastor Payne is dead right in that last paragraph. I never back up what I don't believe with money!

The two Baptist pastors Les mentioned in his response to Payne were the Reverends Weidenaar and Harvey, who agreed to debate

Gadfly

Les about his "Religion Today" column that appeared in the *Casper Star-Tribune*'s magazine section, *Wyoming Weekend*. His January 16th column, which reported Bishop Hugo Montifiore's suggestion that Jesus was a homosexual, created such an outcry that after weeks of being deluged with letters News Editor Phil McAuley decided to publish a ballot with the following headline: "THE REV. KINSOLVING: Keep His Column or Drop It?" Readers could vote "yes" or "no" and then answer, "Briefly, what are your reasons?"

By the end of three days, McAuley received a total of 478 responses. They ranged from the usual fire and brimstone to the very supportive. "I sincerely believe Kinsolving is an infidel and an evil influence." . . . "If you allow a vocal protest to censor your paper, eventually all you'll be able to print are the ads." . . . "Would be the same thing as having a lesbian writing a column." . . . "Much of the time I disagree with him, but he does cause me to examine the motives of my church, my religion, and me!" . . . "He sounds like a communist tool and his views on moral issues are disgusting." . . . "Kinsolving brings up quite interesting points which only the Bible-spouting cretins appear to come unglued at." . . . "He should stick to the bible and keep his nose out of politics. I think he stinks!" . . . "He's one of the few syndicated columnists I read. I like to see a fighter sticking with the church." . . . "He has a dirty mind, and makes unnecessary remarks about Christ." . . . "I hate to see the publication policy of an excellent newspaper determined by a bunch of Bible-belt boobs."

Despite a majority of ballots in favor of dropping the column, there were enough in support to warrant the decision to keep Lester's column. As reported in *Editor and Publisher* on March 6, "In a balloting of this kind, said the editor, those who are against something generally vote more heavily than those who are in favor. Also, there was some evidence of organized opposition to the column."

Editor McAuley sent the ballots off to Les, along with exciting news:

Yesterday, a 16-year-old youth came in with a giant scroll bearing about 160 names (which included several members of The John

Birch society). He threw it at me, screaming, "You are keeping his column but you didn't know about this!" He's a member of a very fundamentalist sect . . . that didn't scare me. What did was that he had an enormous Bible clutched under one arm. I had visions of him hurling it at me. . . . Seriously, I think the next move is a boycott but then again, perhaps not. They would have to identify themselves as bigots and I think many would rally to our side. . . . I think it would be great if you stopped on your way through Wyoming. Both the local television station and the community station want to televise the show. I get the concession to sell stones to hurl at you at the door. . . .

There was talk of Les visiting Casper again in April, where he would address his critics in an open forum. He did, however, appear on KTWO-TV with McAuley in March, when the two debated Rev. Weidenaar and Rev. Harvey, along with three other preachers. As one fundamentalist viewer put it, "The *Casper Star-Tribune* and Station KTWO are to be commended for giving the people of this area the chance to see the real person behind the column 'Religion Today.' . . . I was overwhelmed as I'm sure others were by the rudeness displayed in putting forth his various unscriptural positions. . . . "

During the televised debate, Les scribbled notes on a yellow pad as each of the opposing clergymen shared his view on Hell and damnation. "This really rattled them," he remembers. After the final preacher finished his postulating, Lester announced that he would like to respond with a poem found in his father's scrapbook, from a lady who attended the local Episcopal Church in Rocky Mount, Virginia. As he recited the frightful warnings of hellfire, Les built to a thunderous crescendo by raising his fist in the air which he hurled dramatically toward the moderator, now helpless with laughter. Even the Baptist pastors giggled, while Phil McAuley gazed far off into the studio lights:

Hearken, sinner! Can you tell
Aught of such a place as Hell?

Gadfly

'Tis a furnace where the flame
Roareth day and night the same!
Weeping through eternity
All your tears will make a sea
But that sea, how 'ere it swell
Will not make one drop in Hell!
Tears will make never quench Hellfire
Tears will make it mount the higher!
They will roast your body whole
Till you feel it turn to coal
In this fearful torment o'er
You shall live to suffer more!

Shortly after the hoopla died down, Les received a letter from *Casper Star-Tribune's* publisher, Bill Missett: "We have had a tremendous reaction to your visit here and the TV show. . . . Phil has had all kinds of comments and Truce Llewellyn said at least two-thirds of his parishioners had mentioned it to him. . . . I told Tom and Bill of the great success here and perhaps it might have some effect on their thinking."

Riding on the coattails of Lester's success, the National Newspaper Syndicate created a four-page, fold-out promotional, which was sent to editors across the country. Complete with photographs, Kinsolving Headlines (such as "Was Jesus Christ a Hippie?" and "Scientology: A New 'Religion'?"), and a short biography, the promo also contained numerous quotes, which were separated into three different categories, under a large heading:

KINSOLVING:
THE NATION'S MOST EXCITING RELIGION COLUMNIST

You may *love* him!

"I read you every week in the *Asheville Times*;
if I'm out of town, I have you clipped."
—BILLY GRAHAM

"I Think He Stinks!"

"As I've said before, I like your column very much."
—THOMAS VAIL, Publisher, *The Plain Dealer*, Cleveland, Ohio

"I frequently disagree with him, but Kinsolving is good for the
Church—he keeps us on our toes."
—THE RT. REV. DAVID THORNBERRY,
Episcopal Bishop of Wyoming

You may *hate* him!

"I think 'yellow' describes Kinsolving's kind better than 'pinko' . . .
he exposes himself as the biased liar he is."
—DR. BOB JONES, JR., President, Bob Jones University

"I don't grant interviews to you—you assassin!"
—THE RT. REV. J. BROOKE MOSELEY, Deputy for Overseas
Relations, The Episcopal Church

"You are rotten!"
—"A Born Again Christian"

But you'll *never* want to miss him!

"Readership! The enclosed is evidence. I think your columns are
great and getting better."
—ERIC ALLEN, JR. Editor, *Medford Mail Tribune*

"Your column continues to create much interest in our area
and I am proud to have it appear on the editorial page of
The Post Herald each Saturday."
—DUARD LEGRAND, Editor, *Birmingham Post Herald*

"In addition to these two letters, we had ten phone calls from the
Scientologists—all of them nasty. Keep up the good work."
—BILL TOTTEN, Managing Editor, *Huntington Park Daily Signal*

With the help of the promo brochure, Lester's syndication reached an all-time high of 309 papers. Calling from the road, Les would inform his son Tommy of a new paper that'd bought the column, and Tommy would press an additional pushpin into the large U.S. map that hung next to his father's bed. At times, pushpins in various towns and cities on the map would be removed, since readers would complain about Lester, and cancel their subscriptions. The controversy was lively reading, but sometimes posed a threat to a paper's survival.

After a cancellation, Les would contact the editor either by phone or mail to urge them to reconsider. Inspired by the courageous Phil McAuley, Les sent off a letter to H.W. Greenspan of the *Las Vegas Sun*:

> Earlier this year, the publisher of the *Casper Star-Tribune* in Wyoming considered cancellation . . . but his managing editor persuaded him to run a poll asking readers why I should be dropped or kept. . . . My column was retained. . . . I wrote of my profound gratitude and admiration to them as well as the number of readers . . . whose sense of freedom of the press is a credit to any state. I also expressed gratitude for even my most furious critics in view of their apparent interest. And I know of very few editors or columnists in existence who are without some furious critics.

Although he felt defeated by some or most papers caving in to their readers, Les was easily distracted by the madcap church beat of the Bay Area. After reporting on a pro-Maoist chaplain at Stanford University and Haight-Ashbury's Rev. "Neon Leon" Harris, who created "a sensation by erecting one of the first Episcopal Church's neon signs," Kinsolving zeroed in on Bishop Myers, who was busily raising havoc in the Diocese of California:

> Myers has an absolute genius in alienating all kinds of Episcopalians, by such astounding statements as: comparing Ronald Reagan's sending of the National Guard to Berkeley with

conditions in Nazi Germany; refusing to allow a draft-protest service in Grace Cathedral because "It would be exposing the breaking of the law concerning the national draft"—when only a month previously, Myers had signed a statement of intention to violate this very law in counseling refusal to service; sanctioning threats of violence, as "necessary to get us off the dime," by a band of black militants, and then, when they demanded he provide them funding, offering them no dimes, but rather a suggestion that they go tap Archbishop Joseph McGucken. (Years of ecumenical cooperation went up in smoke as the Archbishop's secretary, when asked about this, shouted: "He said WHAT?")

Conditions in the Berkeley public school system weren't much better. On June 20, 1971, Les reported the firing of a blind teacher from Martin Luther King, Jr. High School, where Laura and Tommy had both attended. Principal Harold Treadwell informed Patricia Munson that she didn't relate "well with the students," and that she "was one of the poorest English teachers in the school" . . . without the slightest substantiation.

Ms. Munson claimed that she, along with four other teachers, were "arbitrarily removed from the faculty" because they were white. She knew "of at least two black teachers without tenure who [were] being retained." Lester further reported that, since Principal Treadwell was black, "the dispute has racial overtones." Allen Jenkins, President of the Alameda County Chapter of the California Council of the Blind, stated, "It was done without any show of cause and appears to be irresponsible, foolhardy, and capricious; suggesting a vicious prejudice." Perhaps the volatile racial climate in the Bay Area was the reason Lester's editors removed his byline from the story.

Returning to Washington since his departure from Pasco ten years ago, Les was invited to speak at Wenatchee Valley College, where he participated in an "Emerging Values" seminar. Although they didn't attend the talk, eleven members of the Wenatchee Valley Evangelical Ministers Association protested Lester's position that, according to a local news report, "an end to disease and a long-term contraceptive pill would end the church's stand on sex before marriage." Remembering how his church burned down a decade ago, Les requested a police officer stand by during his controversial presentation.

During Q & A, one audience member asked, "Why do you wear the cloth if you don't believe in the Bible?" "I believe in it," Lester answered, "I just don't agree with everything in it. . . . Do you condone incest, slavery, concubinage and a flat world?" Without a word, the audience member sat back down in her seat.

Letters, both pro and con, appeared in the local press. Mrs. A.R. Raschda of East Wenatchee, WN, wrote an especially compelling diatribe:

> About 10 years ago I saw Kinsolving divide his congregation in the Tri Cities (He was writing sensational news even then). A "new church" emerged, dedicated to the Kinsolving gospel. . . . Much to their eternal discredit, the Episcopal hierarchy once dismissed heresy charges brought against him . . . "Little Kinsolvings" have been ordained by many other church seminaries, including my own. Whatever the denominations they are a personal affront to every Christian. . . . Conservative adults who tend to view with suspicion and alarm the "new breed" of pastors—who dress "mod" or grow a beard—would do well to note the Kinsolving image. He is clean shaven, close cropped and "properly" dressed—the proverbial wolf in sheep's clothing!

Continuing with his celebration of the Summer of Love into the summer of '71, a modish-dressed and bearded Rev. Cecil Williams was found in a *San Francisco Chronicle* photo where, after hugging celebrants during one of his church services, he "ceremonially stripped himself of his robe and did a dance 'like King David, who danced for God' to chide a pious religion reporter who had called Glide the only morning nightclub in town."

Lester, the *Chronicle*'s former "pious religion reporter," actually referred to Glide Methodist Memorial as "the Nation's only Sunday morning night club," in his September 27th report on Rev. Williams being one of Angela Davis's spiritual advisors. Ms. Davis, "an ardent and self-professed member of the Communist Party," as well as a staunch supporter of the Black Panthers, was being held at the Women's Detention Center in New York City, after being linked to a gun that was used by one of the Jackson brothers in the Marin County Hall of Justice shootout the previous summer. Judge Harold Haley was murdered by escaped inmates who were attempting to kidnap him along with several jurors who were wounded but survived the ordeal.

When Lester questioned Cecil on the fact that the Rev. Jesse Jackson was also a spiritual adviser to Ms. Davis, and if Rev. Jackson was "in any way engaged in 'sheep-stealing,' Rev. Williams replied . . . with the smile of a beneficent Samaritan, 'He was with her for just one hour—I visit Angela every week!'" Les then inquired as to what he thought of a Communist requesting 'the ministrations of Christian clergy rather than comrades.' Cecil, . . . now sounding a bit more like Caesar than Samaritan, responded with, 'Maybe she believes in what Cecil Williams is doing!'"

Additional support from the church world was reported by Les in October, when the United Presbyterian Church's Council on Religion and Race sent a $10,000 grant to the Angela Davis Defense Fund. During the Presbyterian General Assembly in May, it was mentioned in a report by the council that this grant "had been given to the 'Marin County Black Defense Fund.'" When "delegate Deryck Nuckton of Monterey became suspicious and demanded an explanation, the disclosure that the grant was really made to Angela's defense fund made front page news throughout the nation." The Presbytery of San Francisco later issued a report, charging the council with dereliction of duty and impropriety.

Eager for a lighter assignment, Lester accepted the opportunity to interview former Mr. America Walt Baptiste, who was now a burgeoning yogi ordaining ministers. A thirty-two-page, royal purple brochure proclaiming Baptiste as "The Master" asserted that he "is a Guru and Master Guide for tens of thousands of Beautiful People . . . [he]

allows sincere devotees to get glimpses at times of his astral and divine forms—to strengthen faith and engender fresh impulses." The brochure went on to state, "To get the full benefit of Master Power, the disciple must develop receptivity. It is impossible to develop receptivity until implicit obedience is given to the commandments of the Master."

A fourteen-page supplement inside the brochure discussed how "humility is a very difficult talent to come by." During their interview, Lester asked The Master "if he had written of himself as being 'the word made Flesh,'" and if so, just "how did that square with humility? . . . Slightly shaken, The Master admitted that he himself had written the brochure, explaining that 'if you do not tell, who will? You must know yourself without shyness.'"

While Les sat with the pensive Baptiste, "incense permeated the air, which was audibly punctuated by the loud squawking of a parrot on the left, the gutturals of a Panamanian Toucan on the right and the gurgling of a bamboo fountain in front of a large hall with candles, prayer rugs, and a giant tapestry of Moorish arches." Baptiste himself had been ordained "into a denomination called the Liberal Catholic Church, after which 'We incorporated, to ordain, in 1958.'" The process of becoming ordained by The Master went as follows:

> The cost of ordination is $60.00 (paid in advance—or $25 in three monthly installments) explains the purple brochure regarding "the first 60 lessons of The Guidance. If the recipient wishes to be 'ORDAINED' there are 40 more lessons, a balance due of $25 and a required essay to be submitted to The Master. . . . As you begin to receive income by teachings sharing, you will be requested to give a tithing of 20 percent of your gross total earnings." The Master recalls only 14 ordinations since 1958.

Grace Cathedral, once considered by the conservative Episcopal hierarchy to house such "heretics" as Bishop Pike, was now offering up such secular fare as nature worship and hippie festivities. In "'Pagan Rites' at Cathedral," Les reported that in the early morning hours of September 23, 1971, "Living Creatures Association" led a twenty-four-hour vigil on Nob Hill. While Bishop Myers read prayers, a bell was heard ringing, along with the blowing of a conch shell. Thus began "A Vigil for the Great Family—A Celebration of the Autumnal Equinox."

Poets Allen Ginsburg and Gary Snyder, both adorned with animal masks, chanted "The sacred syllable 'OM,'" while "totem symbols [were] erected for every one of the 100 members of the United States Senate—each of which was appointed Godfather of some animal or form of plant life (e.g., Senator Alan Cranston, The Tule Elk; Senator John Tunney, The Brown Bear)."

At sunset, "a chorus of wolf howls, bird calls, and even whale sounds" was highlighted in a "Sensorium," which included a "candlelight procession, [and] images of wolves projected against the Cathedral walls." This cacophonic occasion was comparably mild, given what took place over two years earlier, on January 27, 1969.

"FOUR THOUSAND YEARS—A SENSORIUM ON CELEBRATION OF THE FUTURE" packed Grace Cathedral with 3,000 mostly hippie celebrants. For two hours, incense and marijuana filled the air, while film clips of charging buffalo and skiers flying down a snowy mountain played on opposite screens, projected at the cathedral's ceiling. By the end of the evening, a bare-chested hippie jumped on top of the cathedral's high altar and proceeded to smoke a cigar.

Appalled at this spectacle, Dean Julian Bartlett ran up to the "hirsute youth" and shouted, "NOW YOU GET DOWN FROM THERE!!" at which point the cigar-smoking hippie offered Dean Bartlett "an irreverent finger." As Les and his eldest daughter Laura sat watching, "the dean leaped up and engaged the youth in a brief but strenuous wrestling match, before the two of them plummeted into the applauding crowd at altarside. Two burly cathedral vergers [custodians] then emerged from the congregation to drag the screaming youth outside into the night."

After news of the most recent "Sensorium" spread throughout the Episcopal Diocese of California, nineteen clergy and laity released a letter to the media, protesting "pagan cultic practices" being held at Grace Cathedral. San Mateo rector Rev. Leslie Wilder, "one of the most prominent clergy in the diocese," told Les in an interview, "I think it's high time to protest the Cathedral being turned into a three-ring circus. First the hot pants fashion show at the High Altar and next this nature exhibition. What has become of the concept of the Holy of Holies, the sanctuary of God?"

In their letter the protestors stated, "Grace Cathedral has been consecrated for public worship of God and separated from all unhallowed, worldly and common uses. Any other usage of the cathedral [is] an affront to all sincere Christians, who look to the cathedral for religious guidance and inspiration." Shortly before the opening of the annual convention of the Episcopal Diocese of California on October 22, Dean Bartlett made the following statement: "These are very serious charges and if untrue represent highly irresponsible behavior of churchmen. . . . We are obliged to bring all kinds of God's people into the Cathedral precincts."

The dean went further, to point out "the irony of the protestors singling out an equinoctial festival ceremony motivated by a profound sense of celebration and reverence for all living creatures and things. . . . One wonders whether these churchmen—protestors would have joined those who condemned St. Francis as a heretic, or those who canonized him as a saint!"

Bishop Myers followed up Dean Bartlett's statement with an additional denouncement:

As a rector [chief pastor] of the cathedral, I am deeply concerned with the failure of the critical clergy and laity to inform me of their letter to the dean and chapter [church board] before releasing it to the press. It has been the custom of the Christian Church since its founding that the members of the Body of Christ who are in disagreement go to each other with their grievances to charity rather than air those grievances outside the church.

As Lester speculated that this "raging controversy [might] erupt on the floor of the convention," another was already brewing, as mentioned in "Fireworks Due at Grace Cathedral":

The convention's first sign of controversy appeared last night shortly after it was called to order and a black caucus announced it would hold a meeting. The Rev. N.W. Holland of Hollister asked the convention why there was a black caucus. But he was swiftly ruled out of order by the presiding officer, Bank of America attorney C. Thorne Corse, who explained later: "It was none of his business."

Although Bishop Myers had proved he was radical enough to welcome hippie sensoriums and hot pants fashion shows into the Cathedral, he was adamantly opposed to a resolution allowing women to be ordained Episcopal priests when it was introduced by Rev. Robert Mayer at the convention. The next day, Myers delivered the following statement:

The sexuality of Christ is no accident, nor is his masculinity incidental. This is the Divine choice. Jesus continued that choice in his selection of men to be his Apostles. The overwhelming majority of Christians cannot tolerate the idea of the ordination of women in the priesthood. For Anglicans [Episcopalians] to ordain them would produce a painful ecumenical tension. God is represented in masculine imagery. . . . The male image about God pertains to the divine initiative in creation. Initiative is a male rather than a female attribute.

When Rev. Mayer received word of Myers's denouncement of his resolution, he appeared "visibly shaken—and disclosed that he had previously heard nothing by way of objection from Bishop Myers," according to Lester's convention report "Episcopalians' Mute Row":

Mayer then moved that his resolution calling for women's suffrage in Episcopal ordination be referred to a study committee. This motion passed—but only by the narrow margin of 234 to 207. . . . When it was announced that copies of the Bishop's two-page statement on women would be distributed to all delegates at the close of the convention, one unidentified delegate shouted: "Where?" And a great roar of laughter ensued when Elizabeth La Place, a teacher at Kennedy High School in Fremont, cried out in reply: "In the men's room!"

News of Myers's astonishing statement garnered national attention, including statements from clergy and feminists alike: "An absurd and destructive statement." . . . "To focus attention on the maleness of Christ rather than his being the incarnation of God is a direct contradiction of Bishop Myers' own statement that God is not male." . . . "Absolutely incredible! I had the impression that the bishop was forward-looking on such social issues as race. How could he be so Neanderthal?" In "Women Angered at Bishop Myers," Lester cited that Myers had received "some of the strongest public criticisms ever directed to an Episcopal bishop."

1971, an unprecedented year for controversial news stories in the world of religion, reached its pinnacle on December 1st in Lester's page-one exposé in the *San Francisco Examiner*: "Panther Cleric Elected to Top Episcopal Body." Les reported that "The Rev. Earl Albert Neil, rector of St. Augustine's Episcopal Church in Oakland, which is known as 'the Black Panther church,' has attracted national attention; first as the spiritual mentor of Huey Newton and later for his officiating at the funeral of George Jackson."

It further stated that Rev. Neil had been "quietly elected to the highest ranking governing body of the Episcopal Diocese of California [and that] there has been no public announcement whatsoever of his election, 14 days ago, by the Standing Committee of the Episcopal Diocese." The Rev. Fordyce Eastburn, president of the Standing Committee, told Les, "I don't suppose they [the members of the Standing Committee] thought it was important."

According to the *San Francisco Chronicle* (which reported Rev. Neil's election the next day), "the Standing Committee of the Episcopal Diocese [is] a powerful eight-member body which can act for the bishop when he is absent and can approve or veto clerical ordinations in its jurisdiction." Although Rev. Eastbern stated to Lester that Rev. Neil was not elected by secret ballot, "he declined to disclose whether the election was unanimous . . . he said that he would vote against any member of the John Birch Society, the Minutemen, or the Ku Klux Klan."

During the Episcopal diocesan convention in the previous October, the Rev. Mr. Neil "introduced a resolution deploring racial discrimination and segregation and calling for the appointment of a committee to investigate race relations in the Diocese. His anti-segregation resolution specified, however, that 10 of the 21 investigators must be selected by the Bay Area Union of Black Episcopalians."

Although the resolution passed, Rev. Neil's nomination for election to the Standing Committee at the convention did not. However, he was "elected three weeks later, on November 16, by the Standing Committee itself, which has the power to fill vacancies between diocesan conventions."

Exhausted at year's end, Lester wondered if 1972 would be filled with more, or less, brazen exposés of his own diocese, as it underwent major upheaval at the hands of Bishop C. Kilmer Myers. A few days after covering a Christmas Eve service at Grace Cathedral, where the bishop refused to deliver a sermon because he was "upset" about the Vietnam War, a colleague approached Lester and asked, "Hey Les, ever heard about this church up in Ukiah? They have a swimming pool in the middle of the sanctuary, and it's attracting a large congregation. I think the name of the pastor is the Rev. Jim Jones."

Investigating the Peoples Temple

1972 STARTED OUT with a bang. As early as February, two scathing stories by Les appeared in the *Examiner*. The first, "Storm of Protest Over Glide Pastor Sermon," reported that Rev. Cecil Williams, the infamous pastor at Glide, was tentatively scheduled to preach at the United Methodist Church's general conference in Atlanta that April. Shortly after the announcement, Rev. Irving Smith, chairman of the convention, told Lester, "We have had an unprecedented number of written protests of the Rev. Mr. Williams being invited to preach." Furthermore, "The Atlanta church's pastor, the Rev. Dr. Robert Ozment, told the *Examiner*, 'Cecil Williams will not be welcome in this church unless I can get his assurance that he will do nothing that will be offensive to our people.'"

After inquiring if Williams "would provide Dr. Ozment with such an assurance that he would do nothing offensive, the Rev. Mr. Williams laughed proudly and replied, 'I'm coming to Atlanta to preach the gospel—you better know it!'" Although he was bound and determined to preach the gospel as he knew it, Cecil Williams was "currently under severe criticism by fellow Methodist clergy throughout the country."

The Rev. McGee of Centenary Methodist Church in St. Louis revealed many shocking details of "a seminar led by Williams which took place in his church in 1969":

"Williams may deny this," Dr. McGee told the *Examiner*, "but I'm quite certain that he told that group that 'The qualifications for a secretary at Glide are that she be sexy and wear miniskirts. . . . We haven't had any fornicating during our Glide services, but one young man got so stimulated by our belly dancers that he began masturbating. . . . We hug, kiss, feel and smell one another. And when another young man disrobed, I walked over, patted him on the fanny and said, 'Man, what a beautiful body you have!'"

When Les asked Rev. Williams to comment, he responded with:

"I'm glad to be criticized by McGee. I simply said that church secretaries shouldn't be sexless and that ours aren't and wear miniskirts. As for the masturbating report, I don't want to comment on that." Were there at any time belly dancers at Glide Church? "Not that I know of!" he replied with a chuckle. "As for that disrobing episode. I simply told the group that if a young man would disrobe I'd encourage him not to feel guilty about it. If I had ever patted any young man, I certainly wouldn't use the word 'fanny'—I'd say 'arse'!"

Rev. Clinton McPheters of Central Methodist Church in Phoenix stated that Glide's "present worship services are 'a prostitution of the Christian religion—a complete betrayal of everything Mrs. Glide and my father stood for.' (Mrs. Lizzie Glide, a Kern County oil man's widow, built the church in 1930 as a memorial to her husband)."

Rev. McPheters' father, Dr. J. C. McPheters, was Cecil Williams's predecessor, serving at Glide Memorial Methodist from 1930 to 1948. He added, "Mrs. Glide would turn over in her grave. I was present at the church three weeks ago and what I saw going on was certainly not the memorial she intended."

The second exposé, "Sheriff Names Gay Pastor Jail Chaplain," discussed how Robert Richards, an openly gay man who professed to be a Roman Catholic priest, had recently been appointed by Sheriff Richard Hongisto to counsel homosexual inmates at the County Jail. "I worked for Hongisto's election," Richards explained to Les. "My appointment is a specific indication of the sheriff's own commitment to the gay community. He made this again and again and in certain ways he's come through and shown it to be fact."

Archbishop Joseph T. McGucken stated to Lester that "Richards was never given the facilities of the Roman Catholic priesthood," and that he "recalled having discussed with Richards his expressed desire to transfer from the priesthood of the Antiochian Orthodox Archdiocese of Toledo, Ohio. 'But he asked that nothing public be done about his status at the time . . . because he was wanted by the FBI.'"

Richards was a draft resister who "served for three months at Terminal Island federal prison." His ordination certificate was inscribed with the name "Robert Tato," which Richards stated was his real name. That previous March, a letter from Archbishop Michael of Toledo stated, "Robert Tato has been suspended for many violations, plus leaving here with many debts to many people, businessmen, and churches." Six months later, Richards "announced that he was leaving the Roman Catholic Church, after having founded a homosexual commune entitled 'The Community of St. John the Beloved,' which held services, until forbidden by authorities, at the University of San Francisco."

Shortly after the story broke in the final edition of the *Examiner*, a handwritten telephone message was delivered to Les on February 23, at 4:30 P.M.: "**FOR MR:** 'Rev.' **FROM:** 'Sheriff Hongisto' **REMARKS:** 'Sheriff says "Tell him today's story a piece of trash.'" Six days later, a report appeared in the *San Francisco Chronicle*: "Hongisto Denies Naming Chaplain":

Hongisto said that Richards, 31, a founder of the Community of St. John the Beloved . . . was "merely one of 20 volunteers" at the jail, including a number of chaplains of various religious affiliations. . . . Hongisto said he was aware that Richards . . . once served a three month term for draft resistance [but stated,] "It doesn't seem to be a fact that would hurt his volunteer work at the jail."

During the early 1970s, religious cults were emerging as a world-wide phenomenon. The Church of Synanon, Children of God, Unification Church, Hare Krishna, and the Rajneesh Movement were just some of the organizations run by charismatic leaders who waged mind control over their members. One particular group on the rise was the Church of Scientology.

Founded in 1954 by former science-fiction writer L. Ron Hubbard, the cult was based on Hubbard's book *Dianetics*, which taught individuals to rid themselves of "reactive mind engrams" in several "auditing" sessions until they reached the state of being "clear." Shortly after its publication in 1950, *Dianetics* became a popular commercial success, with the help of members who purchased up to hundreds of books at a time.

In 1968, Paulette Cooper, a freelance writer who had studied comparative religions one summer at Harvard University, began research on contemporary religious cults. She investigated Scientology, and chose it as the subject for her next magazine article. Published in 1969 by the British magazine *Queen*, the Church immediately filed a lawsuit against Cooper, and began waging a campaign of intense harassment after her article was expanded into a book, *The Scandal of Scientology*, in 1971.

Lester's story, "Scientology Sued For $15.4 Million," ran on page one of the *Examiner* on April 2, 1972. He reported that Miss Cooper had "charged the Scientologists with illegal wiretapping of her Manhattan apartment, making obscene phone calls, visiting her home at 2:30 a.m., posing as members of the FBI, reading letters allegedly signed by J. Edgar Hoover and stealing portions of her manuscript."

Five years later, the FBI raided Scientology offices in Los Angeles and Washington, D.C., and located a 1976 document entitled "Operation Freakout," which detailed a plan "to get P.C. [Paulette Cooper] incarcerated in a mental institution or jail, or at least to hit her so hard that she drops her attacks." After the 1977 FBI raid, nine Scientology members were "indicted by a grand jury and charged with theft, conspiracy, burglary, and other crimes."

On August 1, Lester's editor Tom Eastham received a letter from a colleague, reporter Carolyn Pickering of the *Indianapolis Star*. She informed him that her editors were "contemplating sending me out to your grand and glorious state to probe into a religious cult operation in Redwood Valley, near Ukiah . . . called Peoples Temple." Pickering had just interviewed a frantic parent, Georgia Johnson, who was trying to get her two young daughters to return to Indianapolis after the Peoples Temple church relocated its Indianapolis congregation to Ukiah, California. Johnston had informed Pickering that one of her daughters had been forced into a mixed marriage as part of Jones's pledge to create a new race.

The previous October, fellow *Star* reporter Bryon Wells had written an exposé of Jones's visiting "miracle healing services," where the preacher proclaimed, "With over 4,000 members of our California church, we haven't had a death yet! . . . I am a prophet of God and I can cure both the illness of your body, as well as the illness of your mind!" After reading Wells's report, Georgia Johnston wrote a letter to him, which he passed on to his editor, who then assigned the story to Pickering, his top investigative reporter.

Pickering's letter went on to say, "The fraud who conducts this holy organization is the Rev. James W. Jones who once had a small church here. . . . If there is someone on your staff who might have some knowledge of this bunch, or could provide some entrees to state officials who might be interested, I'd appreciate it."

Back in February, Les had made a call to George Hunter, editor of the *Ukiah Daily Journal*, to inquire into what he'd already heard from more than one person: that Peoples Temple was attracting thousands to their Sunday services, besides having a swimming pool in the middle of the sanctuary.

Four days after Les's call to Hunter, *Examiner* editor Ed Dooley received a letter from Timothy Stoen, an attorney-at-law in Ukiah. It was obvious that Hunter had phoned Stoen after he'd spoken with Kinsolving. Stoen's lengthy letter contained ample praises for Jim Jones, such as his past appointments to various positions of public trust, "including Foreman of the Mendocino County Grand Jury," and that Jones was "the most compassionate, fearless, and honest person I know of. . . ."

After looking over Pickering's letter, Eastham called Les into his office, and suggested he contact Carolyn, as well as attend one of the Temple's services with a photographer.

On Sunday, September 10, Les and *Examiner* photographer Fran Ortiz made a two-hour trip from San Francisco to Redwood Valley, ten miles north of Ukiah. As they entered the sanctuary of the Peoples Temple church, they were confronted by Tim Stoen, who was wearing a blue-green pulpit robe, since he assumed the role of (unordained) assistant pastor. After demanding their identities, Stoen informed Les that he was also Assistant District Attorney of Mendocino County. Fran Ortiz was ordered by another assistant pastor, Archie Ijames, to leave his camera at the church entrance—he refused and was relegated to wait outside.

As a great multitude of Temple members stepped off overnight busses from Portland and Los Angeles, Les met the Rev. Jim Jones. Dressed in a black pulpit gown and white turtleneck, he flashed Lester a charismatic smile and praised Les: "I admire your courage in exposing Cecil Williams for the phony he is." Lester later admitted in an interview, "I could feel Jones' magnetic charm."

Later, as Les sat with the Temple congregation during a ninety-minute service, he began to grow weary of Jones's continuous ramblings. He was also nonplussed about an affirmation on the program which stated, "Death was overcome again, through the mighty gift of our Prophet, Jim Jones!" Suddenly, Fran Ortiz approached him and asked if they could leave. Les agreed, feeling he'd had enough, and they walked to the parking lot. As they got into the car, Fran whispered to him, "Let's wait until we're out of sight." Driving up the road onto the freeway, Ortiz said, "I took photos of their busses and the ushers. Les, one of them wore a holster, with a .357 magnum. The other was holding a shotgun."

That night at home, the phone rang at 11:15 P.M. "Was that black guy with the camera with you?" a voice asked. It was Tim Stoen, calling from the Temple. Les confronted him about the late-night call to his home, and why the Assistant District Attorney of Mendocino County would ask such a peculiar question. Stoen shot back with, "Did you know Jim was run out of Indianapolis for faith healing? I read about it in the *Star*." He also informed Les that he'd be sending him financial information, since the Temple treasurer had refused to furnish that to Les earlier, and quickly hung up.

The next day, a hand-delivered letter from Stoen arrived at the *Examiner*, addressed to "Rev. Kinsolving." After elaborating on the Temple's annual expenditures, Stoen continued gushing about "this wonderful group of people and their remarkable pastor Jim Jones. . . . Jim has been the means by which more than 40 persons have literally been brought back from the dead this year":

> I have seen Jim revive people stiff as a board, tongues hanging out, eyes set, skin graying and all vital signs absent. . . . Jim will go up to such a person and say something like "I love you" or "I need you" and immediately the vital signs reappear. . . . Jim is very humble about his gift and does not preach it. . . .

On September 17, "The Prophet Who Raises the Dead" ran on the front page of the Sunday *Examiner*. Les included additional excerpts from Tim Stoen's letter:

> People's Temple does, frankly, have a remarkable human service ministry and is devotedly supported by extensive numbers of people. It is extremely important to us to keep our credibility. The Prophet is supremely and totally dedicated to building an ideal society where mankind is united, life (human and animal and plant) is cherished, and the joys of nature and simplicity are esteemed.

Because he reported the use of guns by Temple ushers, Les ended his first Jim Jones exposé with, "his sturdy sentries lend the temporal assurance that the Temple of the Prophet is the best-armed house of God in the land."

The same Sunday "The Prophet Who Raises the Dead" appeared, Les attended one of the Temple's services, which was held in San Francisco.

"I know that Pastor Jim Jones is God Almighty himself!" cried one of the more than 1,000 people who overflowed the auditorium of Benjamin Franklin Junior High School on Geary Boulevard yesterday morning and Saturday night.

"You say I am God Almighty?" asked the Rev. Mr. Jones, the charismatic pastor-prophet of the People's Temple Christian (Disciples) Church near Ukiah, who was holding special services in San Francisco this weekend. "Yes, you are!" shrieked the unidentified but obviously ecstatic woman, as the audience clapped or waved their arms and shouted approval at Sunday services.

As Jones pontificated that he was "only a messenger of God" and that he had a "paranormal ability in healing," Les scribbled notes on his yellow notepad:

The Reverend Mr. Jones stopped abruptly in the midst of a sermon sentence, shouted "Oh no, not again!" and leaped off the stage, robe flying like Batman on a rope.

Lester described the surrounding scene of Jones laying his hands on two supine women in vivid detail:

He raced to the side of these two ladies, who had become suddenly and apparently stiff. Another unidentified woman began leaping wildly and screeching hallelujahs, while an even more elderly woman commenced a long series of ecstatic hopping.

While Rev. Jones lifted the two women up, "the crowd broke into thunderous applause." Jones then pronounced:

You'll have to understand—she was given up to die; they said she'd never be able to move again. That's the 43rd time this has happened. I just said: "I love you, God loves you, come back to us." The registered nurses around her said it was so.

On Monday, September 18, "Healing Prophet Hailed as God at S.F. Revival" appeared on page four, rather than page one of the *Examiner*. Undoubtedly the editors felt it was a safe decision, since the accompanying photograph of an ominous-looking Jones in dark sunglasses might frighten some newsstand readers away.

Although Lester's first two exposés were considered "gee-whiz" pieces meant to provoke readers' interest, the third one, "D.A. Aide Officiates for Minor Bride," went straight for the corrupt jugular of the Peoples Temple. In an affidavit signed by Mr. and Mrs. Cecil Johnson, Tim Stoen was charged with officiating at the marriage of their daughter Mildred, who was a minor. Mildred was then placed on the Mendocino County welfare and forced to turn over her monthly $95 welfare check to Peoples Temple:

When asked by what authority he had officiating at the marriage of Mildred "Mickie" Johnson (who has now returned to her family in Indianapolis), Stoen contended: "I meet all the requirements of the State Civil Code." When asked which section of the state code permits an attorney (rather than a judge) to solemnize marriages, Stoen replied: "I'll have to ask you to let me go back and check that." . . . He said that he had not known the Rev. Mr. Jones in 1965, when the Johnson affidavit says: "Jones said that the world would end on July 16, 1967, and encouraged the congregation here to pool their money and follow him to California—where he promised they would find a place where only they would be safe from this impending disaster."

In the early hours of Tuesday, September 19, Jones was alerted to this third story by a "sneak" in the *Examiner* composition room and was told that it would appear that morning on page one. Jones realized that it had far more serious implications than the first two. The Prophet rounded up 150 members of his flock and ushered them into buses with placards and signs, bound for San Francisco.

As Les commuted that morning to work, he was overwhelmed by the sight of a long line of Temple picketers in front of the *Examiner*. The line stretched as far as the corner of 5th and Mission Streets, where the *San Francisco Chronicle* was located. The picketers held signs stating, "This Paper Has Lied: They Saw Healing Undeniable and Would Not Print," "Government That Governs Least Governs Best," "This Is an Invasion of Privacy of Religious Services," and "Do You Persecute Him Because He Is Not in the Jet Set?"

A group of newsmen, along with editor Tom Eastham, were already standing at the window watching the picket line three floors below, when Lester came up and joined them. Eastham turned to him and inquired, "Well, Reverend, what are you going to do about this? Aren't you going to go down there and welcome them?" Lester responded with, "I'll do better than that—I'll take up a collection!"

Using a policeman's hat as a makeshift collection plate, Lester paraded through the picket line, pleading for a donation. Local television stations were already on the scene, and began filming the worker-priest in action:

KINSOLVING: I stand as you march by. No one will contribute. *I've* been to two of *your* services that went on for hours, and nobody will contribute anything. We're passing the hat, ladies and gentlemen, an opportunity for sweet charity to come out from among you.

KRON-TV: Reverend Kinsolving, why are you doing this?

KINSOLVING: Because I'm having fun, and I feel very sorry for my colleagues in the fourth estate who are assigned to such comparatively dull beats as politics, science, and crime.

KRON-TV: You have factual information to back up what you've written?

Gadfly

KINSOLVING: I don't print anything unless I've got factual backing.

KRON-TV: You think Reverend Jim Jones is a phony?

KINSOLVING: Yes, I think he is a phony . . . in many respects.

KRON-TV: In what respects?

KINSOLVING: Well, I think that the fact that he made several claims at self-effacement and so forth, and I see hypocrisy there. . . .

The *Chronicle,* owner of KRON-TV, was furious at having been scooped by the *Examiner* once again. That night, as the Kinsolvings watched the 11:00 news report at home, Lester's final response to the broadcaster was cut short as his face ballooned into a freeze-frame, and his voice was turned into a high-pitched shriek. "I sounded," Les recalls, "like Mt. Vesuvius erupting." The camera then dissolved into Jim Jones sitting in the KRON-TV studio, "looking like the Archangel Gabriel, talking sweet nothings with that Fletcher's Castoria voice of his":

KRON-TV: The pastor of the church, the man in question, Reverend Jim Jones, was in our studio tonight, where he talked about the church, faith healing and the charge by the writer of the articles that he is phony in many respects.

JIM JONES: Well, I'm not phony in any area.

KRON-TV: What about this faith healing? This has come up time and time again in the article. Reverend Kinsolving has quoted one of your directors as saying that you have brought back more than forty people from the dead this year alone.

JIM JONES: If I could raise the dead in a clinical sense I would free every graveyard.

After tuning in to the KRON-TV program, *Examiner* publisher Charles Gould sent a stinging memorandum to Les:

> You did not show charity, compassion, or consideration when you harangued the peaceful picketers seeking a collection. You seemed to play the role of bully and bigot . . . they have every right to practice their religion. . . . I caught about one minute of [the] interview with Rev. Jones. He came off as [a] low-key, soft-voiced, convincing believer. A charlatan he may be, however he definitely knows how to make friends and influence people. . . . You should never let another man of God beat you at your own game. Jones did. Yesterday, at least.

The fourth exposé, "Probe Asked of Peoples Temple," appeared on Wednesday, September 20. In March 1972, Ukiah Baptist Pastor Richard Taylor had asked Mendocino County District Attorney Duncan James to investigate Tim Stoen's conduct surrounding Temple member Maxine Harpe's suspicious suicide. Rev. Taylor had also requested that Sheriff Reno Bartolomie investigate the Temple on the suicide issue as well as many others. But no action was taken.

On September 19, one day before the fourth exposé went to press, Rev. Taylor wrote to State Attorney General Evelle Younger with another appeal: "What is of utmost concern is the atmosphere of terror created in the community by so large and aggressive a group . . . I sincerely believe questionable activity is going on. . . . I do request that your office conduct an investigation." This would be the final article to be published, although Les had written four other exposés. They involved further investigation into the Maxine Harpe suicide, the welfare scam, The Prophet accusing a pastor of propositioning two Temple girls, and "survival training," where, on a camping trip led by Jones, four-year-old Tommy Kice was forced to eat when he wasn't hungry. When Tommy threw up, he was forced to eat his vomit. Jones repeated the torture over and over as the little boy continued to vomit.

Shortly after the picket line, Jim Jones and Tim Stoen met with

Gadfly

Examiner editors and threatened the paper with a lawsuit if they didn't allow Jones to tell "his side of the story."

"This is when the *Examiner* stopped examining," Les remembers, "They were already being sued by Synanon, another cult, so they didn't want to bother with this one." However, the *Indianapolis Star* would be handling the Temple matter quite differently. Carolyn Pickering had been busily collaborating with Lester for the last month, filling him in on details of Jim Jones's rise to power in Indianapolis, while Les was informing her of the latest Temple news from California. The *Star* would run a total of five Pickering exposés, starting on September 21, two days after the *Examiner* picket line: "Former City Preacher Feels Heat of Publicity in West," "Family Pleads with Aged Aunt Not to Throw Away Her Bible," "'Prophet,' Attorney Probe Asked," "Two Firms Jones Founded Lax on Filing Tax Returns," and "Woe-Beset Woman Says 'Prophet' Harasses Her and Mate," where Temple assistant pastor Archie Ijames demanded members Marion and Opal Freestone (now Temple defectors) tithe 25 percent or suffer the consequences with their lives.

The *Star* was also harassed with a picket line and threats of a lawsuit, but unlike the *Examiner*, the editors didn't back down, and the Temple never sued. Two days after the fourth exposé appeared, Lester sent a memo to one of his editors, John Todd:

Let me briefly outline my deep concerns at present. . . . One of my very best sources in the Ukiah area phoned me in serious anxiety. The *Ukiah Daily Journal* reported that the Rev. Mr. Jones had been approached by some other *Examiner* reporters who wanted to hear his side of the story. This came on the same day that my articles abruptly stopped. . . . If all my evidence is threatened by even the momentary impression that I have been removed from the story, I wonder how I can possibly do the job which so desperately needs to be done.

Although the *Examiner* editors awarded Lester a $100 bonus, they stalled when he asked if they were going to print the rest of the Temple exposés. They urged him to get more information, such as sworn taped testimony and signed affidavits. For the next few weeks, Lester returned again and again to Ukiah to gather further evidence, not knowing that it was at the risk of his life.

Feeling intense frustration and a need for a respite, Les took his family to a UC Berkeley football game on Saturday, September 23. Returning home after a rousing victory against Stanford, where Cal receiver Steve Sweeney scored a touchdown in the last three seconds of the game, the Kinsolvings walked up to the front door and noticed one of the glass panes smashed in. It looked like a burglary, although perhaps someone had thrown a rock from a passing car.

As they entered the house, their two small dogs were found in a bedroom with the door closed. They weren't hurt, and there were no valuables missing, so it was very perplexing. As Sylvia and the children gathered in the living room, Les came up from his office in the basement. "Copies of my articles and check stubs are missing downstairs," he told them. Although charges couldn't be filed due to lack of evidence, Lester knew the Temple had been responsible for the burglary. It was a warning of the dangers that lay ahead.

That same day, over in San Francisco, *Examiner* editors were perusing a story that would appear in the next day's Sunday edition. Besides canceling Les's Temple series, they assigned reporter John Burks to conduct an interview with Jim Jones, where he would be given the opportunity to tell "his side of the story." While sitting with Jones, Burks considered him a "strange hick preacher who was a real dim bulb." The article, "Prophet Tells How He Revives Dead," included the following excerpts from Burks's interview:

BURKS: Let's say somebody just died in your temple and you have just laid hands on that person in hopes you will revive them. What's your next move?

JONES: It's just spontaneous. I would say "This is Jim." That's my title. No "Reverend," or anything. "This is Jim." If it were someone I didn't know very well, I'd say "pastor." I'd say "This is pastor." But most of them had attended at least several times. I'd say "This is Jim. I love you." When you feel something like this, what do you say? "I love you. We need you. Your family needs you. We care. I'm giving you love." It would never be any magic words. No magic little catechism or prayer. Feeling.

BURKS: Ok, so . . . what are you feeling at that time?

JONES: Deep concern. Deep empathy. At first it frustrated me and I found that this was the worst thing. The most important thing I found was—that they must detect in their mind—is calm. "You're going to be fine. You're going to be all right."

On Sunday, September 24, "Prophet Tells How He Revives Dead" ran in the "bulldog edition" of the *Examiner*, the early morning edition. By the afternoon, the Prophet and Stoen returned to the paper, with more threats of lawsuits. By the *Examiner*'s late edition, Burks asked to have his byline removed, since the original article was butchered beyond the point of recognition. As a result, two versions of the same story ran on the same day, the latter with no sign of an author.

One week later, two letters to the editor from Ukiah were published:

Thank you from the Concerned Citizens of Ukiah and Redwood Valley. Had not your reporter, the Rev. Lester Kinsolving, brought to light the strange events at the Peoples Temple we wouldn't have had a prayer as far as investigation is concerned. Our radio station KUKI and the *Ukiah Daily Journal* have presented only biased stories.

Jim Jones and the Peoples Temple have many of us Ukiah and Redwood Valley citizens very concerned. If it weren't for Rev. Kinsolving and *The Examiner* we probably would be left in the dark, so to speak. . . . The fear in this town is unbelievable. The feeling is everywhere. . . .

The two authors, Brenda Ganatos and Pat Rhea, were members of the Concerned Citizens, a group of residents in Ukiah and Redwood Valley who had banded together in 1970 after hearing disturbing stories about how community members were becoming increasingly fearful of the Peoples Temple members. In addition, Temple defectors were receiving death threats—if they filed a report with authorities, it would end up in the hands of Assistant District Attorney Tim Stoen. Jones had thrown hush money around, infiltrating every branch of government, and even hoodwinked the *Ukiah Daily Journal*, where employees were ordered to throw away any letters criticizing the Peoples Temple. Any pleadings from the Concerned Citizens fell on deaf ears.

After reading the two letters, Lester immediately contacted Brenda, who told him that when his first exposé appeared in the *Examiner*, Temple members bought up all copies from every newsstand and store in Ukiah. Brenda had to make a special request at the local liquors to save her three papers. Les began having meetings with Brenda and the Concerned Citizens, where he recorded sworn statements and collected signed affidavits. When Jim Jones was informed that Kinsolving was returning to Ukiah, he set up volunteers on "surveillance runs." "We would be at someone's home," recalls Ganatos, "and some cars would go up and down the street, and they'd stop and they'd look at our cars . . . as soon as we walked out the door, they'd jump in their cars and leave."

Although Les risked his life and those of the Concerned Citizens to deliver the tapes and affidavits to the editors, the remaining stories would never appear on the pages of the *Examiner*. "It was," Les recollects, "the greatest dereliction of duty in the history of journalism." Ironically, on January 17, 1973, Executive Editor Tom Eastham nominated Les for the Pulitzer Prize, stating in a letter to the Advisory Board:

> Examiner readers today know what is really happening in the church, and they also know why. Readers who a few years ago ignored church news now search the pages for Kinsolving and write to congratulate us for printing him. . . . The pattern set by Rev. Kinsolving is truly a distinguished service, to both religion and journalism.

However, none of the published Temple articles were submitted for the nomination.

"I Saw It–
Kinsolving Did It!!"

SHORTLY AFTER THE Peoples Temple–*Examiner* debacle, Les went east in November to cover the Catholic Bishops conference in Washington, D.C., along with various speaking engagements. Before heading back to the Bay Area, he decided to motor down to southern Virginia to attend a football game between his alma mater Episcopal High and their noted rival, Woodberry Forest. Traveling up a slight incline on a two-lane road not far from Charlottesville, Les never noticed the oncoming truck as he was making a turn in his rental car. "It came roaring over into traffic, and I was hit very hard on the side," he remembers vividly.

Les suffered two broken ribs and a damaged sternum, and was rushed to the University of Virginia hospital in downtown Charlottesville. There he lay for several days, while the broken bones in his chest healed after surgery. A daily smoker, Lester hadn't had a Kent cigarette in over a week. He hardly realized this, since he was distracted by a great deal of pain. When Lester returned home, he went for a check-up where, after an examination, the staff doctor inquired, "Mr. Kinsolving, do you smoke?" Les nodded reluctantly. "Well, do you remember the pain that you had when the anesthesia wore off after the surgery?" Les nodded again, cringing at the thought of it. "Well," the doctor added, "that's what emphysema's like . . . except that it's *slower*." From that moment on, Les never touched another cigarette again. He would stave off nicotine cravings by eating a box or two of Cinnamon "Red Hots" a day.

"The Roly Poly Boy God," published in the *Washington Star* on January 6, 1973, was Lester's reference to the Maharishi Mahesh Yogi, who was quoted in the *Times of India* as saying, "At present, I get the money from where it is in plenty: the United States." Lester further described Maharishi as "one of India's major, if unofficial bogus holy men," who had "recently reached a new pinnacle in blatant pseudo-ecclesiastical flimflammery. . . . The boy god looks as if he is either a pubescent Gautama Buddha suited up for Pop Warner football—or else the world's best fed midget."

Having established "Divine Light Missions in 45 states," the Maharishi, also known as the "Savior of the World," made a return trip to India, where "he was accompanied by seven jumbo jets full of U.S. disciples" along with a briefcase totaling "$80,000 in currency, precious stones and watches. "There is little if any control over the export of fakirs—beyond the Foreign Exchange Control Act, by which the Reserve Bank of India can restrain Indian nationals from accumulating fortunes abroad. Hence the Maharishi ran into trouble in London, recently, where he purchased a $33,000 yellow Rolls Royce."

Les elaborated further on "The American yen for bizarre religion" when reporting on the growing popularity of Satanism in "Devil's First Tactic":

Also overlooked has been a revival of the belief in Hobgoblins, although Satanism—the devil-worship which recently led to a teenager's ritual murder in New Jersey—is widespread. This particularly repulsive and imbecilic movement might have shriveled in the manner of most fads, but for the obviously unintended longevity given it by the alarmed acknowledgements of such world religious leaders as Pope Paul VI and Billy Graham.

Gadfly

Shortly after the article appeared in the *Examiner*, Lester received an irate response from Church of Satan founder and High Priest, Anton LaVey. The following date was written on Mr. LaVey's letter: "4 February VIII A.S.":

You ego-starved nincompoop! Your article in the January twenty-ninth *Ex* citing a murder in New Jersey as your only example of contemporary Satanism displays your typically-theological gift for selective inattention. You fucking well know what the majority of modern Satanists' doctrinal and behavioral approach to life is. *I* ought to, for I have set the standards. I also know sour grapes when confronted with vats overflowing.

Rege Satanas!
Anton Szandor LaVey

Although the *San Francisco Examiner* refused to publish the remaining four exposés on the Peoples Temple, Les still pursued the story in earnest. "Messiah From Ukiah" appeared in the *Washington Star* in early February, which detailed Lester's futile attempts to alert the higher-ups of Jim Jones's denomination:

National leaders of the 1.4 million-member Christian Church (Disciples of Christ) headquartered here, are either unable or unwilling to do anything about one of their pastors in California who has claimed to be the reincarnation of Jesus Christ. . . . The denomination's president and general minister, Dr. Dale Fiers, told me: "There has been no request for any investigation from his region . . . so we are standing behind the church."

Les also reported that he had a copy "of a letter written [by David Conn in 1970] to that regional conference's acting president, Nellie Kratz, asking that the Rev. Mr. Jones' highly questionable healing methods be investigated. Her response to Conn was 'I really don't feel I have any evidence on which to act or even on which to talk to Jim.'"

The previous December, Les attended a meeting of the National Council of Churches and confronted the Disciples of Christ leadership there. They ignored his pleas for an investigation, claiming every church had local autonomy and that "a probe was being done by the district attorney's office [where Tim Stoen was an assistant] and other legal bodies." It would later be revealed that the Disciples of Christ accepted $1.1 million from the Peoples Temple, from 1966 until its demise in 1978, in Jonestown.

After Lester's newest Temple article appeared in the *Merced Sun-Star*, an angry letter to the editor appeared:

We protest the article that was published by the Rev. Kinsolving. . . . We like the truth but we think there were some things more important than looking for something wrong with Rev. Jim Jones, when we who know him find no fault in him. We learned from reliable sources he [Rev. Kinsolving] was kicked out of his church. Why does he find fault with Rev. Jones. . . . He is only doing good for the people. . . . He teaches us brotherhood, love, peace and good will toward all men.

(*Undersigned:* Opal, Eugene and Miles Glover, Robert Burns, Alton Taylor, Miles Mary Salery, Eva Williams, John Craig, Margie and Claude Nutt, Zula Mae Beal, and Lucie L. Woods.)

On February 16, Rev. Edward Murphy sent Les a copy of his letter to the *Sun-Star*, countering the Temple supporters:

Pastor Kinsolving was not "kicked out of church." He has been unacceptable to a number of parishes, but never has he been deposed. That is a very serious matter of judgment which is beyond our prerogative. When you state that you feel "everyone should be able to worship their own God," let us also remember that all Christians worship the same God (this means all denominations). As for your statement, "we who know him find no fault in him" (referring to Pastor Jones), I feel that is a rather broad statement in that we all, as innately rebellious people, "fall short of the glory of God," and that no man is infallible. In short, everyone has faults.

In "How Churches Backed Indian Caravan," Les described the "Trail of Broken Treaties," where a group of American Indian protestors traveled cross-country in the fall of 1972 to the Bureau of Indian Affairs in Washington, D.C., where they "caused $2 million in damage." The Indian caravan "was partially financed by [Los Angeles'] Episcopal Bishop, the Rt. Rev. Ivol Ira Curtis. Bishop Curtis, who is president of the denomination's 8th Province (West Coast) approved the appropriation of $10,000 in National Episcopal funds for the caravan."

Other donating denominations were the Methodist Church ($4,500) and the Mormon Church, which "provided $1,000 in food and $150 worth of gasoline." Caravan coordinator Russell Means was a prominent leader of the American Indian Movement (AIM), a group which "was the recipient of a $40,000 grant from the Roman Catholic Church's Campaign for Human Development . . . despite the extensive criminal records of three other AIM national leaders. For Dennis Banks and the Bellecourt brothers, Vernon and Clyde, have among them accumulated 19 felony convictions for such crimes as assault, burglary, and robbery."

Shortly after Indian caravan members vandalized the Bureau of Indian Affairs, painting "AIM" on the walls and destroying bathroom facilities, "Bishop Curtis wrote of the caravan he had helped finance: 'These people are not hooligans. Many of them are young and a few of them are in college.'" Rev. George Pierce of the Pine Ridge Mission, "in the Sioux Reservation at Pine Ridge, SD . . . refused to have anything to do with the Broken Treaties caravan, because it was dominated by AIM, which was guilty of the following infractions:

Last spring, in Pine Ridge, AIM was responsible for the disruption and demoralization of our local school, as well as the intrusion of our hospital and jail. They also beat a Methodist minister so badly as to put him in the hospital. . . . AIM was also responsible for the takeover of the Fort Totten, ND jail last summer, at which time they released all the prisoners— including two felons convicted of the rape of two Indian ladies. The Rev. Webster Two Hawk, president of the Rosebud Sioux Tribal Council, has taken a strong stand against AIM. . . . "We believe in social justice—but we do object to the Church funding hooligans."

On February 13, Jay Lintner, Program Coordinator for United Ministries, sent off a letter to Ed Dooley, Lester's editor. After inquiring into Kinsolving's background, he made the following statements:

The church, I am certain, will survive such one sided hostility. However, in our nations Indians have not done so well at surviving this sort of racist attack. In seeking some kind of justice for Indians, I am curious to know whether your policy is to print only such vicious and one sided attacks upon Indians as in this article, or whether you also print articles which carry an opposing point of view, and leave it to your readers to sort out the truth between differing positions.

Les took Lintner to task in his response of February 25:

Is it possible that you believe that there is no such thing as an Indian gangster? This is how your letter sounds—and if this is the case, I would suggest that you contact the Sioux reservation in Pine Ridge, or Bishop Harold Jones, the only Indian bishop I know of in the U.S., and ask him about Indian gangsters. For Bishop Jones told me that his sister-in-law was one of the teachers in the Pine Ridge school that these AIM thugs disrupted and demoralized last Spring. . . . Your letter also charges that my article "convicts both Indians and church." I hardly am able to "convict" any churches—although the conduct of some church officials surely needs to be exposed. As for convicting the leaders of AIM, that would be something on the order of gilding the lily.

At Glide Memorial Methodist Church, the high jinks continued: "We'll now say the Lord's prayer," advised the officiant, who was Glide's "Rabbi in Residence," Abraham Feinberg. "Surely somebody will remember it from their school days! This is Glide Memorial Church," announced the rabbi later during the service. "As far as I am concerned you can just drop the Methodist!"

While Cecil Williams was away on "important business" that Sunday, Black Panther Bobby Seale, who was running for Mayor of Oakland, would guest preach that day:

Seales' sermon, an almost completely disorganized and inor- dinately silly ramble, suggests that he is badly in need of some tutoring in the fine art of rabble rousing—from Mas- ter Cecil. For by contrast to A. Cecil's weekly delivery of shrieking pizzazz, Seale's almost low-key growling about "racist-imperialist warmongering-Oakland Rotary Club fat businessmen and police-trying-to-spy-on-us-with-their- technology" fell flat.

Dr. Gregory Yasinitsky, pastor of Calvary United Methodist Church in San Francisco, wrote to Les and thanked him for the lat- est report on Glide: "May I assure you that you are doing great work and we all who are on the other side of the fence are grateful to you." Dr. Yasinitsky mailed the article to Rev. Robert Ozment, who responded with, "I hope Lester Kinsolving will continue to keep the public informed about the activities at Glide. By doing so, maybe the pressure will become so great that someone of authority will feel the compulsion to act."

Other encouraging correspondence came from Billy Graham on March 5: "Dear Les: I am just on my way to Europe and Africa.

Your article 'Peace Ends Billy Graham's Ordeal' as published in the *Asheville Citizen* March 1, 1973 was excellent! Thank you! At the next opportunity, I am going to give it to the President."

After finishing a speaking engagement at the Contra Costa Press Club in late March, Lester received a gracious letter from the club's president, Steven Shelby: "You certainly dispel the image of pious pomposity popularly believed to be vested in high-church Anglicism. . . . The members of the program committee did not invite a speaker known to be controversial and outspoken and then expect to be able to sit back in mellow yellow bliss while wafted in pleasantries. . . . "

In closing, Shelby offered "our sincere thanks for a great presentation, and our best wishes to you and your family in your move to Washington."

By early 1973, Les began to realize that less space was being offered to the religion beat in daily newspapers across the nation. What was red-hot church controversy in the 1960s was now beginning to cool down by the new decade. Thirsty for a new challenge, Lester decided to make a bold move into the world of political news.

"*Star-Tribune* opens bureau in Washington," ran the headline in the Casper, Wyoming, newspaper July 31, 1973. "Wyoming's first Washington bureau in history, due to open officially on Aug. 1, will be headed by the first clergyman in history to be appointed chief of a Washington bureau. . . . He will concentrate on the Congressional delegations from Wyoming and Idaho for the *Star-Tribune* as well as three of Idaho's four largest daily newspapers, in Lewiston, Twin Falls and Pocatello."

Les stated that "there is considerable similarity in covering religion and politics, because religious leaders are all astute politicians—although none of them are ever supposed to admit it." He insisted he would "continue to wear his clerical collar in the Senate and House Press Galleries as well as while attending occasional press conferences or briefings in the White House":

"If anyone questions my garb—and no one has yet," he observed, "I'll refer them to Father Drinan of the Sixth Congressional

District of Massachusetts—who wears his collar on the House floor! He is a good friend and a top congressman."

However, at his very first White House press briefing, Les was cornered by five reporters, including "the most respected of the White House press corps," John Osborne of *New Republic*. They interrogated him, demanding to know who he was and what he was doing at the White House. Les responded, "I'm also a religion columnist. Have you directed any of these questions to Congressman Drinan?" None of them answered back, and the clique broke up. After a year of having "so many of them at my throat," Les decided to forego his collar, which, for him, was "a bit emotional . . . however, the White House is not a religious beat."

The move to the East Coast would not be an easy one for the Kinsolving family. "The only reason I was glad to leave California was that we would be far away from the Peoples Temple," Sylvia recalls. Not only had the cult burglarized their home, but it was also revealed that they had conducted nightly surveillance on the house by hiding in the tall bushes outside a school yard across the street. Years later, the *New York Times* reported that Terri Buford, a former Temple member, testified "under oath before a Federal grand jury" that Tim Stoen and Jones had discussed plans to murder Les, either by beating him to death in a burlap bag, or shooting him with poisoned darts. Stoen "had even used the District Attorney's office of Mendocino County . . . to research the type of poison that could be used."

Since Laura was graduating from high school and Kathleen from junior high, the transition would be fairly smooth; however, Tommy would have to start over in a new high school as a junior, and leave his close buddies behind. Moreover, the political as well as seasonal climate of suburban northern Virginia was the antithesis of the colorfully militant Berkeley scene. According to the UC Berkeley campus newspaper, the *Daily Californian,*

On May 9, 1972, a resolution was proposed to allocate $1,000 in reparations to a bombed hospital in Vietnam. It failed to pass after only two [Berkeley City] council members voted for

it. Because of the intense opposition, the meeting was held at
the Berkeley Community Theater, where 3,000 people filled
the room and the council sat onstage. . . . The crowd streamed
out of the auditorium angry and frustrated, and trashing began
immediately. A large bonfire was set in nearby Provo Park.

Lester was relieved to escape the radical antics of Bay Area politics, and
return home to his native East Coast. Virginia was considered "Kinsolving country"—as his grandfather Lucien Lee Kinsolving once declared,
"This is Virginia, and I love every blade of grass in Old Virginia!" After
arriving at Dulles Airport in July, the family made a temporary stay at
Sterling's Holiday Inn, where they were entertained nightly by lounge
lizard Archie Ashe. They finally settled in their new four-bedroom home
in Vienna, across from a cow pasture on Beulah Road.

Eager to spruce up the new house a bit, Lester decided to try his
luck at gardening, by planting a row of flowers in front of the house.
He drove to the closest nursery and bought several bunches of violets,
which he proceeded to smash into the ground. Terribly frustrated at
his lack of a green thumb, Lester watched the hapless violets wither
and die, and trudged back into the house, where he exclaimed, "I
am GOING to hire a MAN!!" He never followed up with the hiring
process, and gave up the cause of gardening forever.

Editor Phil McAuley was delighted to publish two of Lester's earliest political stories in the *Casper Star-Tribune* during the latter part
of July 1973: "McGee Makes Nixon 'List,'" provided details about
how "Sen. Gale McGee (Dem-Wyo.) has been described as 'a fat cat'
in a memo to former Presidential consul John Dean." The memo by
Gordon Strachan, H.R. Halderman's former assistant, mentions that
McGee's visit to Sen. Edward Muskie is "of interest to you and the
'political enemies' project."

In "House Dumps Congress Raise," Les reported the following:

Consideration of revisions in the controversial Federal Salaries
Act was decisively defeated Monday by the House of Represen-
tatives, 237–156. Wyoming's Congressman Teno Roncalio told

the *Star-Tribune*: "It's not that there hasn't been an increase in the cost of living here in Washington—or any decrease in the amount of work that most Congressman do. It's just that [this] is no time to consider any pay raise for Congress."

Besides covering the political scene, Lester would occasionally return to his old stomping ground of the religion beat for some additional lively copy. Through a press release, he was informed of an illegal ordination of women into the Episcopal Church being held in September at New York City's Riverside United Church of Christ. Inviting his three teenagers along for the road trip and promising they could use the family car for the day, Les was dropped off at the church on Riverside Drive, where a large crowd of reporters and cameramen had gathered in the vestibule for a press conference before the ordination began. Among the general array of questions, Les sounded off with typical controversy: "Why are you taking vows in the Episcopal Church in a church which is not Episcopal?" And "You're taking a vow to obey, which automatically makes you break that vow—would you care to comment?" Although these confrontational inquiries instigated a few groans and disgruntlements, Les was completely unprepared for what was about to take place.

Walking up into the narthex as the press conference wrapped up, Lester heard a nasty remark from the cameraman who trailed behind him. Turning around, Les fired back with, "Why don't you take a long walk on a short pier?!" As the heated exchange escalated into a furious shouting match, the cameraman chose a more drastic measure of combat by flinging his camera toward Lester's face. Thankfully, two reporters pulled at this assailant's shirt before the moment of impact and he fell backwards, exposing a naked, barrel-shaped stomach, which Lester promptly slugged. As his fist hit the cameraman squarely in his paunch, a loud "OOF!!" was heard throughout the church, making every head in every pew turn around.

Suddenly a voice rang through the astonished congregation: "I SAW IT—KINSOLVING DID IT!!!" Les turned and immediately recognized the man with the white Afro in the dashiki, who pointed his finger as he shouted his accusation. He was Donald J.A. Morton, an unfrocked Methodist minister from South Africa whom Les had investigated a few years earlier. In 1971, Morton had abandoned his wife and two children, seduced sixteen-year-old Louise Stack from his youth group, and fled South Africa with the teenager to London, where he attempted to marry her, but was turned down by order of the Archbishop of Canterbury. He then migrated to New York and was later hired as a consultant with the National Council of Churches. On December 7, 1975, Morton made a public confession at American University, that he had been unfrocked by the Methodist Church because, "I was a naughty boy."

Les defended himself with a "YOU'RE CRAZY!!" as two custodians broke up the near-bloody altercation. After a short reprieve, Lester watched the ordination, where, during communion, two bishops administered wafers the size of manhole covers. "Undoubtedly this was meant to attract the attention of the cameras," Les quipped.

Back in the nation's capitol, President Nixon was buckling under the stress of the Watergate scandal. In front of a national TV audience, the disgraced commander-in-chief "seized his press secretary by the lapels, spun him around and shoved him toward a number of reporters," according to Lester's "Deputy Press Secretary Ducks Queries on Shoving," published September 5, 1973 in the *Casper Star-Tribune*.

President Nixon's Deputy Press Secretary, Gerald Warren, repeatedly refused Tuesday to disclose to newsmen whether the President has ever apologized for shoving Press Secretary Ron Ziegler, last month in New Orleans. . . . A number of reporters asked Warren why he had not answered the question—which was initially raised by the *Casper Star-Tribune*.

The next day, a memo enclosed with a clipping was sent to Les from the Wyoming paper: "This arrived from an anonymous reader in today's mail." The clipping was a cut-out section of Lester's article, with this following message scrawled over it: "Whatever happened to fairness? Lay off the President!"

Gadfly

Besides having his column printed in the *Washington Star*, Lester was encouraged to approach its rival, the *Washington Post*, by his own National Newspaper Syndicate. Executive Editor Benjamin Bradlee couldn't have been more warm-hearted when Les called his office in early September: "Why sure, Les, come on over!" After a congenial meeting in which Bradlee was quite complimentary, Kinsolving was told that they'd be in touch with him shortly. After two weeks, Les sent off a couple of nudges to Bradlee:

September 17, 1973
    I so very much appreciate your continued consideration of and gracious comments regarding both my column as well as my view-from-the-pew idea. . . . I am also enclosing four additional weekly columns, including one for release at the end of this month. . . .

September 20, 1973
    I certainly don't want to load up your mail box—but I did think the enclosed might be of special interest to you. Today at the White House press briefing, after three references in a row to a "newspaper of general circulation in the Washington area" (as Warren refers to *The Post*) I could resist no longer, so I asked: "Gerry; have you ever been with the President while he is reading *The Post*? How does he react? Does he moan, or grunt, or curse, or laugh, or what?" Needless to say, this opportunity for Warren to give the nation some real human interest was disdained—with the 37th "No comment" in the past two days. I am not discouraged, however, in remembering that great old Western proverb that Even A Steer Can Try—and also that evasions in the White House still make copy.

A few days later, Les received the following from Bradlee: "I think we'll pass on your column for now. We just are in no position to add columns in any area right now. Please try again in six months." And with that, a long, vitriolic feud between the two newspapermen would launch, for many years to come.

14

"Shut Up, You Bawling Jackass!"

O N NOVEMBER 7, Les sent a letter to Republican Senator Cliff Hansen of Wyoming, in an earnest plea to improve seating arrangements at President Nixon's press conferences. Michael Schroth, an assistant to Press Secretary Ron Zeigler, had promised Lester a reserved seat in the East Room of the White House, only to give it to another, more recognizable reporter. When Les "took this matter up with Schroth" after the press conference, "he appeared singularly unconcerned."

Informed that the preferential seating was due to "tradition" and "seniority," Les expressed hope to the senator "for any assistance you could render in alleviating this discrimination against Western newspapers in sparsely populated states. . . . If the White House is at a loss for some criterion on which to assign these reserved seats, I would suggest that each daily newspaper bureau, each nationally circulated periodical and each network or electronic group be given priority for reserved seats provided they regularly cover the daily press briefings." He also suggested to the Senator that "the remaining seats might be available by a drawing on the day of the press conference."

Gadfly

Les was so incensed by the unfairness that he drew up plans for "A Lottery for Presidential News Conferences: Questions—and Some Possible Answers," which included the following:

QUESTION: What would motivate anybody to attend if all the questioners are selected in advance?

ANSWER: If necessary, after the first 27 minutes of the news conference call for two or three wild card questioners to be recognized by the President, since the equal opportunity goal would have been fulfilled.

QUESTION: Why should those who spend full-time covering the White House have no more chance to question the President than those whose only appearances at the White House are to cover Presidential news conferences?

ANSWER: In the lottery, each media which has at least one full time reporter covering the White House will have three entries. . . . Each media which has had at least one reporter who has for the past year covered either the White House of the presidential campaign on an average of once per week, shall be entitled to one entry. . . .

Although rejected at first, Lester's lottery idea would eventually be implemented, at Ronald Reagan's first presidential press conference. At present, he wasn't faring well with President Nixon, who was grappling miserably with the final months of his embattled administration. By early 1974, Les had resigned himself to joining in with the rest of the reporters, who desperately shouted at Nixon. On March 11, the *San Francisco Examiner* ran a short blurb in their Outlook section with the headline, "He Will Be Heard!"

Lester Kinsolving, an Episcopal priest from San Francisco at one time, who writes on religion, has become something of a minor gadfly in Washington. His screeching sounds of "Mr.

President! Mr. President!" at one Nixon press conference so angered the respected columnist John Osborne of *The New Republic* that Osborne turned scornfully and said: "Shut up, you bawling jackass." Next time out, Kinsolving kept his mouth shut—and instead held up a poster with old English printing saying, "Mr. President." Nixon ignored it all.

Photographs were featured on front pages nationwide, showing a stoic Nixon pointing his finger away from the pesky placard. Captions read, "Newsman Holds Sign to Attract Nixon's Attention," and "Unidentified Reporter Tries Novel Way of Getting President's Attention."

In April, Les was invited to speak at the Rockford Woman's Club in Illinois, where he shared his experience covering both religious and political beats, as reported in the *Freeport Journal-Standard*:

Armed with a booming voice and a vigorous vocabulary, the Rev. Lester Kinsolving, columnist and Episcopal priest, told the Rockford Woman's Club Tuesday that "the White House is conducting war with the press. . . . Nixon sets up his press conferences so reporters are crowded together and must shout to be heard. Nixon comes off like St. Francis of Assisi being pursued by a pack of wolves busily devouring themselves. . . .

Although Les stated, "'I look on my writing as a ministry. That's why I wear the clerical collar,' . . . Some women listening to the speech rustled in their seats agitatedly. Some remarks heard were: 'He doesn't show any religious thinking at all,' and 'He's too critical of America.'"

At the start of June, Les was offered a special column for the celebrity tabloid, the *National Star*. It was entitled, "Test Your Religious IQ." Among some of the questions Les posed to readers were, "Is an apostle related to an epistle?" and "The inventor of bourbon whiskey was a Baptist clergyman. True or False?" (the former question being false, and the latter true). Although the *Washington Star* had dropped his column and the *Washington Post* was no longer interested, Les had already been picked up by his hometown paper, the *Vienna Globe*. It was the beginning of a productive partnership that would span several years.

Still reeling from embarrassment at having been exposed for giving $10,000 to Angela Davis, a moderator for the United Presbyterian Church, the Rev. Clinton Marsh, sent off a letter to Les on May 22, along with a copy of a handwritten memo mentioning one of Lester's articles: "Dear Clint: With your travels I thought you might miss this and I didn't want you to fail to hear this jackass braying!" Marsh's cover letter stated, "The enclosed note accompanied a copy of your recent swill. I have also been complimented by a number of people that I must be doing something right to come up on your wrong side."

Lester responded with, "Your use of the one word 'swill' to describe my column is of note, as this word is usually defined as food for pigs. Pray tell, Mr. Moderator, just how did you know that my column was 'swill' until after you properly digested it?" A few weeks later, Rev. Marsh sent off his rebuttal: "The answer is that your column was so obviously swill that I didn't taste it or much less swallow and digest it!" Although Les chose to discontinue correspondence, the irate moderator sent off a final missive, simply stating, "Just another love letter." Soon afterward, Les received another angry message, scrawled anonymously on his article, "Abortion Problem": "Keen Solver for Satan's Herods. I wonder what will God say to you when you die with your advocacy of sheer infanticide."

"Methodist Church Hosts Whores" ran in the July 20th issue of the *San Francisco Progress*. Needless to say, Lester reported on the further adventures of Cecil Williams:

> Glide has for some years been in the hands of the Rev. A. Cecil Williams, a generally screeching, pseudo-sacerdotal clown with an absolutely insatiable lust for publicity, together with an uncanny ability to sniff the self-promotional possibilities in new and more spectacular outrages. . . . The Rev. A. Cecil has now outdone himself, by using his Methodist Church to host

a convention of whores. . . . The Rev. A. Cecil has not (as yet) announced any plans to turn Mrs. Glide's Memorial Church into the nation's first Methodist Brothel, which may impress his guest trollops as somewhat square.

Olga D. Levene, incensed at the article, fired off a letter to the editor:

I find it hard to believe that the *San Francisco Progress* had the appalling bad taste to print this slanderous, grotesquely ill-informed article—especially on the "religious" page. More strength to the Glide Memorial Church and the Rev. A. Cecil Williams for giving space and money to the "floozies organization." It's due to the sick moral attitudes of Kinsolving and others like him, that prostitutes suffer the unspeakably cruel and unjust victimization of the present legal system. As editor of this paper you should have more integrity than to permit the publication of this vicious filth.

In the Fall of 1974, Globe Newspapers announced it would be running a new eight-page religion section, with Lester as editor. Entitled *Northern Virginia Religion News*, the first issue would appear on Thursday, September 5. Judy Prisley, a former reporter for the *Tampa-Tribune*, would serve as Les's associate editor. Featured articles would include "View from the Pew," where "sermons [would be] reviewed like drama critics review stage and screen," "Test Your Religious I.Q.," "Bulletin Board," and "Guest Editorial."

By the third issue, controversy was already erupting in Northern Virginia, with such headlines as "Inside the Mormon Temple: Pros and Cons of 'Camelot on the Beltway,'" "Anti-Abortion Attempt to Rock Rocky: The Campaign to Block Rockefeller's Confirmation," and "Should Deformed Babies Be Allowed to Die?: The Reaction to a Local Catholic Priest Who Said 'Yes.'" Besides "Jehovah's Witness Calls Martin Luther a Fornicator and Bigamist," which ran inside the October 24th issue, the Unification Church's D.C. appearance made the front page: "Sun Myong Moon Lays Egg in Constitution Hall: Dancing Girls and a Two-Hour Sermon: Clustered Cuties Couldn't Counteract 'Charlie Chan in Convulsions'":

> Mr. Moon preaches entirely in Korean—which he alternately howls, hisses, groans, grunts, roars, screeches, murmurs or bellows . . . he sounded like a drill instructor of kamikaze pilots, auctioning tobacco during an earthquake. . . . I would add the image of the late Peter Lorre with St. Vitus Dance.

> All of this is translated by Lt. Col. Bo Hi Pak [who] is the reported conduit for extensive support from the South Korean dictatorship. . . . What really convulsed the Moonies (while the rest of the crowd sat dazed or amused or asleep) was the Rev. Mr. Moon's announcement, delivered with a great smirk: "Billy Graham is not Elijah; he comes from North Carolina!" Before the end of Mr. Moon's marathon of screeched nonsense, at least 2,000 people walked out, either in apparent fatigue or disgust.

Les also reported that "a platoon of large and muscular blacks wearing 'CONCERT USHER' tee shirts" assisted "the first three to leave . . . when six of them seized one young heckler [they] carried him out, beat him in the lobby, and slammed his body against a truck." The young man who was beat up had thrown a water balloon in the direction of Rev. Moon, while, "minutes later, two other youths stood and shouted 'C.I.A.'—whereupon they were similarly pounced upon." Outside on the street, protestors carried signs (such as "Moon's God Is Money") and chanted, "Down with Park, the fascist goon, down with his agent, Sun Myung Moon." Security guards also escorted an unidentified black evangelist from the lobby after he began attracting a crowd by loudly preaching, "Moo Moo is a false prophet!"

Top stories in November included "Jesuit Compares National Rifle Association (NRA) to the Mafia," "Bishop Blasts Good Shepherd Leaders as 'Subversive'—They Insulted Him—With Smile Buttons," and "Speaking With Tongues: Charisma or Curse?"

The so-called "charismatic movement," including glossolalia (speaking in tongues) and "divine healing," seeks fervently to entice Baptists into its movement. . . . The heretical teachings of this movement create, in adherents, a false sense of piety and superior holiness and creates a breach of fellowship, all contrary to the New Testament.

In his quest to spread the news of Holy Roller Invasion, Lester included several mini-articles on page two: "Even the Episcopalians—Tongues at Truro," "One Virginia Pastor's Formula for Handling Parochial Babbling: 'How Many Tongues Met?'" "Spirit, Snakes, and Strychnine," "Charisma in the Car Pool: 'Arunkek, Tiblick, Sestua, Glbnick,'" and "Boone Booted for Babbling," in which Les interviewed singer Pat Boone, "a devout member of the archconservative Church of Christ." When Boone "began speaking with tongues, he was 'disfellowshipped' by the Inglewood, California Church. . . . Boone recalled that within hours of the news breaking about his 'disfellowship,' he was contacted by both Jehovah's Witnesses and Mormons." Before going to print, Lester's associate editor Judy Prisley resigned from the paper, since she herself was a member of the charismatic community.

On December 6, four months after President Nixon resigned and Gerald Ford was sworn in as the new President, the *St. Louis Post-Dispatch* ran a blurb and photo in their People column:

White House press secretary Ronald H. Nessen gave a reporter a scolding yesterday for what he said had been rudeness toward Secretary of the Interior Rogers C.B. Morton at a press conference. The reporter, Lester Kinsolving, who is also an Episcopal priest, denied that he had been disrespectful, but Nessen said, "The tone of your questions and your constant interrupting amount to incivility in my point of view." What actually happened: Kinsolving, who writes for a group of western newspapers, asked Morton to explain why the Park Police had not given traffic citations in the famous Tidal Basin incident involving Representative Wilber D. Mills. When Morton jokingly replied, "I wasn't there," Kinsolving told him, "I think you are to be commended for that."

Gadfly

By March 1975, Lester was once again heard over the airwaves. Broadcasting from WAVA, "Washington's only 24 Hour News Station," he delivered "Capital commentary every weekday morning at 7:45, along with 'Today in the White House' and 'The Diplomatic Front' at 3:15 P.M. In his broadcast, "How the President First Gets the News," he reported:

> The following was reported on March 25, by United Press International: "President Ford heard of the assassination (of King Faisal) on the radio, about seven A.M." . . . There remains only one question about this marvelous medium, where the President gets his news first—and we asked that on March 25 at Ron Nessen's daily White House press briefing: "Ron, was the President listening to an all-news radio station?" Amidst the chortles of the White House press corps, Nessen countered: "And if so, which one?" Well Ron, since you mentioned it, yes, which one? Lyndon Johnson, as reported by *Time* magazine, "had the Oval Office wired so he could monitor WAVA instantly." . . . Thanks for listening, Mr. President—and everyone else!

WAVA circulated a promotional with a large photo of a smiling Lester in clerical collar, along with the message:

> Expect the unexpected. Les Kinsolving's friends of yesterday may be his bitterest critics tomorrow. Partly because he has a viewpoint that's distinctively his. And partly because he is almost totally unpredictable.
>
> Agreeable. Disagreeable. Les marches to the beat of a different drummer that is uniquely his own. Sometimes controversial but always interesting and enlightening.

Back at *Northern Virginia Religion News*, Les was firing off exposés of the *Washington Post* left and right: "*Post* Refuses to Publish

Conservatives' 'Unfounded' Letter—Until Paid $1800 For Ad," and
"The Post Goofs Again":

> According to the Friday, May 23 edition of *The Washington Post,*
> the United Presbyterian Church's General Assembly meeting
> in Cincinnati, "Gave $90,000 to the ROSCA Foundation in
> Columbia . . . which had been criticized by the church's synod of
> Columbia as Marxist." This news report is simply not true. It is
> another example of this newspaper's incredibly shoddy reporting
> in the field of religion . . . the Presbyterian Convention voted
> down this $90,000 grant by a three-to-two margin. . . . This
> denomination's nearly three million members are entitled to an
> apology from *The Washington Post* for this misrepresentation.

Unrelated to the previous story, Les ran "The *Post* 'Apologizes'":

> *The Washington Post* has only one eighth of the circulation of the
> *National Enquirer*: "I CUT HER HEART AND ATE IT RAW."
> But *The Post* is definitely beginning to overtake *The Enquirer* in
> credibility. Just how irresponsible this newspaper is becoming
> is seen in the ludicrous manner in which it retracted its page one
> report that U.S. planes conducted major bombing raids during
> the evacuation of Saigon. The retraction came forty-eight (48)
> days after this false story was reported on page one . . . . It was
> published during the height of the vacation season in the least
> circulated edition (Saturday) of the *Post*. . . .

On June 17, WAVA ran the following "Capital Commentary":

> A New York weekly, *The Village Voice*, wrote about sneakiness and
> censorship in [a] *Post* story. *The Voice* said that the words 'who lives
> with Sally Quinn' were censored by Bradlee. . . . When this com-
> mentary asked for Mr. Bradlee's office, in order to get either a con-
> firm or deny, presumably from Bradlee's exceptionally courteous
> and congenial secretary, we got instead of this secretary, Himself.

"What the f_ _ _ (An Anglo-Saxon expletive deleted, indicating fornication) are you trying to do, Kinsolving?! I think you're nuts and so do a lot of people I've talked to!" I replied that I was simply trying to verify a report in *The Voice.*

"I've read your venom!" snarled the slayer of *All the President's Men.* "You're just bitter because we didn't take you on! . . . I have no comment for your commentaries!" said Mr. Bradlee, with a tone of loathing. Just before the telephone clicked, I replied as cheerfully as possible: "Thank you, reader!"

In spite of the seething animosity, the *Post* nevertheless ran a feature story on Les in their Metro section, on Sunday, July 6, 1975. Entitled "Priest as Gadfly: Kinsolving Irks Nessen," *Post* staff writer Bill McAllister drew a vivid portrayal of the Irreverent Reverend:

A large, black-haired Episcopal priest scurried into the White House press room, pulled a fresh yellow legal pad from his bulging tan attaché case and squirmed past several reporters to sit sidesaddle on the case at Ron Nessen's feet. . . . His pointed questions, asked in a loud, booming voice and laced with what one reporter called "moralistic overtones," have also bothered press secretary Nessen. . . . Kinsolving's daily five-minute "Capital Commentary" broadcasts on WAVA are equally controversial, which is just the way the station's general manager Wynn Hott wants them. Hott, who hired Kinsolving about 14 months ago, characterized the priest as a "gadfly who pricks your conscience." [Hott] wanted a newsman who would be a personality. . . . [Kinsolving] offered to be just that when he called up Hott looking for a radio outlet. "You like to stir things up?" Hott asked him then. "He said, 'That's what the game is all about.'"

A few days later, Les received a carbon copy of a letter to the editor, signed by Julio O. Feijoo, and addressed to the *Washington Post*:

I heard an editorial two or three weeks ago by Rev. Kinsolving referring to . . . Benjamin C. Bradlee's personal lifestyle . . . it is rather odd that a writer of the Post spends time and so much newspaper space devoting detail to how the "large black-haired . . . priest scurried into the White House" and how he squirmed past several reporters . . . " (Doesn't that make Kinsolving sound like a cross between a rat and a worm?)

Mr. Feijoo went on further to state, "in all the space not once was there mention of Kinsolving's clashes with Mr. Bradlee. . . . This article is dangerous if it is motivated by a powerful individual's desire to protect his private life through abuse of that power." Moreover, Feijoo warned Bradlee, "You will be open to the same sort of judgment that fell upon the gang of corrupt men whom you helped expose in a certain break-in not so long ago." The *Post* article attracted a great deal of interest in Les's radio broadcasts, along with keeping his syndicated column in good standing with over 200 newspapers. In addition, the Associated Press would present a broadcasting award to Les, for his commentaries on WAVA.

Later that month, a WAVA program manager came across a brown envelope sent to "News Director and Assignment Editor." Postmarked from Redwood Valley, California, it contained an endorsement letter from Rev. John Moore. As the program manager looked it over, he thought Les might be interested. Entering the studio after Les finished another "Capital Commentary," the manager quipped, "You know we got the kookiest things in California—some minister is endorsing a church called the Peoples Temple!"

"Who Teaches You
Methodists Ethics?"

"I'VE KNOWN THE Rev. James Jones for a number of years," wrote the Rev. John Moore, a district superintendent of the United Methodist Church. "I have been impressed with the quality of community life of the church. In my judgment, other churches could learn from Peoples Temple. Their concern and care for their members provides the qualities of family life which has been lost in so many churches. . . . "

Lester was astounded at what he read. What was even more irksome was that the endorsement letter was written and mailed on Methodist letterhead and envelope with a Berkeley address, but mailed from Redwood Valley, where the Peoples Temple church was located. Obviously this was an unauthorized and illegal use of Methodist stationary, which was possibly stolen. Les called four Bay Area newspapers that syndicated his column and made appointments. The *San Francisco Progress, San Jose Mercury News, Sacramento Union,* and *Berkeley Gazette* all expressed interest in this developing story on Jim Jones, who was rapidly gaining power in San Francisco.

At the end of July, Les met up with Sylvia and the kids, who were vacationing that summer in the Berkeley Hills, and made his way down to John Moore's home. As Les approached the Methodist pastor in front of his house, Moore told him he hardly recognized him, since he had gained so much weight. "I stopped smoking," Lester acknowledged with a smile.

Sitting in the backyard, Les began confronting Moore on his letter of endorsement of the Temple, and if he was aware that Tim Stoen had claimed Jim Jones had raised forty people from the dead. Moore agreed that the claim was "ridiculous" but that the Temple had performed many good deeds, such as helping drug addicts, the elderly, and offering educational scholarships. "It's all façade, cover for fraud," Les asserted. He also showed Moore the affidavits of former Temple members, and Rev. Taylor's 1972 letter urging the attorney general to investigate Jones.

Although the evidence Les presented concerned Rev. Moore, he grew angry when Les questioned him if the Methodist letterhead and envelopes were stolen. Rev. Moore demanded that Les get off his property. As he gathered up his files, he inquired, "Who teaches you Methodists ethics?" Moore spat out a retaliation: "I don't trust you—Cecil Williams doesn't trust you!" while Les shot back with, "Cecil's a fraud and you know it!!" After fleeing the Moore residence and driving for an hour, Les reached in the backseat and realized that he'd left his briefcase behind. "That was," he recalled later, "about the worst mistake I ever made."

The next day, August 1, Les made his way to his first appointment at the *San Francisco Progress*. There, talking to the editor, were Tim Stoen and another Temple official, Michael Prokes, who were threatening a lawsuit. Because of high legal fees, the *Progress*, along with the other three newspapers, dropped all plans to print Lester's new Temple exposé.

Defeated once again, Les returned to the East Coast on August 2, and found his briefcase waiting at the United Airlines counter at Dulles International Airport. It had been turned in by John Moore right after he met with Jim Jones and staff at the Temple in San Francisco. Moore was called to the special meeting after informing his daughter Carolyn, Jones's mistress, about Kinsolving's visit.

Three things were missing from the briefcase: Lester's confidential memo to the four newspapers, a file containing letters and enclosures from Eugene Chaikin, and a personal letter to Les from Ukiah resident Ruby Bogner. It was obvious why the Temple visited the four newspapers. In addition, Ruby Bogner received a threatening phone call on August 3, when a woman told her, "If you have another negative thing to say, or make a single comment against the Peoples Temple, it'll be your life, your property, or your job."

"Inspired" by John Moore's declaration that Cecil Williams didn't trust him, Les fired-off a two-page exposé, "Is The Methodist Church Sick?" in *Religion News* on September 18. Highlighted by photos of Rev. Williams hosting prostitutes at their 1974 convention and sitting with Angela Davis at a press conference, Lester related the following:

> When the Rev. A. Cecil reached what may be his pinnacle of publicity—by hosting a convention of whores—Bishop R. Marvin Stuart received protests from all over the county. The Bishop explained in a form letter: "I have no authority over any local church facilities. . . . I cannot govern the actual use of those facilities (nor would I want to do so, frankly, if I had that authority). . . . I must express my reservations about the endorsement of prostitution that I believe is implicit in granting permission to a convention of prostitutes to use meeting rooms in the Glide facility. . . . The buying and selling of human sexuality is evil. It is evil for both parties involved. . . . Jesus had compassion for the woman taken in adultery. . . . But he left the woman with the words, 'Go and sin no more!'"

According to Don Shewey's "Spirit Willing" article on Glide Memorial Church, the hosting of prostitutes was mild, compared to another Williams desecration:

When hippies took over the church one weekend for a happening and someone painted on the men's room wall "Fuck the Church," Williams took it not as offensive obscenity but as inspirational verse. Exercise your spiritual libido! Tickle the tushie of your God-love! Impregnate the house of worship with your passionate, orgasmic love for life! Stick it in and wiggle! Just say ooooaaaohhhhh!

On a lighter note, Les reveled in another exposé in early October, this time on his own denomination: "Episcopal Bishop Considers Ordaining Horse." It featured Lexington Kentucky Bishop William R. Moody's photo with the caption, "Nothing in Canon Law Prohibits My Ordaining Secretariat," a triple-crown-winning horse.

The retired Episcopal Bishop of Lexington, KY has announced that if there are any more illegal ordinations of women to the Episcopal priesthood, he intends to seek permission to ordain the race horse Secretariat. "I find nothing in Canon [Church] law that forbids my ordaining this magnificent product of Kentucky to the priesthood," said the Rt. Rev. William R. Moody, "nor can I imagine his owners objecting. . . . There is not one word in the New Testament which criticizes the Roman Emperor Caligula, who reigned from 37–41 AD—at the time of the 12 apostles—and who made his horse a Counsul of Rome."

Les delighted in relating Bishop Moody's follow-up story to colleagues, stating that one reporter once asked Secretariat if he would like to be ordained in the Episcopal Church. Secretariat's answer?— "NEIGH!!"

Since 1976 was a campaign year in which Ronald Reagan challenged President Gerald Ford for the Republican nomination, Les traveled north to cover the January primary. "Reagan Opens in New Hampshire" was the leading story in *Politics and Religion*, formerly known as *Northern Virginia Religion News*.

[Reagan] warmed the sub-zero temperature of northern New Hampshire with a dazzling smile—which intrigued scores of obviously adoring and hovering women from nine to ninety. He wore green ski pants and threw snowballs—each time with an amusing crack about Ford aide Ron Nessen's jibe at New Hampshire's skiing conditions. . . . But there was much more than the magic of a Hollywood star, as the former California Governor waxed eloquent on economics as if he were a reincarnation of both Alexander Hamilton and Daniel Webster. His primary target: Washington D.C. bureaucracy and financial profligacy.

Not all present were privy to the former actor's charm. One sign displayed the message, "IF THE TORIES WERE ALIVE TODAY — THEY'D BE RUNNING REAGAN'S SHOW."

Back in the nation's capital, scandal was brewing between editors and politicians: "Bradlee Involvement in Another JFK Sizzler" ran on page two of *Politics and Religion*'s February 26th issue.

At least in its new gossip column, *The Washington Star* appears to be willing to take on Katherine Graham's Colossus on L Street and Boss Ben Bradlee. For *The Ear* reports a *People Magazine* tidbit that famed Watergate reporter Bob Woodward confronted crusty Congressman Wayne Hays (D-Ohio) to ask when he plans to marry the lady he's living with. "About the same time," countered Hays, "that Ben Bradlee chooses to make an honest woman out of Sally Quinn." *Ear* reported, unfortunately, that Woodward said this was none of the Congressman's business. But a check with Woodward himself disclosed the following: "I didn't say that's none of Hays' business. I said that's a pretty good answer!"

Lester complimented Woodward for his "commendable response, which came on the same day that the *Post* front-paged yet another alleged adultery by Ben Bradlee's very close friend, the late John F. Kennedy."

The Ear, penned by columnist Diana McLellan, contained gritty gossip in and around Washington, D.C. *The Star* was always overjoyed to scoop the *Washington Post*, its rival newspaper. McLellan became a fond crony of Lester's, and would feature him on a fairly regular basis:

The Vicarious Wrath of God . . . The State Department press room, normally a haven of high demeanor, has been set all awry by the arrival of legendary noisemakers Sarah McClendon and Rev. Lester Kinsolving, *Ear* hears. . . . To one Sarah query, spokesman Robert Funseth said he'd provide an answer later if she would leave her name and phone number. . . . Then Kinsolving, interrupted in mid-harangue by Reuters reporter Lars Eric Nelson, later bellowed at him, "If you ever interrupt me again, you'll have more trouble than you'll know what to do with!" Everyone was terribly embarrassed. *Ear* adores feistiness.

Scarlet Gushings . . . Honestly, every gossip columnist in town has been waiting all year for a ketchup item. . . . On the road with the Prez to Springfield, Ohio, Rev. Lester Kinsolving had the bad luck of stomping on a little ketchup package while reaching for a phone at an outdoor pressroom. (Conditions are awful out there.) The ensuing splat hit the pale natty suit of normally contemplative NBC correspondent Russ Ward, who exploded and call Kinsolving "a gorilla in a priest's suit." Kinsolving was all innocence until he found the defunct ketchup cartridge attached to the sole of his shoe (right where Adlai Stevenson used to wear his hole). Apologies followed and Ward withdrew his simian suggestion. . . .

Later that year, Les received the following invitation in the mail:

Because you have been mentioned in
The Ear
and lived to tell the truth
You are cordially invited to attend a benefit
Ear Ball

Gadfly

a Champagne Dansant at the glittering new
Hyatt Regency Washington

With D'arcy and His Orchestra on the dance floor and crepes served at midnight, the benefit for the *Ear* as well as for Galludet University proved to be a most splendid occasion for all those who instigated newsworthy buzz and prattle on the D.C. scene.

On Thursday, March 18, Les and colleague Sarah McClendon, who had covered the White House beat since the Presidency of Franklin Roosevelt, appeared on Tom Snyder's *The Tomorrow Show* on NBC-TV. They were invited by Producer Pamela Burke after Les sent a letter of protest to Barbara Hering, senior counsel at NBC, regarding a previous broadcast in January, where Mr. Snyder had made certain comments along with his guest, Dick Reeves, when discussing the White House press corps:

REEVES: "The cloth"—I mean Lester Kinsolving—one example of people who are there . . .

SNYDER: . . . A sort of "roast rector" . . . out and out mean . . . fight-picking reporter . . .

Les confronted Ms. Hering: "Dick Reeves . . . simply tried to malign me on the NBC network—without ever having talked to me; without any warning; without my being present and able to defend myself. . . . Here Mr. Snyder ties it up. Kinsolving is quite definitely: not nice, not friendly, and not outgoing—and not present to defend himself. Thank you NBC for fairness in action!"

Shortly before receiving a congratulatory letter from Pamela Burke—"What a terrific program! I do hope you had a good time—we did!" Les attended a noon White House press briefing:

Q (PHIL JONES, CBS): Could you please give some reaction to Les Kinsolving and Sarah McClendon's appearance on *The Tomorrow Show?*

MR. NESSEN: When was that?

Q: You didn't watch it last night?

MR. NESSEN: I did not.

Q: You are unaware that they made an appearance on nationwide television?

MR. NESSEN: If I had known that I would have stayed up later.

Q: Doesn't the White House videotape that, Ron?

MR. NESSEN: No, they don't. If I had known about it, maybe I could have asked them to.

Q: Could you get Jones to give us a pool report?

MR. NESSEN: That is a good idea, Phil. Maybe Les could give us a pool report as a participant.

Q (KINSOLVING): No comment. I think it would be inappropriate.

MR. NESSEN: Les, you owe it to the people.

Q: I was very grateful that NBC was fair enough to give me an opportunity to answer charges raised before.

MR. NESSEN: What were the charges?

Q: That I bait you. (Laughter)

MR. NESSEN: Did you refute it or rebut it?

Q: I think it would be inappropriate for me to judge that, Ron.

Gadfly

MR. NESSEN: Don't you think the people have a right to know whether you rebutted it or not? You are a public figure. The people are paying for their television sets—and you don't expect them to pay that money and not get an answer, do you? What happened to the open clergy we heard about?

Amidst laughter, the questioning then shifted to another subject.

On April 22, *Politics and Religion* ran a review, "Nessen, Ford and N.B.C. Degrade the Presidency," which detailed a guest appearance by Ron Nessen on the now-legendary *Saturday Night Live*. "NBC has achieved the most tasteless, witless, repulsive spectacle since it marketed the nuptials of Tiny Tim":

> Nessen as a comedian is something on the order of Earl Butz as Secretary of State. Even with seven or eight costume changes, the President's Press Secretary bombed almost continuously during this utterly dreadful production. Side acts included Bill Crystal (?) who has all the appeal of Frankenstein . . . as well as a quartet of hairy screechers called the Patty Smith Group—with Patty contorting her face into a remarkable resemblance to Lena the Hyena of Lower Slobbovia—with howling to match.

After viewing such *SNL* skits as "The idea of making jam out of hemorrhoids," "The 1976 Presidential Erection," and "How to spruce up douches with carbonation," Lester urged President Ford and Ron Nessen to "hold a joint press conference to apologize to the American people for, in effect, allowing dirty graffiti on the White House walls—and this on the first hour of Easter."

From a White House press briefing on May 21st, the following was printed on page two of *Politics and Religion*, in "Ron Nessen Bombs Again":

The questioning was sharp and the notorious Nessen temper looked as if it might erupt when . . .

SOFT-SPOKEN *CLIFFORD EVANS* OF RKO GENERAL PURRED THE
FOLLOWING INQUIRY: Is it possible that the Attorney General
[Edward Levi] might resign over differences with the President
who opposes bussing?

MR. NESSEN: *JESUS CHRIST!!*

*(Fleeting moment of silence while the White House press corps
assessed.)*

RESPONSE BY SHARP ONE-LINER *JIM DEAKIN* OF THE *ST. LOUIS
POST DISPATCH*: It *is* fascinating how these briefings are always taking on new dimensions!

ADDITIONAL CHIRP BY *WALT ROGERS* OF AP RADIO: There goes
the Baptist vote!

Somehow we have never gotten the impression . . . that "Jesus Christ"
is a possible replacement of Edward Levi as Attorney General [!]

Two days later, the *Washington Post* broke the 1976 scandal of Congressman Wayne Hays and his "secretary" Elizabeth Ray, in "Closed
Session Romance on the Hill": "For nearly two years, Rep. Wayne
L. Hays (D-Ohio), powerful chairman of the House Administration Committee, has kept a woman on his staff who said she is paid
$14,000 a year in public money to serve as his mistress." Incensed at
the hypocrisy, Lester ran a page-one story on June 3: "Wayne & Liz
& Ben & Sally—The *Washington Post* Morality: Mistresses are of no
public interest if kept by powerful editors; only if kept by powerful
Congressmen."

The volcanic temper of the Executive Editor of the *Washington Post* has been known to erupt with horrifying consequences
to anyone so rash as to even titter at his Very Special Relationship with his subordinate editor, Sally Quinn. And, quite

conveniently, both the *New York Times* and the *Washington Star* have apparently agreed that the sex life of powerful editors is entitled to a sacrosanctity of concealment which is unavailable to elderly Congressional chairmen, who may be afflicted with either hyperactive prostates or second puberty.

Les disclosed further scandal, which instigated yet another of Ben Bradlee's frothing eruptions:

The Post has reported in titillating detail the conduct of Congressman Wayne Hays . . . yet there was no *Post* follow-up of the report of WAVA News and P&R that on the night of July 9, 1975, a blue Chevrolet Vega was parked—on the sidewalk—outside Sally Quinn's $100,000 mansion. An alert neighbor got the tag number of this vehicle . . . which was registered in the name of Antoinette Pinchot Bradlee. What was Mr. Bradlee's second ex-wife's car doing parked all night long in front of Sally's? Is it possible that the ladies were comparing notes on Benjy?

Les added even more fuel to the fire, in alerting the public of Bradlee's tactics, which would never be mentioned in the *Post*: "His having lobbied to have the *Post* receive the Pulitzer Prize—instead of Woodward and Bernstein," and referring to a reporter applying to fill the vacancy of *Post* Los Angeles bureau chief as "a gifted journalist who is a pain in the ass. . . . None of us wants a pain in the ass out there," and "his peddling of his own book *Conversations With Kennedy* on the *Post* premises."

The following February, Lester's friend Henry Hinck sent him a copy of a response he received from the *Washington Post*: "I am glad to hear of the qualities that Les Kinsolving showed to you. He has not shown them to me. Sincerely, Benjamin C. Bradlee."

Delighted to continue down this path of unabashed needling, Les attended a Washington, D.C., rally against the South African government in early July.

Perhaps the high point of the rally—at least of any nationally known or even locally known speakers—came when Washington's renowned City Councilman and Methodist minister, the Rev. Douglas Moore, was introduced (the introduction included no mention of his arrest record for assaulting his girlfriend's car with his car, using false license plates, and for biting an 18-year-old tow truck operator on the back).

During his speech to 500 participants, Rev. Moore "announced that a recent commentary on South Africa, as broadcast by WAVA News, was nothing but (the vernacular for bovine excrement). Such an accolade from the Rev. Councilman prompted us to obtain the following interview, just after his epochal speech":

KINSOLVING: Excuse me, Councilman, I was just wondering—you mentioned something about WAVA. What was that?

MOORE: That guy's a right-winger over at WAVA and I think people ought to go on the air to challenge him for that garbage he puts out.

KINSOLVING: I see. What garbage are you talking about? What's this guy's name?

MOORE: I don't know his name. I wouldn't even dignify to remember his name.

KINSOLVING: What was the garbage you're talking about?

MOORE: He's defending South Africa.

KINSOLVING: Defending South Africa? What did he say to defend it?

MOORE: He's saying that blacks in South Africa should look at other African countries and realize that they're the best paradise. And that's b***s***.

KINSOLVING: I see. Well, what other countries would you suggest in Africa are much better in so far as—

MOORE: Who are you from? Who are you with?

KINSOLVING: Who am I? I'm from WAVA.

MOORE: (after a slight pause) Are you the man?

KINSOLVING: I'm the man.

MOORE: O.K. Well, you're a SORRY person to be putting that garbage out on the air. I'm going to respond to you. I'm going to respond to you.

KINSOLVING: I appreciate your interest.

MOORE: I'm going to respond to you: you're a hypocrite!

KINSOLVING: I appreciate your interest.

MOORE: The airways do not belong to you.

KINSOLVING: I realize that. We do appreciate your interest. Did you hear the broadcast?

MOORE: I heard of it.

KINSOLVING: You heard OF it? You mean you haven't heard it firsthand? Councilman, are you accepting information secondhand?

MOORE: I'm going to do you in! Cause you're a whole white racist! You always have been!

KINSOLVING: I see. Are you going to bite me?

MOORE: No.

KINSOLVING: Oh, good.

MOORE: I'm going to whip you in an election.

KINSOLVING: Whip me in an election?

MOORE: Yeah. There's no question.

KINSOLVING: I see. Well, thank you Councilman Moore.

Excerpts of the WAVA broadcasts Moore was referring to were reprinted in the *Washington Star,* shortly before the anti-apartheid rally:

When asked about . . . black nationalist terrorists, President Ford's Ambassador to the U.N., William Scranton, noted that U.S. credibility in black Africa depends on "our help and abetment in the liberation of southern Africa." Does Mr. Scranton mean "liberation" in the sense of the 19 military dictatorships and 22 one-party governments in the black Africa where he yearns for U.S. credibility?

. . . Such rioting in Soweto, if continued, could result in massive black deportations—in the manner in which Field Marshall Amin drove Indians out of Uganda. It would be really tragic if the blacks of Soweto were deported to any of a number of black African dictatorships where wages are microscopic and where the bloodshed makes Soweto and Sharpeville minor skirmishes by comparison.

News of Lester's South African stance was heard in newsrooms across the nation, which *Californian* City Editor Eric Brazil reported in "From Salinas to White House Gadfly: The Rev. Les is making his mark": "Those who recall the Salinas Kinsolving as a man of liberal, leftish persuasion, may be surprised to learn that he seems up to his clerical collar in apologetics for the South African and Rhodesian governments."

Brazil also reiterated what was now common knowledge regarding Lester's stature in the White House: "It wasn't long before reports started coming out of the capital about Kinsolving's impossible, obnoxious, often incomprehensible questioning of Presidents and press secretaries. Whether regarded as a jackass or a gadfly, Kinsolving is the most conspicuously individualistic newsperson in Washington."

As Brazil attended one press briefing, where Nessen "said he was unable to respond" to Lester's question "whether President Ford found the prospect of a 'bloodbath' on the nation's death rows next October less distasteful than pardoning former President Nixon." UPI's Richard Growald guffawed. Kinsolving tartly suggested that his question was a serious, civil one that merited an answer. "I find it funny," Growald said. "Well I don't," Kinsolving said, adding that he'd be pleased if Growald would refrain from interrupting his questions.

After the press briefing, Brazil sat with Lester and Sarah McClendon, who both gave their opinion of the current press secretary. While Sarah had a generally "low regard," Les asserted "that if Ford were to win reelection in November, Nessen would probably be the first in the administration to be fired." The following altercation then took place:

NESSEN: What was that? What did you say, Les? (Nessen's voice cracked across the room like a rifle shot.) Say it loud. Haven't you got the nerve to say it loud? (Nessen rises from the couch where he had been shooting the breeze with some reporters.)

KINSOLVING: (standing up as Nessen walks toward his table to confront him) Do you want me to?

NESSEN: Yes, I really do.

KINSOLVING: Fine, Ron, what I was saying is that if Ford is elected in November the first thing he'll do is fire you and replace you with

Greener (William T. Greener, Jr. is deputy press secretary to President Ford.)

NESSEN: I'm glad you finally found the nerve to say it to my face.

KINSOLVING: I didn't just find it, I've always had it.

NESSEN: I just wanted to know what my press room is being used for. (turning away) Character assassination.

KINSOLVING: And eavesdropping too, Ron.

After this unnerving scuffle subsided, Lester told Brazil that "Nessen is . . . an arrogant punk . . . he likes to bully certain people and I'm one of them, but he knows I'm not going to take his crap. I've been in the White House three years, and hell week should be over."

Since 1976 was an election year, it was expected that President Gerald Ford would be choosing a vice-presidential running mate, as he intended to win the election in November. In a large front-page photo in the *Washington Post* on Saturday, July 10, the President was surrounded by reporters in the Oval Office, where he announced, "I exclude nobody." Readers scanning this leading weekend story were undoubtedly intrigued by the stoic newsman in the clerical collar, busily scribbling notes on a large yellow pad not far from the commander-in-chief.

Besides the election, America would be celebrating its 200th anniversary on July 4. Massive media coverage on celebratory events ran every day and thereafter, including Lester's report, "The 'Peoples Bicentennial' Bust," which was *Politics & Religion*'s top story on July 8:

Months ago, about the same time his boss, Jeremy Rifkin, was obtaining a permit for 250,000 people to "March on the Capitol" on July 4th, Randy Barber was busy in New Hampshire, following candidates (mainly Ronald Reagan) in order to needle them at every whistle stop, as "The Candidate of Big Business." On July 4th near the Tidal Basin, this very same New

Gadfly

Hampshire Needler, Randy Barber, began issuing orders on his bullhorn, in order to form the line for the Big Parade—the long anticipated "March on the Capitol."

When reporters examined the Big Barber Parade, the most optimistic of estimates would venture no more than 2,500—or one (1) per cent of prediction. . . . "Where are the other 249,000?" I asked Randy, pleasantly. "Oh they're waiting for us," . . . Mystified as to where they were keeping this great bulk of the announced quarter of a million, I inquired further: "Are they in the bushes? Or are they up in the trees?" Randy the Dandy treated me to a sneer that was straight vinegar. Then he plunged forward, shouting more orders over his bullhorn.

Then a new figure moved into prominence—and seemed to take over the Big Parade from young Barber . . . an elderly man with rather wild eyes who tried to warm up the rather slim crowd by asking them to join him in singing that old labor favorite, "Solidarity Forever." The march then began during which I attempted to engage Mr. Solidarity in conversation, which he quite angrily disdained. Almost as if on signal, Randy Barber immediately approached my flank, informed me precisely what part of the anatomy he believed me to be a pain in, and suggested that someday we must discuss things at lunch. (He did not say to bring a taster, but I will.)

One of the advertised stars of this rally, the Rev. Jesse Jackson, didn't even show up—and no explanation was announced. The *Washington Star* described the event as something that "looked like a Central Casting staging of the 1960s anti-war protests."

Besides the nation's capital, other landmarks of history were being shaken up that summer, most notably the Naval Academy at Annapolis, and Lester's boyhood home, West Point. On October 8, 1975, President Ford "signed into law a bill that would admit women into America's service academies," according to the USMA Public Affairs Office. Taking particular umbrage to this radical threat of the masculine tradition of "Duty, Honor, Country," Les traveled to West Point on the opening day of Plebe Week, and was particularly pleased when he "pressed" cadet Gay Gray after a press conference, in telling him just how many push-ups she actually did during her first day: "Well, I can only do 25 or 30—but my boyfriend can do 100."

Over at Annapolis, Lester observed how Midshipman ("there are no midshipwomen") Barbara Webb "stepped on the scales to be weighed—by a huge First Classman (senior) named Jack Gavin [and] made the very bad mistake of answering Midshipman Lt. Gavin improperly. 'SIRRH!' roared Lt. Gavin in a voice which could be heard across Severn River—and which is not likely ever again to be forgotten by Midshipman Webb."

Several photos of apprehensive females marching in the ranks and carrying heavy duffle bags graced the pages of *Politics & Religion*, along with one shot of Cadet Gray at the press conference, with an overpowering portrait of General Dwight Eisenhower looming over her. Although Lester was resistant to this feminine infiltration, he was fair in offering up some credit: "None of West Point's largest incoming Plebe class in history (1,481) dropped out that first day. Moreover, the women cadets evoked what should be a cherished compliment from a giant Cadet Captain . . . named Stan Ford."

When asked by reporters how the women were doing on their first day—and if there is any tension between the sexes, Cadet Capt. Ford replied, quite seriously: "Basically the women have had less problems than the men today because often they're more coordinated. As for tension, between the sexes, nobody has time for things like that."

One hour later, after the Coed Corps of Cadets marched with traditional precision onto the Plain for the swearing-in ceremony, Father Thomas Curley, one of the Academy's Catholic Chaplains, in delivering the invocation, mentioned "Our brothers, and sisters, of the Corps."

The 1976 Democratic National Convention, held at Madison Square Garden for four days in July, was a rollicking bastion of color and pomp, brimming with delegates who were hell-bent on ousting the long-standing Republican stronghold in the White House. They would nominate Jimmy Carter, former governor of Georgia, who was also widely celebrated as a wealthy peanut farmer.

Les was accompanied by his sixteen-year-old daughter Kathleen, who would serve as his photographer for the *Politics & Religion* Democratic Convention Special Issue. Relegated to standing in long lines to obtain thirty-minute floor passes, Kathleen was nevertheless elated to photograph countless celebrities, politicians, and delegates in showy apparel who were cruising the convention floor. Hollywood star and devoted Democrat Warren Beatty afforded Kathleen a handsome close-up as he smiled when answering a reporter's questions.

Les was less fortunate in his quest for one particular interview. Convinced that a certain blonde was none other than Elizabeth Ray (Wayne Hays's former "secretary"), he ran behind her as she trotted along the convention perimeter, prodding her with the question, "Miss Ray? Miss RAY??" The disgruntled young woman turned around and faced Les for the first time, snarling, "You ought to be ashamed of yourself!" She turned out to be a television cohort of Leslie Stahl's. Lester blushed and vehemently apologized for the grievous error to the fellow journalist.

Lester's son Tom, a budding journalist who would vote for the first time in November, served as "*P&R*'s Editorial Assistant." He would pen the special feature "Convention Panorama," where he described some of "the colorful and almost equally pompous ceremonies that occurred outside on the street":

Oddballs included the Hare Krishnas, whose shaved heads and orange robes set off their dancing and chanting of their endless repetition of the Krishna song. Another group in action was the Marijuana Advocates, who carried black flags bearing the familiar weed leaf. They even had a three piece band, which sang verses such as "I Pledge Allegiance to the Bag of Marijuana." . . . Perhaps the most amusing happening of the entire four-day peanut convention occurred on the final day. I was strolling along the sidewalk, when suddenly a 7-foot Dinosaur stomped around the corner and shoved a pamphlet in my hand. It read: GODZILLA FOR PRESIDENT.

The Republican National Convention in August offered much the same colorful regalia. Held in Kansas City, Missouri, at Kemper Arena, President Ford won the Republican nomination over Ronald Reagan. As the balloons and confetti fell upon the screaming crowd, large banners declaring "BEDTIME FOR BONZO RONNIE" and "ONE SCHWIEK AND YOU'RE OUT RONNIE" appeared everywhere, the latter referring to Reagan's liberal choice for vice-president, Senator Richard Schweiker of Pennsylvania.

Outside the arena, the protests were in full swing. In his second "Convention Panorama" spread, Tom Kinsolving reported the following:

Outside in the parking lot of the Convention each night, assorted groups gathered to protest the Republicans. One group leader was arrested 3 times in the four days for disorderly conduct and disturbing the peace. . . . One young demonstrator wore a grinning Jerry Ford mask, complete with a hang rope around his neck, asking "Anybody want a pardon? Only a buck!" while another strutted around in circles swaddled in an American flag diaper and storm trooper boots.

Alongside the hordes of yippies was the clashing of Christian Evangelicals with the National Coalition of Gay Activists, who would fling barbs at each other, such as, "Same Sex—Try It Next" and "Don't Be Gay—Be Saved—Turn to Jesus." This noisy spectacle was fairly mild, compared to what was taking place right then in Kemper Arena's press gallery. While Lester was gathering his things and walking down a long corridor en route to his car, he came upon Ben Bradlee, followed by his entourage, with Sally Quinn in tow.

Lester gleefully seized this most golden opportunity and yelled, "WHY, IT'S GENTLE BEN!!" As Les's exclamatory reference to the popular television series about a 650-pound black bear was heard throughout the premises, Mr. Bradlee looked straight ahead, didn't flinch a face muscle in response, and proceeded on to the convention floor.

At year's close, Lester read of the news that movie legend Elizabeth Taylor had married for the seventh time—this time to John Warner, who would be running for a senate seat in Virginia. In *P&R*'s front-page story, "Liz Taylor's Holy Matrimony in Middleburg," Les reported that on December 4, 1976,

> The Rev. S. Neale Morgan had gone into a field on the estate of American Bicentennial director John Warner and officiated at a service of Holy Matrimony by which Mr. Warner became what Admiral Elmo Zumwalt has described as "Mr. Elizabeth Taylor, The Seventh."

The Rev. Mr. Morgan, rector of Emmanuel Episcopal Church in Middleburg, greeted the many reporters when they attended next day's Sunday service, where he asked them, "Why don't you reporters ask me about my sermon this morning?" Having arrived only in time for the post-service coffee hour, Les inquired if by chance he had preached on the Gospel according to St. John's account of Jesus and the woman at the well, to wit:

> The woman answered and said, "I have no husband." Jesus said unto her: "Thou hast well said I have no husband. For thou hast had five husbands; and he whom thou now hast is not thy husband."

The Rev. Mr. Morgan "did not appear to think that this was either humorous or apropos, as he replied: 'No! I preached on the Kingdom of God!'"

Bishop Robert Hall, who headed the Episcopal Diocese of Virginia, "sanctioned this ceremony upon the recommendation of his assistant, Suffragan Bishop John Baden of Alexandria." Les, awestruck at this decision, felt a bit of righteous needling was in store:

Suppose, I asked the bishop, that Miss Taylor tires of Mr. Warner and decides to try a third round with Richard Burton—and then tires of Burton again and wants to return to Middleburg. Would the Episcopal Church "solemnize" her ninth marriage as it has her seventh? Would the Episcopal Church seriously proclaim Miss Taylor's ninth as well as her seventh weddings to be as the Rev. Mr. Morgan intoned: The bond and convenant established by God in creation and adorned by Our Lord Jesus Christ?

"I don't know," laughed the bishop of Virginia. "But our church is now designed to look to the future rather than the past."

For ten marvelous years, Lester enjoyed tremendous success as a muckracker, always striving to expose monumental hypocrisy in the worlds of religion, politics, and the media. But the wrath of some who were exposed would soon wage their vengeance, and Les would suffer the greatest smear of his life as a professional journalist.

The 1977 South African Scandal

I N 1975, AFTER the *Post* ran their story "Priest as Gadfly," Les
sent off a letter to the editor, where he explained, in one of his
quotes, that "rich man's ethics" were "the *Post* and *Times* opposition
to reporters' accepting expenses-paid trips to foreign countries," and
that "the *Post* has earned enough from those full page ads bought
by North Korea for Kim Il Sung to pay for 25 trips overseas, or a
reporter's wages for an entire year."

In regards to Lester's "expenses-paid trips to foreign countries,"
The *Post* reported the following:

> One of the things that has most troubled some of Kinsolving's
> critics has been his open acceptance of press junkets to Israel
> and South Africa. Kinsolving readily admitted he took the trips
> at the expense of the governments of the two countries, but said
> he promised to do nothing in return for the trips.
>
> He also acknowledged he was offered stock valued at about
> $200 and travel expenses to attend stockholder meetings of
> International Business Machines Corp [IBM], International

Telephone & Telegraph Corp, and the Southern Co. Each company was beset by a church group seeking to curb its investments in South Africa because of the country's racial policies.

Kinsolving said the stock and the travel money came from a Washington lawyer hired by the South African ministry of information and the funds he received were "about half" his normal speaking fee. Although he said he made no promises to the lawyer about what he would say at the meetings, he did speak against the church group at each session.

The church group the article referred to was the National Council of Churches (NCC), which Les had taken to task several times, ever since the first *Northern Virginia Religion News* was published. "NCC Executives Fired" exposed General Secretary Claire Randall who, on June 14, 1974, fired five top executives. According to the *Washington Post,* the NCC executives had similar physical attributes: "all of them male, all of them white and all of them over 60."

Lester also made special mention of James McCracken:

Another white male [and] one of the world's most knowledgeable and competent authorities on feeding and clothing the hungry, was fired as Director of the renowned Church World Service . . . by the Rev. Eugene Stockwell . . . alumnus of Chicago's Ecumenical Institute, whose leader, Methodist minister Joseph Matthews, has said: "Let any church send us 30 laymen for a weekend and we will send back 29 awakened revolutionaries."

. . . The six fired executives would appear to have a solid case if they were to choose to appeal to the New York State Division of Human Rights, since the State's antidiscrimination law applies not only to all races, but to sex and age as well. (The only black executive removed by Miss Randall was the Rev. Maynard Catchings, a communications officer with no media experience whatsoever, who was immediately rehired as a "minority communications" officer.)

Gadfly

Other exposés followed in early 1975, most notably, "NCC Clergy Deplore Alleged CIA Destablizing of Chilean Marxist Gov't," "The Shepherd Is a Wolf: Ex-Methodist Minister, Unfrocked for Seducing 16 Year Old, Now Employed by Nat'l Council of Churches," and "South Africa Condemned While Uganda Condoned by Liberal Protestant Churches," where "the NCC as well as the Lutheran Council and United Presbyterian, United Methodist, United Church of Christ and Episcopal Church national headquarters have been focusing their attentions instead on condemnations and boycotts of South Africa and Rhodesia," while the following was taking place in other parts of the African continent:

- Liberia, where racial segregation has been retained in Article 5 of the Constitution for more than a century by the black government.
- Nigeria, where the black government conducted a campaign of systematic starvation against the Ibos of Biafra.
- Chad, where black dictator Engarta Tombabye has been burying black Christian ministers up to their necks in ant hills.
- The Central African Republic, where authorities of another black government punish larceny by cutting off either ears or hands.
- The Sudan, where the white Arab government in Khartoum has slaughtered more than half a million blacks in South Sudan.
- Burundi, where the ruling Tutsi tribe slaughtered more than 75,000 of the Hutu tribe.
- Zaire, where President Mobutu ordered the people to divest themselves of all Christian names.
- Uganda, where critics of the black dictator, Major Gen. Idi Amin ("Big Daddy") Dada, have been thrown to the crocodiles, and where more than 60,000 Asians were deported and their property expropriated.

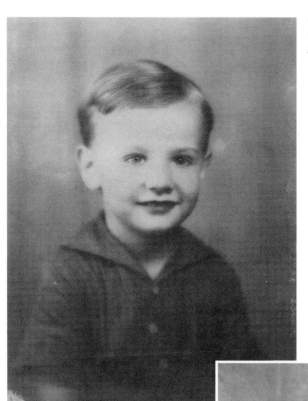

Three-year-old Les, West Point, New York (1931).
Source: Kinsolving Family Collection.

Brothers Arthur and Charles Kinsolving, World War I (1918).
Source: Kinsolving Family Collection.

Seventeen-year-old Les, Fort Knox, Kentucky (1945).
Source: Kinsolving Family Collection.

The Kinsolvings at Arthur's consecration as Bishop of Arizona, Pittsburgh (1945).
Source: Klingensmith.

Sylvia beaming and Les snarling after their wedding (December 1953).
Source: Kinsolving Family Collection.

Les greeting his congregation at the mission church of St. Thomas, Rodeo, California (1953). Temporary quarters were in the Rio movie theater.
Source: Barry Evans.

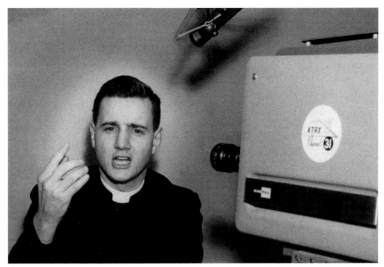

Les delivering one of his *Cross and Crisis* sermons, KTRX-TV, Pasco, Washington (1958). *Source:* KTRX-TV.

Damage from the second fire at Church of Our Savior (February 16, 1961). Les in fireman's coat. *Source: Tri-City Herald.*

"A New Dimension in Religious Reporting":
Les interviews naked hippie in San Francisco for
the *San Francisco Chronicle* (1968). *Source:* Jerry
Telfer, *San Francisco Chronicle.*

n in the black suit is Rev. Lester Kinsolving on the job as a reporter in San Francisco.

Yea,
though I walk
through the valley
of the shadow
of death
I shall fear no evil :
for I am the meanest
son-of-a-bitch
in the valley

Les at the *San Francisco Examiner* (1972). *Source: San Francisco Examiner* photo staff.

Worker-priest on the job (1973).
Gift from *San Francisco Examiner*
cartoonist. *Source: San Francisco Examiner.*

THE REV. MR. L. KINSOLVING, JOURNALIST, AT WORK

NEXT!

Ronald Reagan welcomes Les to the White House Press Corps Christmas Party (1981).
Source: White House.

Les as Brigadier-General William Barksdale and son Tom as his aide-de-camp on the set of *Gods and Generals* (2003). *Source:* Turner Pictures.

Les poses another question, White House Press Briefing (2005). *Source:* Uli Loskot.

The Les Kinsolving Show, WCBM-AM in Baltimore (2005). *Source:* Uli Loskot.

Les with George W. Bush at the White House Press Corps Christmas Party (2007). *Source:* Chris Greenber.

Donald E. deKieffer, an attorney with the Washington, D.C., law firm Collins, Shannon, Rill, Edwards, and Scott, was also registered as both agent and lobbyist for the South African government. He approached Lester after he'd heard of and read his reports citing African atrocities, which were completely ignored by the National Council of Churches, while South African policies were always the subject of their vehement protest. Les had just returned from a ten-day government-sponsored trip to the country in February, after he exposed Rev. Donald Morton, in "The Shepherd Is a Wolf" page-one story for *Religion News.*

DeKieffer made the proposition for Lester to attend stockholders' meetings where NCC Executive Director Tim Smith was pleading with companies such as IBM and the Southern Company to divest from South Africa, due to its racial segregation and oppression. Les responded with interest, since he was eager for an additional opportunity to confront and expose the NCC's hypocrisy. He insisted that he would speak his views only, and never be told what to say by anyone. DeKieffer agreed to this completely and would provide travel expenses to the stockholders' meetings, and $200 in stocks, in order to gain admittance. The payment would also be equal to Lester's usual lecture fee, something akin to payment he received when he spoke at Israel Bond rallies in California as religion writer for the *San Francisco Chronicle* and *Examiner.*

According to Mostert Van Schoor's "Politics" report in *Pretoria News,* the following exchange occurred at an annual meeting of the Southern Company:

TIM SMITH, NCC: A contract to purchase coal produced in South Africa under such frightful circumstances is indeed a contract with a Mafia-like political order.

KINSOLVING: I would pose this question. Are the stockholders for whom they hold proxy—this information centre for the National Council of Churches—are they prepared to give back their dividends on 6,489 shares, which amount to 6,000 dollars, of this company which does business with South Africa, the allegedly slave-driving Mafia? If they are not prepared immediately to give back the dividends, I suggest they are accessories of the fact.

Incidentally, this is the same traveling road show that did the same thing at the IBM stockholders meeting, where their 54,000 shares of IBM—which also does business in South Africa—netted a take of $957,000 dollars.

When this group, the same individual as a matter of fact, appeared in Pittsburgh at the IBM annual meeting, in which they asked IBM to stop selling computers to South Africa, this request mentioned not one word about IBM's business dealings in Uganda, of all places. If you want to talk about racial discrimination, talk about any of the more than 50,000 Indians who were not only discriminated against, they were thrown out—brutally deported—simply because of their skin pigment, by the Ugandan government. . . .

Instead of accepting no money from the Southern Company or IBM, these church bureaucrats accepted dividends at the same time that they were protesting against business with South Africa. So I suggest a rather obvious hypocrisy in all this profit by alleged prophets.

At the same IBM annual meeting in Pittsburgh, held in April 1975, Tim Smith announced to 3,000 stockholders that Lester "was a South African agent." Les's response (on "point of personal privilege") was that Smith "was a liar." It was possible Mr. Smith had a motive to fling such accusations since, on April 10, by far the most damning exposé on the NCC made the top story in *Religion News*: "Alleged Ex-Nazi on Council of Churches Board: Justice Dept. Probe" reported such details as:

Rumanian Orthodox Bishop Valerian Viola D. Trifa of Detroit— who was identified 20 years ago as a "former Rumanian Nazi" by columnist Drew Pearson—is now slated for court action to revoke his U.S. citizenship by the U.S. Attorney's office in Detroit. The case of Bishop Trifa, who allegedly lied about his wartime activities, has been featured in such newspapers as the *Detroit Free Press* and the *New York Times*. But thus far largely unnoticed is the fact that Bishop Trifa has for the past three years been a member of the General Board of the National Council of Churches.

The Jewish Telegraphic Agency has reported that Trifa was a leader of Rumania's Iron Guard, which, in cooperation with the Nazi occupation forces, murdered at least 1,000 Jews in Bucharest. 200 of these were taken to that city's municipal slaughterhouse, stripped and led to the chopping blocks. Here their throats were cut and they were hung on meat hooks while their bodies were stamped "Carne Kosher" ("Kosher Meat").

. . . Five years ago, a past president of the National Council of Churches was asked what the NCC would do if it were discovered that its General Board members included a foreign agent. Dr. Cynthia Wedel, now living in Alexandria, replied that member denominations are entitled to appoint their own delegates without question from the NCC.

I can recall that I never suspected at that time that such ecumenical laissez-faire would include Nazi war criminals. The Congress, as well as the public in general, should therefore take cognizance of the standards which apply to membership in the directorate of the National Council of Churches, and judge all pronouncements of this body accordingly.

After Lester was the first to blow the whistle on NCC, he began the second round of stockholders' meetings, beginning in March 1976. That summer, a blurb appeared in *Church as Shareholder,* issued by the United Church Board for World Ministries:

A right-wing journalist in clerical collar managed to divert the attention of the press and many stockholders by his disruptive tactics. . . . He launched into a vicious attack upon the National Council of Churches and the United Church of Christ in particular. His speech was always the same: (1) the Republic of South Africa is the freest country on the continent of Africa and is a "utopia" for its black inhabitants; and (2) the NCC and UCC are actually fronts for Communism and black dictatorships.

On July 19, 1976, Tim Smith sent a letter to Brian Ahern, an official with the Foreign Agent Registration of the Department of Justice:

I am writing to inquire if Lester Kinsolving is in violation of the Foreign Agents Registration Act of 1938 since he is personally not registered as an agent, yet he has taken money on a number of occasions by agents of the South African Government to speak against critics of South Africa at stockholders' meetings. At these numerous stockholders' meetings, Mr. Kinsolving used a great deal of the logic that the South African Government uses in disparaging its critics. In addition, Mr. Kinsolving wears his clerical collar but never reveals that he is a journalist when he speaks. He thus seems to be acting in contradiction to his role as an "objective journalist" when he speaks as an advocate.

Copies of the letter were sent to Congressman Charles Diggs (D-MI), Senator Richard Clark (D-IA), Harrison Humphries (Chairman, Standing Committee of Correspondents), Senate Press Gallery, and Lawrence O'Rourke of the White House Correspondents Association.

Lester got wind of Smith's letter, when, on August 11, two White House press corps members informed him that he was "being accused of being an agent of a foreign government." Donald deKieffer's letter to the Standing Committee of Correspondents on August 12 went on further to state:

I trust that your committee is well acquainted with the legal definition of foreign agent, or lobbyist, as one who works under "the direction and control of a foreign government." Any allegation that he has—or would do so is unadulterated libel. While my client has never made any attempt to conceal his opinions, they have been seized upon by various groups whose activities he had exposed in the course of his duties as a journalist.

On August 25, deKieffer received a response from SCC Chairman Harrison Humphries, who enclosed a copy of Tim Smith's letter, which he had received, along with the explanation that, "Since the letter was not addressed to the Standing Committee of Correspondents, it has not been brought to the attention of the Committee and no action has been taken or is contemplated." Press Gallery Superintendent Roy McGhee, echoing Humphries's response to Tim Smith's inquiry, explained, "We often get complaints, of a wide variety, from non-members. We simply don't have the staff to investigate them all."

On Friday, November 17, Les received a registered letter from Joel S. Lisner of the Foreign Agents Registration Unit at the Department of Justice. The letter stated the following: "Information at our disposal indicates that you are required to register with this Department pursuant to the Foreign Agents Registration Act as an agent of the Government of South Africa. There are also indications that you are acting for the Government of Rhodesia and of Israel."

The next Monday, Lester sat down with Harold Webb of the same unit along with Don deKieffer, who was now acting as his attorney. Les asserted that he was not an agent of either South Africa, Rhodesia, or Israel, and if "my lecturing for stock at Israeli bond rallies made me an agent of Israel, then surely the Department of Justice would be obliged to register several thousand rabbis and hundreds of Christian clergy as foreign agents." Accepting this as a valid argument, Webb suggested he "write these views at length." Lester did, and a few weeks later spoke to Webb. After their conversation, he never heard from the Foreign Agents Registration Unit again.

As Bishop Trifa faced indictment and the National Council of Churches stood stalwart, Jewish groups began staging demonstrations at NCC board meetings and headquarters, as Les reported in

Gadfly

"Rabbi Confronts NCC on Ex-Nazi," published in the *San Francisco Progress* on November 19, 1976:

> When the NCC Governing Board members returned from lunch during its October 8th meeting, they found the platform of the grand ballroom of Manhattan's Roosevelt Hotel had been occupied by three dozen robust and angry looking young men wearing yarmulkes. . . . Following the Jewish demonstration, Rabbi James Rudin of the American Jewish Committee issued a statement that the AJC believes the continuance of Bishop Trifa on the NCC board is "an affront" about which "millions of Christians and Jews throughout the United States" are seriously concerned. The millions of Christians whose denominations belong to the NCC could show serious concern by withholding their church offerings until this Nazi is ousted. But few of such Christians are that seriously concerned.

A month later, Les covered yet another demonstration "of some 500 Jewish youth and rabbis outside the Manhattan headquarters of the National Council of Churches." It was then he was informed that Tim Smith "was distributing to various denomination headquarters copies of deKieffer's reports of stocks . . . which had been public information for more than a year" (as mentioned in the *Post*'s "Priest as Gadfly"), on which the Standing Committee of Correspondents never followed up. The reports of stocks contained the following information:

> Registrant arranged for Rev. Lester Kinsolving to speak at various stockholder meetings of corporations. Rev. Kinsolving was paid a regular speaker's fee for these appearances as follows:

> 4-19-76 Expenses $500.00
> 4-19-76 Stock purchase $1,629.50
> 4-19-76 Speakers fee $225.00

Registrant emphasizes it did not at any time prescribe what Rev. Kinsolving could or would communicate at such stockholder meetings, did not in any way exercise any prior review of Rev. Kinsolving's comments, or control his activities.

In mid-January, a month before the National Council of Churches would finally acquiesce to intense pressure and urge the Orthodox Church of America to suspend Bishop Trifa's membership on their Governing Board on February 9, 1977, Les received a call from Peter Pringle, a reporter from the *Sunday Times* in London. After being interviewed for ninety minutes, Mr. Pringle included a tidbit in his story the following Sunday: "And, in one odd episode the Washington Law firm paid an Episcopalian minister, the Rev. Lester Kinsolving $1,600 to buy shares and infiltrate stockholders' meetings of large corporations such as IBM and ITT and to combat criticism of their South African operations," along with Lester's tongue-in-cheek comment, "If I'm an agent, I've been grossly underpaid."

After reading Pringle's story, Alexander Cockburn of the *Village Voice* in New York shot off an editorial, where he commented on Lester's quip: "Kinsolving reckons he's not had enough money." Lester's letter to the editor was published in January 24, stating:

> My rather apparent jest, "If I'm an agent, I've been cheated [grossly underpaid], has been twisted completely out of context by Mr. Cockburn in order to convey the idea that I wanted more money, which is totally false. If Mr. Cockburn had made any effort to contact me (as Mr. Pringle did) rather than practicing Xerox journalism with the *London Times*, he would have learned that the Justice Department also suggested that I might wish to register as an agent for Israel, as well as South Africa. While this is an unintended honor, the definition of an agent requires that one be under the control and direction of a foreign power, which I have never been and never will be.

Cockburn replied:

Kinsolving took money from a Washington law firm to appear at stockholders' meetings and argue the case of the white minority South African government. Kinsolving will undoubtedly reply that it is not his fault if his views happen to coincide with those of the South African government. This is the classic response of any journalist charged with being a paid lobbyist.

Starting in London and making its way into New York City, the South African scandal would soon land in Washington, D.C., where it would fall into the waiting clutches of Ben Bradlee. Three days after Lester's letter appeared in the *Village Voice*, the following front-page story ran in the *Washington Post*: "South Africa Is Waging Extensive Publicity Drive." Reporter Walter Pincus, citing a dozen American journalists who accepted subsidized trips to South Africa, put Les in the lead, and repeated facts from the *Post*'s 1975 "Priest as Gadfly" feature:

> In 1975 and 1976, Lester Kinsolving, Episcopal minister, colum-
> nist, White House press corps gadfly and local radio commentator,
> got over $2,500 worth of corporate stocks from a lawyer-lobbyist
> working for the South African Information Department. . . . The
> clergyman-journalist, who normally appears in clerical garb, said
> he was never asked by the law firm to speak at the meetings. He
> would speak only to counterattack anti-apartheid groups who
> attended the stockholder gatherings, Kinsolving said.

The "anti-apartheid groups," more accurately known as the National Council of Churches, remained anonymous throughout the article, and in one of the closing paragraphs, Pincus referred vaguely to Rev. Donald Morton, who had fled South Africa with his teenaged lover:

> The clergyman-journalist took a subsidized trip in February, 1975,
> after he had "exposed" an alleged refugee from apartheid. . . .
> After a 10-day visit, he returned and wrote an attack on an
> anti–South African church group. . . .

If Mr. Pincus had dug more thoroughly, he would've found Lester's story, "South Africa Condemned While Uganda Condoned By Liberal Protestant Churches," published in January, before he ever traveled to South Africa. Lester's "attack on an anti–South African church group," (the National Council of Churches) written after his "10-day visit," may have referred to one of the exposés, "National Council of Churches Report Accuses FBI, CIA," written in March, or "Alleged Ex-Nazi on Council of Churches Board," written in April. Neither of these newsworthy stories could fairly be considered "an attack."

In a follow-up to the *Washington Post,* "Press Colleagues May Collar Kinsolving Pass" appeared three days later, in the Sunday, January 30 edition of the *Washington Star.* Reporter William Delaney focused solely on Lester, opening his story with, "Lester Kinsolving, a brashly unorthodox minister-columnist who appears to have few admirers among his Washington press colleagues, soon may need all such friends he can get."

Delaney didn't hide the identity of the National Council of Churches as the *Post* had, and stated that Lester was "opposed to South Africa's racial separation, [and] was on record as a more vociferous critic of the lack of civil liberties under black-run African nations. . . . " The reporter also mentioned that "in the same section" of the *Post* story, "was a full-page ad featuring photographs of interracial athletic competition, paid for by Olympics-barred South Africa's Committee for Fairness in Sport."

In one quote, Delaney allowed Les to explain his attendance at the stockholders meetings: "I'm against the hypocrisy of the National Council of Churches . . . always pointing to South Africa but never calling attention to the dreadful record of black dictatorships all over Africa. Why is it that they say nothing about these?"

Mentioning that "at least two formal complaints against Kinsolving were reported to be en route to Capitol Hill's Standing Committee of Correspondents, following a report late last week that he accepted corporate stocks from a South African lobbyist," Delaney concluded that "The Kinsolving matter is expected to come up at 1

P.M. tomorrow when the committee, with three new members and new chairman Madden, holds its organizational meeting." The two complaints reported were as follows:

RALPH DENNHEISER, REUTERS: The *Post* story raises serious allegations about Lester Kinsolving . . . more than $2,500 in return, Pincus suggests, for public defenses of South African racial policies.

JOHN S. LANG, *NEW YORK POST*: Reconsider the credentials of Lester Kinsolving. Here are some points of inquiry which I have heard alleged: That the Justice Department has asked him to register as a foreign agent—That the State Department has refused his credentials—That he had had arrangements with the Rhodesian government similar to those reported with South Africa.

On the afternoon of January 31, the Standing Committee of Correspondents met, without notifying either Les or his attorney, who had explicitly requested that "he be notified in advance of any dealing with Kinsolving's case." The Committee requested the Counsel of the Senate Rules and Administration Committee to consider two issues:

1. Has Rev. Kinsolving been requested by the Department to register as a foreign agent?
2. Has Rev. Kinsolving been denied credentialing by the State Department?

On February 9, 23 out of 350 members of the State Department Correspondents Association met. "The organization never notified me that such a meeting would take place," Les recalls. "They never invited me to be present to defend myself, never identified my accusers, and never informed me of the nature of the charge." SDCA President Richard Valeriani would later apologize for the "oversight" of not informing Lester of the meeting.

According to the March issue of *The Quill,*

He did hear about it in advance only by way of a phone call to his home in Washington from his son in California. Kinsolving's son had learned that an ouster meeting might be held from reading a story about his father in the *San Francisco Chronicle*. At the suggestion of his attorney [David Harquist], Kinsolving did not attend the meeting.

Before a vote was called, two respected journalists, Marvin Kalb of CBS and Barry Schweid of Associated Press, raised their voices in protest:

KALB: The *Tass News Agency* correspondents are allowed to remain, even though they earn their entire incomes from the Soviet government! What about members taking fees from the U.S. Information Agency and the BBC?

SCHWEID: There are many accredited Washington journalists who've spoken for honorariums for such causes as Israel Bonds!

The Quill further reported, "Kinsolving's defenders also said other American correspondents, unnamed at the ouster meeting, on occasion had accepted transportation and lodging from the Saudi Arabian and Jordanian government during former Secretary of State Henry Kissinger's Middle East shuttles."

Although the Association's President Richard Valeriani of NBC admitted "a double standard," which violated the rules of the association, he still went ahead with the procedure, ignoring Harquist's pleas for a roll-call vote. *The Quill* noted later, "The request was declined because members feared individual lawsuits."

The vote of 9–7, with seven abstaining was cast, and Lester was expelled. It was then that Marvin Kalb wrote his letter of resignation, citing the association's "improper procedure" and their attempt "to play God." *The Quill* also noted, "He would ask to be reinstated only after it adopted a more explicit and fair code of behavior. Kalb also asked for Kinsolving's reinstatement." Later, he would tell *Broadcasting*

magazine, "So many people in the association are technically in violation; why take it out on one person?" Barry Schweid added, "We have
no right—legal, moral or otherwise—to decide who is a legitimate
reporter and who isn't."

Over at the Senate Press Gallery, the Standing Committee of Correspondents convened, and later informed Les of the following:

> We've decided, for the time being, not to issue you new creden-
> tials until we've had an opportunity to pursue questions that
> have been raised about your activities. This action in no way
> prejudices whatever decision the committee may eventually
> take in the matter. Also, your existing press gallery credentials
> will remain valid through the end of this month.

On Wednesday, February 16, David Harquist wrote a response to
the Standing Committee:

> In my opinion, there would be no justification whatsoever, legal
> or otherwise, in failing to renew Father Kinsolving's pass on Feb.
> 28 if by that time the Standing Committee has not acted. To do
> so would deprive Father Kinsolving of a basic right directly con-
> nected with his ability to perform his occupation and would, in
> effect, constitute a finding of guilt without a hearing. For that
> reason, I request that Father Kinsolving's credentials be issued
> immediately. If this is not done, we intend to take immediate
> legal action to require the issuance of renewed credentials.

The next day, as Les was hand-delivering Harquist's letter to the
Superintendent of the Press Gallery, he was approached by Dean Levitan, a reporter with Madison, Wisconsin's *Capital Times*. Levitan also
carried a letter, which he had written to the Standing Committee of
Correspondents on February 14:

Dear Standing Committee:
   Hate to cause any international incidents, but—do foreign

press have exemption to rule-banning association with government agencies? If not, I believe the several TASS reporters should have their credentials revoked, inasmuch as Ambassador Dobrynin has declared TASS to be an organ of the Council of Ministers of the U.S.S.R.

Yours down the two-way street of détente,
Stuart Dean Levitan

In its April issue, *The Quill* reported the following:

For the first time in nearly 30 years a newsman is appealing to the Senate Rules Committee and to the Speaker of the House for the restoration of his U.S. Capitol press gallery credentials and privileges. . . .

On March 18, the Rev. Lester Kinsolving was stripped of his press gallery privileges by a 3–2 vote of the Standing Committee of Correspondents of the Senate and House press gallery. On March 9, the committee had held an open hearing to decide whether Kinsolving's press pass would be renewed or revoked. . . .

Kinsolving is taking the appeals route prescribed by law for expelled reporters. "I will exhaust all remedies before going to court," he said. Among the charges Kinsolving makes in his appeal is that the correspondents' committee denied him the right to confront his accusers (two reporters who complained about his alleged South African ties, thus initiating the review).

At the open hearing, *Christianity Today* reported,

Kinsolving denied that he was an agent or employee of the South African government, as [Tim] Smith suggested in his original letter to the Justice Department. . . . Kinsolving likened his appearances at the corporation's annual meetings to his occasional pulpit engagements. He said he was a believer in freedom of the pulpit and that he no more took instruction on what to say at stockholder meetings than he did when he accepted preaching engagements. He also insisted that the fees of about $200 per meeting were, in his opinion, like any other honoraria for speaking. His main purpose at the meetings was to "expose the hypocrisy" of the NCC and its African policies.

Shortly after the scandal broke in the *Post* and the *Star*, Les received a letter from Rev. Paul Douglas, pastor of United Church of Christ in Waubay, South Dakota:

Kinsolving:
Listen you ##%--097&%#"+"! tell me it ain't so . . . that you've sold your ministerial standing for a few pennies on behalf of racist policies in South America and South Africa. . . . Does the profession of minister have on its hands yet another lower class, second rate, cheap shit type who will do anything for money? . . . Say it ain't so, Kinsolving. Say you didn't sell out for a few cheap pennies. Tell me, Kinsolving, that you cherish the good opinion of your fellow clergyman. . . .

The Rev. Cecil Williams of Glide Memorial also sent a letter, but not to Lester. He wrote to the Rev. Jim Jones on February 4, three weeks after he had presented Jones with the Martin Luther King, Jr. Humanitarian Award. The Peoples Temple now had a large church on Geary Boulevard in San Francisco, where the letter (and *Post* article) was addressed:

Dear Jim:
Enclosed is an article on our "friend" Lester Kinsolving.
Thought you might enjoy seeing him getting some of his own stuff.
Walk That Walk,
Cecil

News of Les's expulsions was carried in national headlines, including "Reporters Reprimand a Minster," "Lester Kinsolving Ousted From Reporters' Group for S. African Payments," "Columnist-Priest Stirs Flock of Controversies: Kinsolving Credentials Revoked for 'Lobbying' Speeches," "Kinsolving Sees Stock As 'Lecture Fee,'" and, "'This is a despicable smear: I do not believe in segregation.'" According to Jack Briggs of the *Tri-City Herald,* "One day, Kinsolving was roaming the press room of the White House in his clerical garb without noticing that someone had pinned on his back a notice reading, "Made in South Africa."

The editors at the *Buffalo Courier-Express* in New York made the following announcement in their paper:

The *Courier-Express* will discontinue publication of the columns of Lester Kinsolving, an Episcopal priest and member of the White House press corps, because, to this newspaper's dismay, he sees nothing wrong in having accepted stocks from a South African lobbyist in Washington in return for defending that country's government and its policies at stockholder meetings throughout the United States. . . .

Another editor, Ernie Williams of the *News-Sentinel* in Fort Wayne, Indiana, offered words of encouragement: "Dear Les: Oddly enough, neither your detractors (particularly the Misery Lutheran Synod) nor your admirers (wherever and whoever they might be) have come out of the woodwork to celebrate or commiserate, each in his own way. At this desk, we know you're pure in heart and run the best unlicensed taxi service in the Capitol." And Alvin P. Oikle, editor of *Greenfield (Mass.) Recorder,* sent a quick note: "Les—Keep Smiling!"

As Lester waited on word from the Senate Rules Committee and whether it would review his appeal, he bided his time by attending press briefings at the State Department (which he was still allowed to attend) and the White House (where, according to *Religious News Service,* "he was known as 'Father Bother' by some of his colleagues").

Gadfly

Since he owned one share of stock, Les covered the *Washington Post's* annual stockholders' meeting, where he looked forward to needling his nemesis, Ben Bradlee.

"*Washington Post's* Concealed Salaries" was the leading story in the May 19th issue of *Politics & Religion*, where Les asked the following questions to *Post* publisher Katherine Graham, after she received a $110,500 bonus, along with her $150,000 salary:

KINSOLVING: How much bonus has the *Post* paid to its two Pulitzer Prize winners [George Will and William McPherson]?

MRS. GRAHAM: Mr. Bradlee, did you give them any bonus?

MR. BRADLEE: We gave them a bonus, and damned if I see why it's any of your business.

(Mr. Bradlee, I am bound to note, was glaring at me, not his publisher, when he said this, and Mrs. Graham subsequently announced, "I agree with Ben.")

McPherson was out of town, but George Will later confirmed my suspicion that the *Post* hadn't paid him a dime in bonus. But almost as if he had been warned suddenly by an electronic sixth sense, Will added vehemently: "I didn't EXPECT anything from the *Post*! I'm not ASKING for anything from the *Post*!

I thanked George for this information, even as he continued to protest—too much, I think—his vehement non-desire for any bonus. Mr. Bradlee, when contacted later about the discrepancy in bonus info from himself and Mr. Will, declined comment.

On May 27, a small news blurb ran in the *Post*:

KINSOLVING IS "TARGET"

State Department spokesman Hodding Carter III playfully succumbed yesterday to a temptation to deal with far-out questioners. He "pulled a gun" on one of the most far-out questioners in town, the controversial Rev. Lester Kinsolving, who wears clerical garb to news conferences. But it was a toy that fires rubber bands, and Carter missed his target. Kinsolving, grinning back, hurried to a phone to report a near-miss to Arlington radio station WAVA.

Over at the White House, the *Washingtonian* published the following exchange in the press room:

KINSOLVING: Does the President have any comment on news reports that his brother Billy was seen in the company of Farrah Fawcett-Majors at a Hollywood premiere?

JODY POWELL: You can't be serious.

KINSOLVING: I most certainly am serious. Just answer the question. Does the President have any comment—

POWELL: No, he doesn't. Next question.

KINSOLVING: Wait just a minute there. You say the President has no comment—

POWELL: Correct.

KINSOLVING: Despite the fact that Farrah Fawcett-Majors is a married woman?

POWELL: Yes.

KINSOLVING: Yes, the President has a comment?

POWELL: No, I mean, yes, he has no comment despite the fact—

KINSOLVING: Despite the fact that the motion-picture was X-rated?

Gadfly

Jody Powell, who had inherited the diligent task from Ron Nessen in fielding Lester's questions, later remarked, "In Georgia, you have gnats. In the White House, you have Lester Kinsolving."

On September 28, 1977, *Religious News Service* reported the following:

> The Senate Rules Committee has voted unanimously to review an appeal by the Rev. Lester Kinsolving, nationally syndicated columnist and editor of two local weeklies, whose application from renewal of membership in the Senate and House daily press galleries was denied earlier this year.

> Mr. Kinsolving told Religious News Service he "expects to win, but I can't be sure, of course." But winning this case would "by no means be the end of the matter," he said. "That's only the first part. I do not intend to rest with the decision. There will be legal action," he said, but declined to elaborate.

The Ear alerted gossip aficionados of the latest on the Irreverent Reverend in its December 1 column:

> Remember how the Rev. Lester Kinsolving, hell raiser extraordinaire . . . had his congressional credentials snatched away a while back? *Ear* now hears: The Senate Rules committee has agreed to Think It Over, and even toss a little hearing in January.

In the minutes of its meeting held on Thursday, February 23, 1978, the Standing Committee of Correspondents "today reviewed an application for credentials and an accompanying letter from Father Lester Kinsolving. Based on the promise of compliance with gallery rules stated in Father Kinsolving's letter (copy attached) the Committee favorably, and unanimously, accepted Father Kinsolving's application for membership."

Lester's February 7 letter to Joan McKinney, Chairperson of the Committee, stated:

RE: *Lester Kinsolving* v. *Standing Committee of Correspondents*
Since the Senate Committee on Rules and Administration has
provided the opportunity for both parties to reach an understanding respecting matters at issue in my appeal, I am glad to reaf-
firm that I have not accepted any fees to appear at stockholders
meetings since May 1976. Furthermore, I will not do so during
the period in which I hold Press Gallery credentials. Addition-
ally, I confirm that I will abide by the Rules Governing Press
Galleries and the provisions of the enclosed application.

Therefore, I would appreciate the renewal of my credentials to
the Congressional press galleries.

Les would comment later, "My letter to the Standing Committee
in no way acknowledges any violation whatsoever of the press gallery
rules." He was greatly assisted by Senator Mark Hatfield of Oregon,
who served on the U.S. Senate Committee on Rules and Administration, as well as its Chairman, Senator Claiborne Pell of Rhode Island.
On March 9, Les wrote a letter of deep gratitude to Senator Pell and
members of the committee:

I believe your action in this regard has demonstrated that your
committee is a great deal more dedicated to the First Amendment's provision of freedom of the press than is most of the
press in Washington.

Les went on to mention that "your intervention in this case has
had at least three beneficial effects so far," including:

The Standing Committee of Correspondents has finally concluded
that a reporter's participation for a fee on a program sponsored by
a government agency (in this case, the Voice of America) does not
necessarily mean that he is promoting the government's interest for
pay. This action came three months after the Standing Committee,

during my hearing, was unable to demonstrate that anything I said at the stockholders meetings promoted any policy of the South African government. . . .

Since he was in possession of his credentials and could participate as a reporter on Capitol Hill once again, Lester breathed a deep sigh of relief; however, he couldn't resist firing off "An open letter to the editors of the *Buffalo Courier-Express*" on March 28, 1978:

Thirteen months ago, in a column entitled "C-E Drops Columns By Kinsolving," you charged me with what you termed a "breach of ethics."

Despite my having written for you for a number of years, you gave me no chance whatsoever to defend myself before you went into print with this accusation. Fortunately the United States Senate Committee on Rules has an infinitely higher regard for due process and basic equity than you editors. For it was due to their intervention—the first such instance since 1948—that I have been able to win a year-long battle to regain my Congressional press credentials. . . .

Your editorial charged that I "accepted stocks from a South African lobbyist in Washington in return for defending that country's government and its policy at stockholders meetings throughout the United States."

The utter recklessness of this falsehood is clearly demonstrated in the evidence secured by the Standing Committee of Correspondents, who contacted several of the corporations at whose stockholders meetings I appeared. In the transcripts of exactly what I said at these meetings, the committee was unable to find a single instance of my defending any South Governmental policy, whether apartheid, or separate development of racial homelands.

But the *Courier-Express* accused me of doing so—without any contact of me; without having sent anyone of its reporters to cover any of these stockholders meetings. . . .

Looking back over this grueling experience, Les could only be grateful for a kind tribute in the Central Conference of American Rabbis' News Letter, dated March, 1977:

THANK YOU FATHER KINSOLVING
It was the Episcopal priest-radio commentator-newsman, Rev. Lester Kinsolving, who first blew the whistle on the National Council of Churches allowing the notorious war criminal Archbishop Trifa to sit on its executive board. Keeping up his prophetic indignation to this day, he is probably more responsible than anyone else in unseating Trifa, with Henry Siegman of the Synagogue Council delivering a most eloquent coup de grâce at the recent meeting of the NCC which suspended Trifa.

If the South African scandal proved to be a price for ousting Trifa, it was definitely worth it.

"Get This Son of a Bitch Out of My Seat!"

B ACK IN FULL unbridled swing, Les attended a State Department press briefing on March 14, 1978, "which was only five minutes long," according to *The Ear:*

> It was a humdinger. Honcho Hodding Carter III told Joe Poliakof of the *Jewish Telegraph* he didn't like his voice; Lester Kinsolving, the Priest of Panax, asked snippily if Hodding felt the Israelis were justified in retaliating against the Arabs on the precedent of the Jeffersonian response to the Barbary Pirates; Reutersperson Roy Gutman cackled; Timesman Bernie Gwertzman snapped to Kinsolving, "You're wasting time"; Kinsolving cried he didn't need any advice from *The Times*, thanks, and besides, Bernie was a pompous ass. It looked like fisticuffs time, Earwigs. Hodding hastily declared the briefing closed. (Thank heavens, after Les and Joe had stamped off, he finished it in the closet.)

"The Priest of Panax," *Ear*'s new moniker for Les, referred to *Politics & Religion*, now under the auspices of Panax Corporation of America, with John P. McGoff officiating as publisher. Lester, assuming the role as National Editor, ran Panax's first *P&R* issue on May 5, 1977. By July, a new nameplate appeared on the front page: *Washington Weekly*, along with the leading story, "Transition—and Intention":

Three years ago this September, Northern Virginia's Globe Newspapers began publishing a weekly supplement, originally entitled *Northern Virginia Religion News*, and later, *Politics & Religion*. This editorial venture was something of a rarity in the nation's weekly and suburban press. For it contained editorials and features which were not only controversial (i.e. of interest to readers with strong convictions) but which focused upon issues beyond the county line. . . .

People in this area . . . deserve an antidote to the almost tedious sameness of the lockstep liberal editorial policies of American journalism's Siamese Triplets, the *New York Times,* the *Washington Post*, and the *Washington Star*.

. . . Three years ago, *The Globe's* General Manager Walter Dowie embarked on this editorial venture, despite an initial tidal wave of resistance. Last month, Publisher John McGoff told the editors of 40 Panax Newspapers that weekly newspapers too often abdicate national and international editorial leadership to the big dailies downtown. . . .

Featured columnists included Accuracy in Media's Reed Irvine, Patrick Buchanan, Andrew Greeley, and Dorothy "The Dragon Lady" Faber. Along with his regular editorials, Lester wrote an occasional movie review, a tradition he started with the *Crucifer* in Pasco, Washington. That summer, he made a special trip up to Radio City Music Hall with daughter Kathleen, who was looking into acting schools for next year. They attended the premiere of *MacArthur,* starring Gregory Peck as the famous five-star general of the U.S. Army. Douglas MacArthur was also one of the most celebrated graduates of

West Point Military Academy, so Lester felt a personal kinship with the great World War II leader.

Before the film started, the Rockettes performed, riveting audiences with their sensational line of kicking legs. They were followed by a religious spectacle, complete with angels and saints filling the stage among stained-glass panels. The finale featured a tribute to Disneyland which lingered on a bit longer than it should. Les, growing impatient as the actors danced around in either giant rabbit ears or mouse costumes, was so anxious to see the great military leader's cinematic bio that he wriggled in his seat and whined loudly: "Can we get on with IT??!!"

Finally, the screen fell, where it presented an inspiring and moving portrait of General MacArthur in all his glory. The closing scene, where he gave his most famous speech at West Point, ended with the immortal words: "Today marks my final roll call with you, but I want you to know, that when I cross the river, my last conscious thoughts will be, The Corps—and The Corps—and The Corps—and The Corps. I bid you farewell." Watching the cadets jump up and cheer, Lester sat in his seat as the credits rolled, absolutely stunned. He then rose to his feet, marched up the aisle of Radio City, wiped a tear from his eye, and announced, "That was MAGNIFICENT!!!!" Needless to say, his review for *MacArthur* offered nothing but raves.

In early 1978, *Washington Weekly* ran such scintillating stories as "Carter Fiscal Integrity Up in (Tobacco) Smoke," "'Mr. Elizabeth Taylor' Seeks Senate Seat," and "A Widely Respected Member of the Washington Press Corps," where Lester related the following incident with *New Republic's* John Osborne (who earlier had called Les a "bawling jackass" at a Nixon press briefing), at the Executive Office Building:

Osborne, who has covered the White House since the Nixon administration, either knows—or he certainly should know—that the reserved seats for the regular White House correspondents are held until 5 minutes before the presidential news conference begins. At that time, any unoccupied reserved seat may be taken by any reporter present.

The seat assigned to *New Republic* was second row, two from the aisle. . . . Since this seat was still not occupied when all seats became open, I moved up from row six. With the presidential news conference scheduled for 2:30, Mr. Osborne arrived at row 2—at exactly 2:39.

With a gesture as if he were an umpire proclaiming me out at home plate, this "widely respected" reporter growled: "All right, get out!" I explained briefly the rules that all seats had been open. And I did not move. Mr. Osborne's eyes flashed and his face flushed as he shouted—across the auditorium—an order to a member of the White House staff: "ALL RIGHT, WALT— GET THIS SON OF A BITCH OUT OF MY SEAT!"

No one on the White House staff obeyed Mr. Osborne's order; and I did not respond in kind. Instead, I suggested he find seating in the rear.

By the spring, Les was welcoming additional writers to the *Washington Weekly* staff. Ronald Reagan had already joined the growing ranks, and on April 6, a front-page story announced "Beginning Next Week: Two New Columnists: Lofton and Lasky Will Drive You MAD." The story provided photographs of the two journalists, one of Victor Lasky gleefully grinning, and the other of John Lofton angrily snarling.

Despite his rather ferocious photo, John is actually capable of smiling, which he does briefly on Christmas, Easter and the birthday of Louis XIV. . . . Victor Lasky is the author of the current best-seller "It Didn't Start With Watergate," as well as another best-seller in 1963, "JFK: The Man and The Myth." . . . Lasky has therefore been recurrently denounced, especially by Big Media's top-heavy roster of Kennedy worshippers, who have, however, been unable to keep his books off the best-seller lists. . . .

Frequenting the State Department press briefing on a regular basis, even after having rubber bands shot at him by Hodding Carter III,

Gadfly

Les was still adamant to prod the State Department spokesman for answers to important questions. In "State Department's Wild Reaction to Andy Young's Latest Blunder" on May 18, Lester was unprepared for the following, when inquiring about Ambassador Andrew Young's "appearances in a Congressional chairman's district . . . without knowledge of the White House. . . . When news of this Young involvement was first telephoned to Hodding Carter, a presidential aide, all that could be heard on the other end of the line was screaming":

KINSOLVING: Oh, you don't think he was campaigning? You think it was appropriate for him to make public appearances?

CARTER: No, no. I am not making judgment on what is appropriate. I am saying that the premise of your question is that he was campaigning for a man; and I am saying that it is not clear to me that he was. . . .

KINSOLVING: I really am puzzled by your statement "It's not clear to me that he was campaigning." This primary election in North Philadelphia is on May 16. To my knowledge, there is no segment of the United Nations in North Philadelphia. I don't believe there is anything international in North Philadelphia. He went into North Philadelphia and appeared with a candidate who is running against a Congressional chairman. Can you, really, with a straight face—

(Ed. Note: At this point, State Department Spokesman Carter's face erupted in a great grin.)

KINSOLVING: Well, obviously you can't. Let the record show that you can't [say that] with a straight face.

CARTER: (Removing what appeared to be a dead chicken from under the podium and slapping the bird against the podium) You have plucked me, and plucked, and plucked me enough!

(Whereupon the bird was flung through the air at the questioner.) (Laughter)

KINSOLVING: This is the second time I have been assaulted!

During the next press briefing, Les made certain he was properly armed when delivering one of his questions. A photographer caught the earnest reporter donning a catcher's mask, courtesy of the Alexandria Dukes baseball team, as he held up his arm up high, pen in hand.

On June 14, *The Ear* added another Kinsolving News Flash:

HOME TO ROOST . . . Mark June 25 in le notebook, darlings. That day, Lester Kinsolving, the Priest of Panax, last spotted here on the receiving end of a rubber chicken at a State Department briefing, plans to hit the pulpit again, at St. Thomas Church in Silver Spring.

Relgious News Service contributed additional information on July 11:

The controversial priest and columnist C. Lester Kinsolving announced he has left the Episcopal Church to serve an independent parish there. . . . Mr. Kinsolving made it clear that he is not "renouncing the Episcopal Church. . . . I have served it for 22 years, but I am deeply disturbed about many things in the Episcopal Church today."

Besides objecting to the ordination of women and the revised 1928 Book of Common Prayer, Lester also stated, "There is no way I can worship in a church that solemnizes Elizabeth Taylor's seventh marriage." At St. Thomas, "We rejoice in being able to worship from a prayer book which does not sound like Shakespeare rewritten by a committee headed by Mickey Spillane."

In "His Admonishments Backed by Experience," the *Washington Star* reported on July 15 that "Withdrawing from the Episcopal

Gadfly

Church may not be that easy for Kinsolving. The Diocese of California has put off for a month any decision whether to honor his request to withdraw." However, on July 29, the *Salinas Californian* reported:

> The standing committee of the Episcopal Diocese of California in San Francisco recommended Kinsolving's suspension [July 21] after Kinsolving reportedly wrote in a letter that he was withdrawing from the Episcopal Church to become rector of the independent St. Thomas' Church in Silver Spring, Md. Bishop C. Kilmer Myers interpreted Kinsolving's letter as a notice of resignation and authorized his suspension. . . .
>
> Kinsolving yesterday called his suspension "utterly disgusting. . . . If Myers is the providence of God, then God help us."

The *San Francisco Examiner's* "Kinsolving battles back, airs bishop's dirty linen" further stated:

> Bishop C. Kilmer Myers . . . has initiated a process that could result in defrocking syndicated columnist-priest Lester Kinsolving. Kinsolving, calling the action "a massive hypocrisy. . . . It's the first time in ecclesiastical history a bishop has suspended a priest while drying out in an alcoholic ward. . . . I doubt very much that the secular courts would regard me as more deserving of deposition than the late [Bishop Joseph Minnis] who was formally charged with repeated public drunkenness and sexual conduct in six states and Juarez, but was not unfrocked."

Determined that the threat of being defrocked "would not deter or scare" him, Lester faithfully served communion to the small congregation, which met every Sunday at 11 A.M. at the Auditorium Perpetual Building, at 8700 Georgia Ave. Such sermon topics included, "Should We Always Turn the Other Cheek?", "Does My Dog Have a Soul?", "Why Did God Take So Long to Send Jesus?" and the infamous "Damnable Doctrine of Damnation."

St. Thomas thrived, independent of the traditional Anglican Church. When they applied to become part of that denomination, they were rejected, since Lester was an adamant supporter of legalized abortion. When questioned as to how they would handle such matters as needing a bishop for confirmations, Lester replied, "The Anglican Church functioned in America from 1607 until 1784 without a single bishop, and our brother Anglican, George Washington, a churchman and vestryman of some note, was never confirmed."

According to the *Christian Challenge,* Bishop Myers notified Lester that "he was being inhibited from performing priestly functions, and would be deposed at the end of the six-month period stipulated in the Canons of the Church if he did not retract his abandonment of the ministry." Lester shot back with the following letter:

Dear Bishop Myers:

I received your quaintly-worded inhibition one day after the *San Francisco Examiner* telephoned to inquire about it. Apparently your boys at 1055 Taylor (diocesan headquarters in San Francisco) are leaking again.

I might also suggest that your wording, "We, by divine providence, Bishop of California," is in far greater need of modernizing than the 1928 *Book of Common Prayer.* For such pontifical wording suggests that you believe your administration of the Diocese of California has been providential.

I feel sure that you will understand—even if not appreciate—why I do not feel inhibited about celebrating the Holy Communion this Sunday and in the future. For I believe it is evident that your inhibition should have been more equitably directed toward such of your colleagues as Joseph Minnis and Robert DeWitt, among others.

Bishop DeWitt, according to the *Boston Globe,* ordained eleven women without seeking permission, and thus, "roiled the Episcopal Church, from its leadership to its laity." The *Christian Challenge* further reported:

Gadfly

What Fr. Kinsolving overlooked in his response to Bishop
Myers' letter of inhibition is that it is customary for bishops of
the Anglican Communion to use the phrase, "by divine permission," in such Communiqués. Only five bishops are permitted,
under ancient custom and usage and English canon law, to refer
to themselves as bishops "by divine providence." . . . These are:
The Archbishops of Canterbury, York and Armagh (Primate of
All Ireland) and the Bishops of London (Premier of England)
and of Meath (Premier Bishop of Ireland).

NO American bishop of the Anglican Commission has ever
been entitled to use the phrase employed by the Bishop of
California.

Back at the newsroom, *Washington Weekly* ran another Bradlee
brouhaha on August 3, 1978: *"Washington Post's* Strangely Delayed
Report of Alleged White House Cocaine-Snorter":

The *Washington Post* on July 26th published the following
report, by its own ombudsman (house critic) Charles Seib: At
a party thrown last December by a group favoring the legal-
ization of marijuana [NORML] Dr. Peter Bourne [President
Carter's drug policy advisor] not only smoked marijuana, but
also used cocaine, a very illegal and very expensive drug. . . .

A *Post* reporter . . . said he saw Bourne snort cocaine through a
rolled piece of currency, as is the fashion. Two other *Post* people
were in the bedroom, which must have been a crowded one,
at the historic moment, but apparently they did not supply
material for the *Post* story. If the incident is such big news now,
didn't their reporter consider it news last December?

Seib actually went so far as to conclude that the *Washington Post*
had not come "totally clean with its public." Yet when asked
about the identity of these three *"Post* people" who the *Post*
reported as having watched this cocaine-snorting, journalistic

ethics pundit Seib adamantly refused to "come clean" with their identities. *Post* Executive Editor Bradlee refused to comment, as did Managing Editor Howard Simons. . . .

While the cocaine-snorting of this top Presidential drug advisor was not a felony, it raises a question as to whether the *Post* would have delayed so long in reporting such drug use, had the user been John Mitchell or H.R. Haldeman or John Erlichman. . . .

In Richmond, Pulitzer prize–winning cartoonist Jeff MacNelly portrayed an obviously drug-inebriated White House official floating in air five feet above a podium, while one reporter noted: "There is NO widespread drug use in the White House, according to a high government official."

During the August 11th White House press briefing, Lester and Reed Irvine prodded the press secretary, which was later reported in "Jody Powell Makes Big Joke of Reported White House Narcotics Violations":

QUESTION: A couple of former high government officials said that government officials who are guilty of illegal acts which would put their jobs in jeopardy are peculiar subjects to blackmail. Do you agree with that?

POWELL: I don't generally comment on anonymous statements.

QUESTION: All right, Pat Buchanan and Bruce Herschenson.

POWELL: They ought to know (laughter).

QUESTION: Do you agree?

POWELL: I really haven't ever thought about it that way.

Gadfly

QUESTION: Could I follow up? Think about it while I am asking my next question. Three senators, including the Senate Majority Leader and nearly a dozen Congressmen that I know of, have asked for an investigation of allegations of drug use on the part of the White House staff.

POWELL: Are you back on that again?

QUESTION: The number of people demanding this is increasing. And I was just wondering—

POWELL: Have they asked for their staffs to be investigated?

QUESTION: Let me ask the question.

POWELL: I thought a little give and take here (laughter).

QUESTION: You think it is funny, Jody? You think this is a big joke? You are reading Doonesbury?

POWELL: No, that is not what I think about it, but go ahead.

QUESTION: . . . It is a serious matter. We now have several Senators and including one announced Presidential candidate, Phil Crane, who are asking for an investigation. Now my question—

POWELL: That certainly lends credibility to the request (laughter).

QUESTION: . . . Would you agree that there is that danger if there are people on the staff who are known to their suppliers to be drug users and to people like Keith Stoup [founder of NORML], that they are subject to blackmail?

POWELL: I suppose they are. I am not going to get involved in that.

QUESTION: Let me ask you: are you grateful to the news media for not publicizing these demands for an investigation?

POWELL: Am I what?

QUESTION: Grateful to the news media for not publicizing that demand from the Hill on the investigation of this matter?

POWELL: I am not aware they were unpublicized. I remember reading about them three weeks ago and remember you asking me about it three weeks ago.

(At this point, the subject was changed. And no other reporter in the White House press pressed this issue of narcotics violations on the staff of the president of the United States).

After exposure of his drug use in the media, Dr. Peter Bourne, according to Reed Irvine of *Accuracy in Media,* "resigned his post as White House adviser on drug abuse, after it was alleged in print that he had been observed snorting cocaine, [and that] he told a [*New York Times*] reporter that there is a 'high incidence of marijuana use' and 'occasional' use of cocaine by others on the White House staff." Numerous members of Congress, including Senators Howard Baker, Pete Domenici, and Congressman Henry Hyde called for a full investigation by the Department of Justice. Reed Irvine went on further to state:

The chances are that you have not heard much about these demands for an investigation of the White House staff, since the news media have shown virtually no interest in seeing the matter pursued. There have been no thundering editorials from *The Washington Post, The New York Times* or *The Washington Star* demanding that Dr. Peter Bourne be required to tell under oath what he knows of illegal drug use by members of the President's official family. The media, which were so zealous in insisting that the White House should set an example of strict obedience to the law in the Watergate days, have seemingly abandoned that insistence in this case.

By late September, as reported in *Washington Weekly*'s "Civiletti Coverup of Dr. Bourne" on November 2, 1978,

Deputy Attorney General Civiletti responded to a letter of July 24, 1978, written by Republican Congressman Henry J. Hyde. Rep. Hyde's letter asked Attorney General Griffin B. Bell to conduct an investigation of widespread allegations of drug use by employees on the White House staff.

How did our Department of Justice respond? It responded nearly two months later. How did our Department of Justice investigate? Mr. Civiletti tells how, in his letter:

"During August, a responsible official of the Department who is knowledgeable about drug enforcement talked with Dr. Bourne and asked him whether he had made the statement in the *New York Times* article. . . . Dr. Bourne responded that he had not made this statement. Further, Dr. Bourne stated that he did not have any personal knowledge of drug use by the White House staff members, that he had never seen them using drugs, and that he was not aware of any drug abuse incident involving White House staffers."

End of "investigation."
By the Department of "Justice."

Outraged at this unmitigated injustice, Les demanded that Civiletti be fired and insisted that the entire Bourne affair was "certainly a scandal which endangers our national security, not to mention the national morality."

On November 18, drug use at the White House would seem like a distant memory compared to the news Lester would hear on the radio as he drove home from an Army-Pitt football game that evening. The top story involved California Congressman Leo J. Ryan being shot and killed by gunmen in Guyana, along with four members of the media. It took place on an airstrip in Port Kaituma, not far from a community known as Jonestown.

Lester immediately knew, and said to himself, "My God, it must be the Temple."

Number Two
on the Peoples Temple
Hit List

R ETURNING HOME THAT night, Les was greeted by a shaken
Sylvia as he walked through the front door. It wasn't long
before the FBI had called to inform Les that he was "number two
on Jim Jones' 'hit list'" and that he should protect himself. According
to *Religion News Service*'s report on a *San Francisco Examiner* story,
"Jones had a fund of $3 million and bragged of his contacts with the
Mafia which he said would help him eliminate his enemies of the
Peoples Temple."

Headlines raged across the world, with news of hundreds of Temple
members who were poisoned, either by drinking cups of Kool-Aid
laced with cyanide, or having it injected into their arms, as were the
276 babies and children. Those who attempted to run were shot by
guards. Jim Jones ordered the mass killing, after Congressman Ryan
left Jonestown with Temple defectors and a news crew. As Ryan and
his party attempted to board two small planes, four gunmen drove up
on a tractor and started shooting. While others fled into the jungle,
Ryan was murdered, along with three journalists: NBC's Bob Brown
and Don Harris, and twenty-seven-year-old *Examiner* photographer

Greg Robinson. Patricia Parks, a defector, was also shot to death. The assailants then reported back to Jones, who proceeded with his plans.

As the death count rose from 400 to over 900 men, women, and children, the Kinsolving household was gripped in fear. Eldest daughter Laura, who was living with her parents at the time, was so terrified by the thought of her family being murdered by a hit squad that she was busily finding another place to live. "The only consolation we had at the time," Sylvia recalls, "was our big Labrador, Brandon. He had a thunderous bark which would scare off any intruder."

Jim Jones had ordered his flock to Guyana after an exposé, "Inside Politically Potent Peoples Temple," appeared in *New West* magazine on August 1, 1977. Here, defectors who escaped the cult told stories of fraud, beatings, and torture which were so unsettling that when Board of Supervisors President Quentin Kopp read the article he stated to one interviewer, "I almost fell out of my chair." Since Jones had been appointed Commissioner of the San Francisco Housing Authority, Kopp had Clerk of the Board Gilbert Boreman send an urgent letter to Mayor George Moscone, which included the following:

> The supervisor is quite concerned about the allegations raised in the article particularly those set forth on page 38 under the caption, "Why Jim Jones Should Be Investigated." It is respectfully requested that the Mayor review this article and furnish information as to the Mayor's intention relative to the conduct of any inquiry or investigation into the allegations contained in the article.

A few days later, Mayor Moscone issued a press release that stated, "The Mayor's Office does not and will not conduct any investigation" [over] a series of allegations with absolutely no hard evidence that Rev. Jones has violated any laws, either local, state, or federal. . . . I will not comment upon the alleged practices of the Temple, as it is not my habit to be a religious commentator." Since Jones had helped elect George Moscone, with scores of volunteers voting fraudulently in the November 1975 mayoral election, Moscone refused to investigate.

On November 19, the day after the Jonestown massacre, Les attended a packed State Department press briefing, where he encountered his former editor, Tom Eastham, who was now working for the *S.F. Examiner*'s Washington bureau. Here was the man who was responsible for bringing Lester into the Temple investigation over six years before, and who didn't protest when the Temple exposés were stopped. Eastham slowly approached Lester, and with obvious remorse, said, "Les, I'm so sorry."

Two months later, while attending the American Association of Newspaper Publishers convention in New York, Les found himself in the elevator with Charles Thieriot, publisher of the *San Francisco Chroncile*. Inevitably the subject of Jonestown came up, and Lester became incensed, since Thieriot had accepted a substantial check from the Temple (for their campaign "In Defense of a Free Press" in 1973) and then forwarded it to the Society of Professional Journalists, Sigma Delta Chi. After a heated discussion about the Temple, Lester angrily confronted the publisher: "Don't you realize you have blood on your hands?!"

Along with a plethora of news reports on the Temple, an ironic editorial would appear on the *Examiner*'s pages in San Francisco, written by Publisher and Editor Reg Murphy. In "A Pledge: We Will Not Stop," Murphy asserted:

> The work of reporting cannot be stopped by violence. . . . We will not stop until we have answered the question—dispassionately, professionally, straightforwardly. Greg Robinson loved the clear, crisp, strong picture that captured the critical moment. . . . The way we can pay tribute to his memory is to *continue the investigation* that cost him his life. *He did not lose his life in vain.*

In *Religious News Service*'s "Kinsolving on Peoples Temple 'Hit List,'" reporter John Novotney included quotes from Lester:

> "I am honored to be No. 2 on this maniac's 'hit list.' [It] so effectively exposes the efforts of such big media as the *San Francisco*

Chronicle and the *Washington Post* to cover up their disastrous failure to follow-up on what Carolyn Pickering of the *Indianapolis Star* and I exposed at length on front pages of two major daily newspapers six years ago."

. . . Asked if he was seeking police or other protection now, the 50-year-old clergyman-journalist said he was not. . . .

"If in the line of duty," Kinsolving continued, "you risk your life, then you risk it. This was my duty.

"I only wish to God that the many other journalists whom I begged to follow-up on this (six years ago) had done so—columnist) Jack Anderson, Ralph Otwell, editor of the *Chicago Sun-Times*, as well as the Religion Newswriters Association and Sigma Delta Chi [the journalist society]."

Kinsolving said the "major news media have an enormous guilt on this [Guyana tragedy], and so do the Disciples of Christ, who certainly should be sued for the cost of returning the bodies of victims of one of their ordained clergymen from whom they accepted money for years.

"Why should all U.S. taxpayers be saddled with this expenditure?" he asked.

For his *New Republic* column, "White House Watch," John Osborne added his own comments on the Jonestown affair:

A press room zany and publicity seeker asked Press Secretary Jody Powell why the taxpayers instead of a church (not the Peoples Temple) with which Jim Jones was said to have been affiliated would have to meet the cost of bringing home and processing the bodies of the American dead in Guyana.

At a Nixon press conference in 1974, I called this character "a bawling jackass" and was applauded by colleagues for doing so. He and Powell almost came to blows, not so much over the question as over the unctuously righteous tone in which it was asked. In these times it's never safe to deride such deridable performances.

By early 1979, as the danger of a hit squad began to ease, the Kinsolving family returned to some semblance of normalcy. Brenda Ganatos, whom Les considered "one of the bravest people I've ever known," sent a scroll on parchment paper, signed by her and fourteen other Ukiah residents:

January 13, 1979

Dear Les:

We wish to express our sincere appreciation for your sole support in our efforts to expose Jim Jones' Peoples Temple ten years ago, in its earliest stages of madness. We commend you as a journalist, friend and fellow American for risking your life and job, because of your belief in our futile attempts to protect our community by your relentless investigative reporting and personal guidance.

Although our pleas for investigation were ignored by our local media and government officials, our small group of defectors and concerned citizens do not feel the guilt that the many reporters and other citizens now feel, since the senseless tragedy in Guyana, knowing it could well have been prevented right here in Ukiah.

The only satisfaction we can feel now, after all these years of sharing a personal nightmare, in seeking help of local, state, and federal officials to no avail, is the present investigations of similar organizations being done by our government, as well as other news media.

We thank you again, Les, from the bottom of our hearts. You are a fine example of what "true American journalism" is all about!

Les later proclaimed, "I'd rather have this than the Pulitzer Prize."

"ON WEDNESDAY, JAN. 31, *Washington Weekly* (as announced in its January 18 issue) is increasing its content 50 percent, moving onto 250 newsstands and vending machines in D.C., MD. & VA." Dubbed by then-Congressman Trent Lott (R-MS) the paper that was "once a week, but never weakly," the announcement included a highlight and photo of one of its columnists—Pat Buchanan: "From countless comments—nasty, neutral, and nice—the appearance of my column in *Washington Weekly* is having an impact in both the journalistic and political communities of this Capital City." Additional impacts included:

- At the request of the White House, *Washington Weekly* is mailed each week to the editor of the President's Daily News Summary. It is also mailed to all embassies and all Congressional offices.
- The *Washington Star*'s nationally syndicated and avidly read gossip column *The Ear*, has featured *Washington Weekly* twice within one 10-day period in December of 1977—the only time in *Ear's* three-year existence that any weekly newspaper in the nation has been so featured.
- After *Washington Weekly's* editor asked a State Department briefing why the Carter administration proposed an arms embargo on South Africa with no similar action regarding U.S. imports of two-thirds of Idi Amin's coffee crop, U.S. Ambassador Andrew Young telephoned a special answer for Kinsolving from New York.

In other breaking news, "Panax Corp. announced today the sale, for an undisclosed price, of the *Washington Weekly* to a new corporation which will be headed by the *Weekly's* present editor, Lester Kinsolving . . . effective Jan. 24." Besides "the use of UPI photographs to illustrate lead stories, features, and syndicated columnists" in the new format, Lester added that "We will also increase our use of freelance material, particularly in regard to one of our stated purposes: "ALL THE NEWS THE DAILIES WON'T PRINT."

This provocative pronouncement now appeared on page one, which so delighted one subscriber that he sent off a fan letter: "I was most impressed by the editorial tone and subject material and would like to continue reading of such articles. Particularly I look forward to 'ALL THE NEWS THE DAILIES WON'T PRINT'—the public needs this coverage. I wish you success in your new venture."

Although the majority of letters were positive, such as "The *Weekly* is just outstanding. Enclosed please find check and application for gift subscription," and "I always look forward to receiving your publication. It is the most informative of the ones I read," Les received his usual share of hate mail, which was published in *Washington Weekly*'s Letters to the Editor section:

PURE UNADULTERATED
BOVINE FECAL EFFLUVIA

Lester, this publication is pure, unadulterated, bull----!! I understand completely why you have to give it away. This makes most political demagogues pale!

Arnold Woodrick(?)
Address illegible

Editor's note: See below: Voluntary Paid Circulation will provide you a way to help pay for a newspaper which so obviously fascinates you. Cheers.

. . .

SELF-SERVING CRAP RAG

Dear so-called journalists:

I just bought the first and last copy of your rag I ever will. It must be so pleasant to live in that nether world of black/white, liberal/conservative simplicity. I have read high-school papers with more substance and far less self-serving crap than yours. Sorry I bothered to give you the benefit of the doubt.

Jim Sharp, Jr.
Matt Reese & Associates
Washington, D.C.

Editor's Note: Mr. Sharp thoughtfully returned his copy of Washington Weekly—which he had cut into thirty five (35) pieces. This demonstrative means of correspondence makes it all the more sad that he did not reveal which high school paper it is that he prefers for his reading.

Although Les was officially the editor and publisher of *Washington Weekly,* it was funded by Wilson Lucom, who headed such groups as Concerned Voters, Committee to Restore Internal Security in the House and Senate (CRISIHS), and Council Against Communist Aggression (CACA). Full-page advertisements paid for by Luchom began to appear in the weekly, where some would target Senator Edward Kennedy. The ad headings read: "What Do Mary Jo Kopechne and the Senate's Internal Security Unit Have in Common?", "Ted Kennedy: A Man of Failed and Flawed Character," and "Why Did 'Chappaquiddick Ted' Have the Body 'Snatched'?"

In yet another of Lucom's organizations, The U.S. Anti-Communist Congress, an ad featured a photo of Jane Fonda, with the heading, "C = C : Communism = Cancer." The ad included the following information:

The U.S. Anti-Communist Congress believes that we should treat communism like we treat cancer. Get it out of our system before it gets out of control. Do you agree? Use the coupon to give us your answer. Enclose 25 cents to cover postage and handling, and we will send you FREE 100 "America, Yes, Communism, No" stamps. Use them on your letters.

Another financial supporter of *Washington Weekly,* Frank Fusco, was also chairman of the Mary Jo Kopechne Memorial Society. In July 1979, ten years after the young secretary's death at Chappaquiddick Island, Massachusetts, the Memorial Society held a special service in her honor. They placed a historical marker at the foot of the bridge, which read:

On July 19, 1969, Mary Jo Kopechne, a pretty 28-year-old, was found dead at the bottom of Poucha Pond in a car owned by Senator Edward M. Kennedy. Senator Kennedy said he had driven the car off Dyke Bridge, after turning down this road by error, thinking it led to the ferry. He escaped unscathed, but he left Mary Jo trapped in the car and did not report the accident to the police for more than 10 hours. Nor did he seek any professional help to rescue Mary Jo.

The evidence indicates that Mary Jo may have lived for several hours, breathing air trapped in the sunken car. No autopsy was performed to determine the cause of death. There are many questions about the death of Mary Jo Kopechne that were never satisfactorily answered by Senator Kennedy or his companions.

Mr. Fusco invited Lester to officiate at the ceremony, which he did obligingly. As Les spoke of Kopechne as a "victim of royal negligence—for which men of lesser means and lesser fame have been sent to prison," a *Washington Post* reporter, Stacey Jolna, stood nearby; however, no coverage of the event ever appeared in the *Post.* In her article, "Kopechne Memorial Censored By Pro-Kennedy Media," *Washington Weekly* intern Meg McConahey mentioned that a "Gazette reporter stonily contended that the event was a 'fizzle' although the pathway leading to the bridge was accommodating as many people as space limitation would allow. . . . Reed Irvine, chairman of Accuracy in

Media countered her criticism by reminding her that the turnout was astounding considering the fact that the *Gazette*, owned by *New York Times* Columnist James Reston, had refused to accept any advertising about the event." In an advertisement for the memorial service marked "Censored," a note was printed at the bottom:

> The *Vineyard Gazette* showed its contempt for your right to know by refusing to run this announcement as a paid ad. The other paper that James Reston is connected with has run many propaganda ads for Kim II-Sung, one of the world's worst dictators.

As the historical marker was unveiled and a wreath adorned with yellow flowers was thrown into the waters of Poucha Pond, McConahey noted that the "onlookers nervously shuffled, perhaps uncomfortable at being reminded of an injustice that time had almost allowed them to forget." By the end of the ceremony, Les included his commentary on the local media, before he concluded the service with a prayer:

> We are grateful that here on Chappaquiddick Island the constitutional provision of freedom of assembly and worship still prevails—even though the constitutional provision of freedom of the press does not apply in Mr. Reston's newspaper on Martha's Vineyard.

Along with coverage of the Kopechne Memorial Service, Les ran the following announcement in July: "Washington Weekly Honored By Washingtonian Magazine":

> The *Washingtonian* is an Annapolis-owned monthly magazine which has saluted *Washington Weekly* as the worst weekly newspaper in Washington.

> *WW* is deeply touched, just as we were recently, when *The Washington Star* (a New York–owned daily newspaper) hailed us—in

its best read column, *The Ear*—as "The Wee Weenie." . . . We bask in associated glory. First "The Wee Weenie" and then "Washington's Worst Weekly." Our cup runneth over.

When the announcement ran in the magazine, the editors mentioned that the paper earned the accolade because it was "the weekly goings-on of Les Kinsolving's mind."

By year's end, *Washington Weekly* received another "worst of" award, this time from Ron Nessen: in "a brand new periodical called 'Media People,'" Nessen listed "six of the Washington press corps as 'The Worst'":

Tom Wicker of the *New York Times*, Columnists Evans and Novak, and Nicholas von Hoffman of the *Washington Post*; Frank van der Linden of the *Nashville Banner*, and Modesty Forbids of *WW*.

Mr. Nessen also describes UPI White House bureau chief Helen Thomas (whom he includes in this "over-rated" category) as an ill-informed, "rude, raucous, pushy witch." (He made no mention, however, of the number of times Helen pinned him to the wall and exposed his frequently sleazy evasions.)

John Chancellor of NBC is categorized by Nessen as "a superdud" who is "dull, dull, dull" and "pompous." (Judge Nessen failed to mention, however, that NBC decided not to rehire onetime reporter Ron Nessen, after watching him in action as Gerry Ford's news secretary—where he functioned in a manner so efficient that *Time* magazine once reported of Nessen: "He could screw up a sunset.")

As for Your Obedient Servant, Nessen reports that I ask "unanswerable questions" (like: "Why was Solzhenitzyn not invited to the White House by President Ford?"—at which Mount Nessen erupted so violently that the event was featured by both *Time* and *Newsweek*).

. . . It is interesting, if that's the word for it, that the editor of this new periodical would select Ron Nessen of all people as his initial issue's media evaluator—since Ron was surely one of the most wretched White House news secretaries in American history.

The first *Washington Weekly* of 1980, published on New Years Day, featured a full page of letters to the editor, including one entitled "Fascist Oriented Puke Periodical":

First, I enjoy your newspaper (*sic*) very much. It is really garbage of the highest odor. . . . I resent the insulting things that people are saying about your piece of printed vomit. Recently, a man called it a crap rag . . . and now in the Dec. 4, 1979 issue some freak calls your paper a smear sheet. It is not either of these it is basically a FACIST ORIENTED PUKE PERIODICAL.

Last again I enjoy reading fascist puke sometimes and you certainly fill the bill. Have a wonderful new year 1980 and may all your investments collapse and the benefits go to the people.

(Name Withheld)

Editor's Note—Dear Garbage Collector of Printed Vomit Puke Periodicals: While WW *generally declines to publish anonymous letters, rarely do we receive such culturally inspiring letters as yours.*

Later that month, Les congratulated *Time* magazine "for its strong critique of the *Washington Post's* despicable hatchet job on Dr. Zbigniew Brzezinski—which was written by Mrs. Ben (Sally Quinn) Bradlee," in "The Washington Post Lets Shelby Coffey—Not Bradlee—Take the White House Heat":

For TIME published the photograph of the President's National Security Adviser, which Quinn reported as showing Brzezinski unzipping his fly in front of a female reporter. The photograph showed no such unzipping, although the *Post*—in its retraction—claimed weakly that there were "poses, shadows and background of this picture (which) create an accidental 'double entendre.'"

Even sleazier than this attempt to crawl out of its own gutter was the *Washington Post*'s action in responding to an invitation from the White House (and reportedly Brzezinski's attorney) to discuss the situation—about which President Carter was reportedly furious.

The Washington Post Co. did not send its board chairman, Katherine Graham; or its publisher, her own son Donald Graham; or its executive editor Benjamin C. Bradlee—husband of the writer, whose story he defends as "a son of a bitch of a good story." (Mr. Bradlee would be well advised to avoid his earthy, female canine references for the time being.)

Reporting that Style editor Shelby Coffey was sent to the White House as "a sacrificial lamb . . . to which Mr. Bradlee has assigned Mrs. Bradlee to do her character assassination pieces," Les phoned Coffey later at home, "where he was polite but dedicated to absolutely no comment—albeit with a tell-tale tone of anguish in his voice." It might've proved unfortunate if "Gentle Ben" was fired for allowing this story to go to press, for "*Washington Weekly* would be deprived of one of its most frequent and entertaining features."

While Wilson Lucom continued waging his battle against Ted Kennedy with a full-page ad in March, claiming "A $1000 Contribution Awaits Ted Kennedy's Campaign: All you have to do, Senator, is take and pass a simple lie detector test," another anti-Kennedy ad ran that month, promoting a boardgame entitled "Chap Acquitted":

No, it's not Chappaquiddick misspelled but the name of a party game designed to give the players an objective in-depth knowledge of the incident. A BRIDGE GAME OF SORTS, it is played by 3 active players and a dummy.

The gameboard is a detailed map of Chappaquiddick upon which the players maneuver their cars in response to questions asked by the dummy. Three decks of cards, entitled "QUESTIONS," "EVASIVE REPLIES," and "CHARISMA" are used to surface the fact. Enclosed is a 273 page reference book relating discussions with eyewitnesses, scuba divers, media, medical and legal experts.

A MUST FOR THOSE INTERESTED IN FINDING OUT WHAT REALLY HAPPENED AT CHAPPAQUIDICK THAT NIGHT—AND LATER! © Copyright 1980 ALUCARD LTD

In late April, during the American Society of Newspaper Editors' annual convention in Washington, Les distributed complimentary copies of *Washington Weekly* to the 600 members in attendance. The April 15th issue's front-page headline, "WASHINGTON POST COVER-UP OF CONGRESSMAN'S STRANGE SEX SCANDAL," drew mixed reactions, from "uniform courtesy" to "enthusiastic interest." However, the managing editor of the *Post*, Richard Harwood, when offered the complimentary copy, snapped, "I've already read that." Donald Graham, *Post* publisher stated likewise, albeit with a gracious smile.

Minutes later, "along came the man who made Jason Robards famous," along with his wife, Sally Quinn Bradlee:

KINSOLVING: Hey Ben! Have you seen the news?

BRADLEE: (looking at WW's headline with withering scorn and growling) I DON'T READ THAT SHIT!

KINSOLVING: (noticing a *Washington Weekly* tucked under Sally Quinn's arm) Well, obviously someone does!!

BRADLEE: FUCK YOU!!!

Other notable journalists also expressed their disrelish for the weekly, such as CBS's Washington bureau correspondent Lesley Stahl. As Les was delivering it to the CBS booth in the White House, Lesley took the paper and crumpled it up in front of him. Les responded accordingly: "Why Lesley, I thought you could read!" *WW* contributor Sarah McClendon offered her own eyewitness account on April 29, in "Lesley Stahl Shows Her Temper":

> Colleagues are shocked and grieved over this. . . . The narrow, confining little booth of CBS in the White House Press Center was the scene of a nasty mess recently. . . . Lem Tucker, wiry, thin, black reporter got mauled by quick, angular, highly-tensed Lesley Stahl, who had been covering the White House beat for some time when Lem was added to the staff there.

> There came a day of harrowing, screaming, high-handed bullying, ordering around by Stahl. Then matters got worse. Dashing into the narrow booth, believing she had a scoop on Hamilton Jordan being in Panama, Stahl hurled Tucker physically out of her way and against the wall. In doing so, she elbowed him in the crotch in her haste to get to her typewriter and the telephone. She also turned on the television to get an early newscast over Channel 2. Since the reception was poor, he turned the channel to No. 7. She became more angered and screamed at him. . . .

> Whereupon he notified his office he was leaving the assignment and vacated the booth and the job . . . with some choice four-letter words hurled back at her as he strode through the Press Center. Horrified colleagues looked up to hear Lesley getting it loud . . . not surprised that it was Lesley. . . .

> The end was he got a reprimand for leaving his assignment and was suspended for a day . . . for not carrying out assignment

orders. . . . But no one blamed him for objecting to her treatment. . . . She has told two, the vice president, and many more that she was wrong, that she was high-handed and she is sorry. . . . Both are still working at CBS. . . .

For the July 14 "Special Convention Daily Edition" of *Washington Weekly*, Les ran a full-page ad in hopes of attracting more conservative readers who were attending the 1980 Republican National Convention. Excerpts from the promo read:

An Antidote for Washington's Daily Siamese Twins

Washington's two daily newspapers, along with the *New York Times*, have an undeniable effect upon the TV networks and the wire services in the process of determining what news will be reported and what news will be ignored—or even distorted.

Not only are these newspapers distinctly liberal, but in Washington, the *Post* and the *Star* have editorial positions which repeated surveys have demonstrated to be virtually identical.

. . . For nearly two years, Washington has had a small but very well read (and cursed, or blessed) antidote to the Daily Siamese Twins It is the only weekly or daily in Metropolitan Washington which dares to critique the Big Media—and to publish a considerable volume of the news which the *Post* and the *Star* refuse to report (even when such news is carried by UPI).

Maybe this and our irreverent style is why—with no funds for national promotion—we now have paid subscribers in all 50 states along with avid readers all over Capitol Hill and throughout 1600 Pennsylvania Ave. and the National Press Building. Maybe that's why you would value receiving All the News the Dailies Won't Print—Once a Week, But Never Weakly.

Gadfly

The convention, held at Joe Louis Arena in Detroit, Michigan, had nearby hotels completely booked that week, so the only rooms available were outside of the city. After a full evening at the arena, Les drove to the hotel in the early hours of the morning, along with daughter Kathleen, son Tom, and intern Meg McConahey. After a restful night of sleep, Kathleen drew open the curtains in her hotel room and noticed a large touring bus in the parking lot, with a sign on its side that read BUDDY RICH'S BIG BAND. Looking down the hallway, she discovered many musicians heading to the lobby for a morning meal.

After breakfast in the hotel café, a solo Buddy Rich stepped into the elevator with Les, who cordially asked the famous drummer, "Are you here for the convention?" A frowning Mr. Rich snarled, "WHAT convention??" Like their boss, other members of Rich's band generally kept to themselves. Fortunately the brassy sounds of practice sessions from their hotel rooms could be heard during the Kinsolvings' early afternoon swims. The curtains were always carefully drawn to ward off curious fans.

Color at Joe Louis Arena was fairly lively, according to Lester's report on various convention sideshows. "Outside entertainment" was provided by "The Yippies—those gawky, exhibitionist anachronisms of the far left sixties [who] paraded about with such witless anti-Reaganisms as to bring to mind small boys penciling smut on the gents room wall." The delegates happily ushered in a new era by nominating Ronald Reagan, who would soon win in a landslide victory in November. The final daily issue provided an ad bearing a caricature of Ted Kennedy wearing an "I ♥ NY" shirt, with the words, "Send a Message to 6,000 Democrats in Madison Square Garden Next Month. A Full Page Ad for Only $300."

On August 11, *Washington Weekly* greeted conventioneers with the following salutation: "Welcome to the Democratic National Bloodbath: Can the Democrats Beat Reagan With Either Billy's Brother or the Chap of Quiddick?" The following Wednesday, Tom Kinsolving penned the leading convention story, "'Reagan Will Win' Says Ron Dellums; Carter 'Breaks Promises'":

"I maintain that this November the Democratic Party is going to get blown out of the water," said the Congressman from Berkeley, who went on to charge fellow Democrats with "selling themselves out."

Dellums noted that these people whom he regards as sellouts are supporting a President "who refused to debate party opponents, and who is ignoring significant issues such as poverty and racial unrest."

. . . Dellums went on to predict the election of Ronald Reagan, whom he described as "a Neanderthal Man." . . . The California Congressman also stated that he does not intend to endorse President Carter's reelection, because of what he terms a "faulty platform and a candidate with a record of broken promises."

Tom took a special interest in this assignment, since he had recently seen a group of African American D.C. residents gathered near Capitol Hill in some sort of protest against poverty. Dellums, a well-dressed, well-paid member of Congress, had his fist raised and was yelling at the crowd, "I'm With You In That Struggle!!!"

Publishing and distributing *Washington Weekly* in New York City on a daily basis was a frantic experience for Les. Dashing off editorials, sending the final copy to be printed, and later rushing to the printer in Long Island to pick up bundles of papers after midnight was extremely taxing. As Les was struggling through the traffic snarl surrounding Madison Square Garden to make his first pick-up of the papers, he accidentally bumped into a yellow checker cab. The irate behemoth behind the wheel lunged out, and before he could spit out an infuriated speech, Les yelled, "THERE'S NO DAMAGE AND I APOLOGIZE!!" as he spied an opening in the traffic and sped off toward Queens Midtown Tunnel.

Delivering the bundles that morning to daughter Kathleen's East Side apartment to be distributed on street corners surrounding the convention, issues of *Washington Weekly* remained piled high outside of the building, which Les later discovered, to his chagrin. As he yelled up to the apartment on the intercom, "LET'S GO!!!" Kathleen, Meg, Laura, and Tom sheepishly walked down to the street, where they were greeted by a pleading Lester, who held out his hands in earnest: "WHERE WERE YOU??!!"

To help distribute the papers, Kathleen had recruited fellow acting students from the school she was attending, The American Academy of Dramatic Arts. Les had promised that everyone would be paid $7.50 per hour, a hefty sum in 1980. One of the paid workers was not an acting student, but a rather shady roommate of an acting student. Discovering that the paper he was distributing featured a column by Patrick Buchanan, he yelled, "GET YOUR FASCIST SHEET HERE!!" Fellow reporters witnessing this sight reported it to Lester, who later gave the young man a stern lecture and refused to pay him. Walking away empty-handed, the enraged youth asserted, "Pat Buchanan IS a fascist!!" and then shouted, "REVENGE IS SWEET!!"

Another *Washington Weekly* distribution conflict involved a clown who was passing out leaflets on one street corner adjacent to the Garden. Dressed in an orange wig, white makeup, and red nose, he attempted to bamboozle Lester's eldest daughter Laura into giving up her space, which was closer to the throngs of conventioneers crossing the street. Yelling for brother Tom to intervene as she struggled to pass out *WW*'s bearing the larger-than-usual headline, "THE DEMOCRATIC PARTY IS A CORPSE: FIVE GOOD REASONS WHY IT DESERVES TO DIE," the clown shot off like a rocket as Tom decked him with the back of his hand, in a noble effort to protect his sister from the nefarious intruder. Needless to say, the clown ended up on the other side of the street for the remainder of the convention. Although logistics such as these were challenging, Les was able to sell 15,000 copies of the convention issues on newsstands all over Manhattan.

With party nominations in place and an eventual win for Ronald Reagan in November, Lester was seeking another publisher for *Washington Weekly*. Wilson Luchom, who'd bankrolled the paper, as well as Reed Irvine's organization Accuracy in Media, objected to an exposé Tom and Meg McConahey had written on a Vietnamese refugee who held a demonstration in Lafayette Park, demanding that an atomic bomb be dropped on Hanoi. Irvine, who served as a liaison between Luchom and Lester, refused to let the article go to press, and thus revoked Lester's editorial control over content. As later reported in the *Post,* "The situation frustrated Kinsolving so much that he dreamed of Irvine one night and punched a hole in the sheetrock over his bed next to the portrait of Jesus." Soon after, Luchom, Irvine, and Kinsolving parted ways.

"NEW PUBLISHER FOR WASHINGTON WEEKLY" ran the headline on November 11, 1980, but by November 25, another headline appeared: "After Six Years *Washington Weekly* Suspends Publication." William Dunham, the aforementioned publisher, declared himself "an engineer and business investor whose conglomerate holdings include a printing house in Rockville, MD." Les later discovered that Dunham had no such access to printing facilities, and appeared to be somewhat of a con artist. With no other leads, the only choice was to fold the paper.

Lester's farewell in the final issue of *Washington Weekly* included the following:

> It has been an honor to edit some of the ablest writers we know, who surely deserve a Washington outlet. Two of our former columnists are now writing for the *Washington Post,* which we consider a fair exchange. For that newspaper's executive editor and his love life, towering rages and outrages, ludicrous foul-ups, and amusing—even charming—arrogance, has provided us with an almost inexhaustible source of hot copy.

> We will continue to watch and prod Gentle Ben, over another medium with a wider audience. [We were] dedicated to the somewhat Herculean task of trying to keep the *Post* and the *Star* fairly honest.

Gadfly

Such grappling with two Goliaths at once is surely no sinecure. But we have always been inspired by Teddy Roosevelt's exhilarating admonition:

"Aggressive fighting for the right is the noblest sport the world affords."

It goes without saying that *Washington Weekly* was not always right (such as in headline typos). But we surely have enjoyed trying.

—Lester Kinsolving

Mike Gilbert and Other Knaves

ALTHOUGH LES STILL had his columns carried by such papers as the *Sacramento Union*, Greensburg's *Tribune-Review*, and the *Austin Citizen* (and was occasionally picked up by the *Christian Challenge* and *Presbyterian-Layman*), he was actively seeking another local opportunity in print media. After perusing the *Washington Guide*, a tourist magazine owned and published by Mike Gilbert, Les made contact. After a congenial discussion, Gilbert offered him a position as a contributing editor.

In the May–June 1981 issue, Lester's new column, *Capital Opinion,* featured seven mini-articles, including "The *Washington Post*'s Pulitzer Prize—For Fiction":

On Tuesday, April 14, the *Washington Post* reported with pride that one of its newest reporters, Janet Cooke, had won the 1981 Pulitzer Prize for feature writing.

The *Post* published nearly one half a page of the photogenic Miss Cooke, along with her feature story about an eight-year-old heroin addict which story, the *Post* noted, "led to a fruitless search for the boy by District of Columbia officials."

Janet Cooke lied. And the *Washington Post* provoked this fruitless search because it published her lies without ever having checked into her alleged sources, an editorial irresponsibility of spectacular proportions.

There was no such eight-year-old addict. The quotes in this story were also made up by this journalistic cheat—who also lied about the credentials in her resumé. Executive Editor Ben Bradlee has apologized to Washington's mayor and this city's police chief. I believe the City of Washington would be fully justified in suing the *Washington Post*. . . .

Eight years ago, Bradlee & Co. drove a President of the United States out of the White House—for lying. It is high time that *Post* Publisher Donald Graham demonstrates his leadership and tries to restore the *Post*'s credibility—by applying the same standard to Bradlee & Co. . . .

Although Gilbert was impressed by Lester's journalistic savvy, he expected him to not only sell advertisements, but to assist in deliveries of *Washington Guide* to Embassy Row, the White House, and local hotels. He also offered the paltry monthly salary of $500, promising Lester that even though he couldn't pay much now, the magazine would be going into franchise and that he'd be able to offer him a much bigger paycheck in the near future.

After a rewarding radio stint on WAVA Radio (which changed its format to rock in the late '70s), Les was hired by Stan Karas at WEAM in 1979, where his popular Capital Commentary continued over the airwaves. By August 1981, Karas told Lester, "Get the hell out of here—you're off the air, as of now." Karas accused him of abusing his eating credits with restaurant owners who advertised on the radio station, most notably Alexander's Three. It was later determined that this accusation was unsubstantiated, which prompted Les to send Karas a letter demanding a "written assurance that [I] did not make any such unauthorized purchases, and that you [will] intend to refrain from any and all such defamatory references to [me] in the future."

While working for WAVA, Les enjoyed similar advertising privileges and took his family to such fine-dining establishments as Caesar's Forum, The Devil's Fork, and Top o' the Town. The Lamplighter, a new advertiser, was located in Fairfax, Virginia, and offered an enticing fare which Les was eager to sample. Accompanied by his three kids in the family station wagon, Lester soon discovered that his directions were not leading him to The Lamplighter as promised. Circling around the same block more than twice, Les stopped and asked a taxi driver for assistance. Stomping back to the car, he jumped in and exclaimed, "I don't know what he said, I think he was drunk!" After scaling the block three more times and shouting "THIS IS MANURE!!" Lester finally (and happily) arrived at the destination, and enjoyed a succulent, if not well-deserved, dinner with his family.

In January 1981, Les was bestowed two honors. On the 20th, he received the following letter from the National Committee to Bring Nazi War Criminals to Justice:

We are pleased to invite you as an honored guest to receive a YIZKOR AWARD . . . on March 31, 1981 at the Waldorf Astoria. Two outstanding Nazi hunters, Dr. Simon Wiesenthal and Dr. Charles H. Kremer, will be honored.

It is very appropriate that you be honored together with Dr. Wiesenthal and Dr. Kremer, for through your courage, as expressed in your written words, you helped to bring the attention of the world the work of these once lone voices in the wilderness who have dedicated their lives to exposing Nazi atrocities and bringing to justice the perpetrators of those atrocities.

Along with carrying Les's column, the *Austin Citizen* carried an announcement, "Kinsolving Due Honor":

He will receive one of the Yizkor Awards for having been the first journalist to expose Rumanian Orthodox Archbishop Valerian Trifa, a member of the Governing Board of the National Council of Churches. Trifa recently agreed to surrender his U.S. citizenship rather than face a federal trial on charges by the U.S. Department of Justice that he lied about involvement in Rumanian war crimes, including the killing of Jews, when he applied for citizenship.

On January 27, the following transcript in the 97th Congress Congressional Record appeared, in a floor speech by Virginia Senator John Warner:

MISTREATMENT OF DIPLOMATS—AND THEIR GOVERNMENT'S REACTION—SERMON BY THE REV. LESTER KINSOLVING

MR. WARNER: Mr. President, one of the most patriotic sermons I have ever encountered was delivered by the Reverend Lester Kinsolving on this past Sunday, January 25, 1981, at both St. Andrew of Scotland Anglican Catholic Church in Alexandria, Va., and St. Charles the Martyr Anglican Catholic Church in Annapolis, Md.

The topic of the sermon was "Mistreatment of Diplomats— and Their Government's Reaction," with references both to King David of Israel, circa 1000 B.C., and to President Carter of the United States in 1979, 1980, and 1981.

The text taken by the Reverend Kinsolving was from the First Epistle to the Corinthians—"Ye are bought—with a price." While some might term this sermon "political," it was received by the parishioners of both churches as "patriotic"— and I commend it to my colleagues as very fine reading in this time which many have termed "our national humiliation."

. . . Mr. President, I commend the sentiments of this sermon to all my colleagues because, while I may not agree completely with every point raised therein, its message is one of which all of us must be mindful—"that our land will remind 'of the free' only as long as it continues to be the 'home of the brave.'" I ask that this sermon be included in the Record.

On March 5, White House Press Secretary Jim Brady distributed a notice to the press, announcing that a special presidential press conference would be held. It read, in part: "As is traditional, the first two questions will be asked by the Associated Press and United Press International. . . . The order of questions for the remainder of the press conference will be determined by a lottery." Names would be drawn at the next day's press briefing where reporters would be "given the opportunity to enter the lottery, and the sign-up will continue until one half-hour after the conclusion of the briefing."

Lester was delighted that Brady had followed up on his suggestion of his 1973 idea, "A Lottery for Presidential News Conferences," and also attributed it to a Q & A session after Reagan announced he would be running for President in 1979:

KINSOLVING: If you are elected, would you continue the system whereby all of the best seats and most of the recognition for questions at Presidential news conferences are reserved for the big and rich media?

REAGAN: Well, I never did that while I was Governor, in Sacramento, where it was "catch-as-catch-can."

KINSOLVING: Would you be willing to conduct a lottery, so everyone might have a chance?

REAGAN: I think that would be a good idea.

KINSOLVING: Is that a campaign promise?

Reagan's campaign manager John Sears laughed, and reassured Lester that it was.

Gadfly

After Jim Brady's announcement of the lottery, Les eagerly signed up, and to his absolute glee, was the fifteenth name drawn for the press conference, where President Reagan picked thirty-two questioners from a jellybean jar. His March 11 Capital Commentary broadcast included the following:

> For more than a quarter century, Allan Cromley has been attending Presidential news conferences in the course of covering Washington for the *Daily Oklahoman*. This newspaper is by far the most widely circulated periodical in the entire state. But President Carter recognized Cromley for questions only three times in four years—despite his Inaugural Address:
>
> > "We have learned that 'more' is not necessarily 'better' . . . We are striving for equality of opportunity."
>
> This democratic ideal was apparently not shared by news secretary Jody Powell—who reserved all the front row seats at Carter's news conferences for the Eastern Media Establishment. . . . Reporters like Cromley were rarely recognized, because Powell assigned them seats in what as known as the "Siberia Section."
>
> Any reporter condemned to this outer darkness had only one fleeting hope of being recognized for a question by joining that desperate chorus of howling jumping jacks who shouted, "Mr. President!"
>
> This provided the same sort of video excitement as a fire, or a mob. It was fully exploited by President Nixon, as well as by some commentators, who loftily deplored the indignities of these screeching Plebians.
>
> President Reagan changed all this, by selecting questions from a reporter's lottery. Nine out of the nineteen recognized reporters whose names were drawn on March 6th were *not* Big Media— including Allan Cromley, and me.

Some of those front row regulars walked out; or boycotted; or deplored; or viewed with alarm. But the Candor Award goes to Leslie Stahl of CBS, who said: "I don't like the new system because my name wasn't drawn."

Jimmy Carter never dared to incur such dangerous displeasure in order to be fair to the mere State of Oklahoma [Cromley]. But now, amazingly, a Presidential news conference has been infused with democratic principles—by a Republican President.

Playfully coined by the president as "Reagan Roulette," the lottery story was carried nationally, where the *Washington Post* reported the following complaints from the White House Press Corps:

Time correspondent Larry Barrett said it was "ridiculous," and NBC's Bill Lynch termed it "capriciousness by design." Susan King of ABC, the token television correspondent who asked a question, said it removed the spontaneity of presidential news conferences. . . .

The lottery was supposed to give the many news organizations which cover the White House an equal chance to be recognized, minimizing domination by television networks and the big national newspapers. . . .

Judy Woodruff of NBC and Walt Rogers of AP radio left the news conference room when their names weren't drawn. Sam Donaldson of ABC, another non-fan of the lottery, and NBC's Lynch chose not to come at all. . . .

The first name drawn by Reagan from the jellybean jar was that of *Newsweek* correspondent Tom DeFrank. The second was that of Tim Schelhardt of the *Wall Street Journal*, prompting Reagan to remark, "I'm glad to see that the little people are getting a chance."

Gadfly

Post reporter Lou Cannon speculated that "This change is likely to become a permanent feature of Reagan news conferences, even though the lottery may not have survived yesterday's session." Sadly enough for Lester, Cannon was right, since, as Les would later report, "the Big Media screamed bloody murder, and before the next Presidential news conference, Jim Brady was shot by John Hinckley. So the lottery idea was buried."

To the President's disgruntlement, Les needled him with questions on such issues as abortion:

KINSOLVING: [Mr. President], you said during the campaign you noticed that all the advocates of abortion are already born. And since this also applies to all the advocates of contraception, are you opposed to contraception which also denies the right-to-life?

THE PRESIDENT: No, I am not.

KINSOLVING: Thank you. Do you want to explain it? (Laughter.)

THE PRESIDENT: . . . I think the idea of human life once it has been created and establishing the fact, and maybe I should have just taken your thank you and left here on this, is the whole issue that we have to determine. . . . Thank you.

and the Middle East:

KINSOLVING: Mr. President, on the Golan Heights, do you believe that the Golan Heights should be returned to Syria, given Syria's record of bombarding the Israeli farms for so many years?

THE PRESIDENT: Well, now you're getting into the area of what is trying to be settled in the talks under 242 and 338 in the peacemaking talks regarding all of the territory that might be held. And therefore, it's not proper for me to comment on this. This is the very matter that's being negotiated.

KINSOLVING: To follow that up sir, your own opinion—did you ever object to the Arab legion's occupation of the West Bank or the shelling of Israeli farms?

THE PRESIDENT: Well, you're going back a long way and it's hard for me to remember what my position was. I know where I was during the Six Days War: I was in the Hollywood Bowl at a mass meeting in support of Israel. And at that time there were only two political figures or officeholders there—that I recall—former Senator George Murphy, then a Senator, and myself, as Governor of California.

Four months after the assassination attempt on Reagan, Jim Brady's replacement, Larry Speakes, held a press briefing on July 23. One item on the agenda involved the folding of the *Washington Star*. It was obvious, from the following banter, that Reagan had grown weary of Lester's prodding:

MR. SPEAKES: The President says it is an extremely sad day when a newspaper announces it will cease publication.

KINSOLVING: This isn't you, this is the President speaking?

MR. SPEAKES: Yes. That's really the extent of what he said.

KINSOLVING: Does he mean any newspaper or what?

MR. SPEAKES: He didn't say that about Kinsolving's paper. (Laughter.)

KINSOLVING: When I kick off don't ask him to say anything about me either. (Laugher.)

President Reagan could be seen on televised press conferences, pointing his finger in one direction and Les shouting his question from another. Realizing who it was, the President shook his head and murmured, "No . . . no!!" He once told his press secretary, "My

Gadfly

finger must be crooked; every time I point at someone, Les Kinsolving starts to ask a question!"

In an earnest attempt to protect his boss from further embarrassment, Larry Speakes made a rash decision, as reported in the *New York Post*'s the *Washington Ear:*

SHOCKER AT THE PRESS PARLEY

Scandal at the President's White House press conference.

We are shocked to hear that White House press secretary Larry Speakes muzzled a member of the press. The victim of this strange behavior is ultra-right wing columnist Lester Kinsolving, who frequently asks rather curious questions of Presidents.

Before the press conference, Speakes looked rather sternly at Kinsolving, and ushered him into the back of the East Room. There he put his finger to his mouth and bluntly told the reporter, "No questions."

While many of the White House press corps are sure to applaud the move, Kinsolving is screaming for his First Amendment rights, of course, of course.

Enjoying a much-needed August respite from the DC scene, Lester decided to partake in some historical sightseeing and traveled south to Jamestown, Virginia, where he anticipated an edifying tour of the national park. As he waited with a small group of sightseers, Frank Bradby, a part-Pamunkey Indian and tour guide, appeared in full native apparel and led the visitors to the first point of interest, Jamestown's Anglican Church.

With an angry scowl, Bradby turned to the group and declared, "We wanted no part of this religion or their church. We knew our creator was not inside the building here, but is out here in nature. The church seemed more like a prison to us. . . . We knew the English were forced to attend their church five or six hours a day, every day, or be killed." Barely believing what he was hearing, Lester was awestruck when he heard, "They [the Englishmen] would never bathe . . . they felt if the dirt and earth built up on their skin, the sickness would not enter. These English smelled very bad. They would rub perfume all over their bodies instead of bathing, to take away this awful odor."

Les waited until the final landmark of the tour, before he spoke up. Completely incensed with Bradby's further pronouncements such as, "You white settlers brought disease which we had no immunity against," Les could hardly contain himself as he took the frowning young man to task: "I've never heard such outlandish inaccuracies in my life. . . . We've come here to pay tribute to our ancestors and appreciate American history . . . this is an absolute outrage!" He demanded to speak to the park director, and, after registering his complaint, gathered literature in preparation of another scathing exposé.

"Tourguide Debates Historical Records" ran the headline in the *Sacramento Union* on September 5, 1981. Lester quashed Bradby's claims with formidable evidence:

When we asked Park Service officials for some documentation to back up this report of a 35-to-42-hour worship week, they produced a mimeographed paragraph from a book entitled *For the Colony.* . . . But this quotation had not one word about the length of daily services.

When we reached [author] Dr. Flaherty and asked about this alleged 35-to-42-hour worship week, he replied, "Hilarious! There is no mention of the time of those daily services which were probably morning and evening prayer, which last about twenty minutes."

Another top specialist in colonial Virginia history and Tidewater Indians is Dr. Frederick Fausz [who] described Bradby's report as "bizarre and ludicrous." . . . Dr. Fausz noted that there is no evidence whatsoever that the English colonists never bathed and that certainly some of them knew how to swim. . . .

Les then posed the question: "Is it possible that prior to 1607, disease was known only in Europe, while the North American continent was disease-free?"

Not quite. Dr. Fausz noted the Smithsonian's archeological digs at Nanjemoy . . . where they found 600 Indian skeletons in one burial pit, which remains, he said, indicated "either syphilis or TB."

Bradby's speech was approved by the National Park Service's historian, Douglas Thompson [who] has never written a book or an article or even a term paper about colonial Virginia.

Les gladly reported that "Thompson's superior, Superintendent Richard Maeder of Yorktown, has ordered revisions on Bradby's speech," and that the Secretary of the Interior's office "issued the following statement: 'The National Park Service is not in the business of misrepresenting history. We will investigate.'" Much to Lester's relief, American history was once again fully restored.

Later that fall, Les received a call from a reporter at the *Washington Post.* His name was Chip Brown, and he had been assigned to write a feature story on the Irreverent Reverend for the Metro section. Les was bowled over that Gentle Ben would even consider giving him more publicity, especially after their jocular exchange at the ASNE convention in 1980. After a few weeks of interviews and a tour of his home office, Les was photographed by the *Post* at the State Department, where he was surrounded by quizzically faced journalists as he asked another of his infamous questions.

On November 17, 1981, "Lester Kinsolving: Raising Cain in the Press Corps" ran on the front page of the Metro section. Brown minced no words and shined a piercing spotlight on the ever-controversial "Mad Monk":

Not too many newsmen like him; even fewer take him seriously. For eight years, he has bobbed around Washington like a peppercorn in the federal soup. . . .

Kinsolving has been called a horse's ass, a gorilla in a priest's suit, "the price we pay for democracy," and a dozen unprintable animadversions. Not long ago a reporter said to his wife, "You're a lovely person but your husband's a jerk."

. . . In one sense, Kinsolving is that classic Washington character, the outsider in a city of insiders. Washington, after all, is a city where the mere investment of power can make a bore seem like a fascinating fellow and eccentricity of Kinsolving's kind is discouraged. . . .

"I realize being what I am makes me kind of a leper," Kinsolving says. "But journalism is my ministry. I'm going to ask the questions I think are important and anybody who doesn't like it can take a long walk off a short pier."

. . . Each morning Kinsolving rises at 7:30. After a bowl of Wheat Chex, he sits down with a legal pad in the cluttered upstairs study hung with plaques and pictures of stories. . . . He doesn't just pencil out his questions ahead of time, "I *hone* them," he says. . . .

"Just one more question," Kinsolving said at a recent briefing at the State Department, and from the back of the room a voice quipped, "Promise?"

Pleased with the copy, Ben Bradlee approved it, with one exception. In the sentence describing Les as a "peppercorn in the federal soup," Bradlee scratched out the word "peppercorn" and replaced it with "roach." Although new to the *Post* staff, Chip Brown was unwavering, even in the omnipotent presence of his executive editor. His original copy remained intact before it went to press.

After the article appeared, Bradlee received a frothing letter:

Are you so very stupid you cannot see what a hero you have made of the priest-journalist, Father Lester Kinsolving?

Gadfly

And you forgot to tell the redeeming part about how he goes home at night to beat his aged mother, already a victim of stroke.

. . . Thank you for your "assassination" of Lester Kinsolving. Just as ADA approval is the kiss of death for a politician, your "Judas kiss" of your brother newsman has canonized him to an eternal stature. . . . May the backlash snap you fully in two.

With great disgust,

David C. Bonds-Kemp

By the end of 1981, son Tom had joined up with the *Washington Guide* staff as a contributing editor, after returning from an overseas trip in Europe. His article, "Medieval Ghent," highlighted some of the more unusual sights of Belgium's quaint city:

The Castle of the Counts, near the canal, was built in 1180 by Phillip of Alsace. This ominous fortress was constructed by the 16th Count of Flanders, who modeled it after the Roman fortresses he saw in the Holy Land, during the Crusades. In that same spirit, he and later counts used part of the castle as a huge torture chamber. For the equivalent of 30 cents you can climb one of the gloomy narrow towers into the torture museum, to see some of the Count's sadistic instruments.

Like Lester, Tom would be expected to sell ads and deliver the magazine to various locations. Mike Gilbert demanded that Tom sell ads by "cold calling." During one afternoon, he walked the entire block of Maple Avenue in downtown Vienna, Virginia, and didn't sell a single ad. When Tom explained the tremendous difficulty of such a task to Mike, he was taken aback by the publisher's response: "Don't worry, I just wanted to test you out." Tom began to wonder if Gilbert might be distantly related to the Count of Flanders.

In his new assignment as *Washington Guide*'s National Editor, Les decided to investigate into Children, Inc., after seeing one of their heart-wrenching ads of a little girl living in third-world squalor. The caption under the photo read, "Tina has never had a teddy bear." Given that CI's (and its sister organization, Christian Children's Fund) total 1981 revenue was over $49 million, Les scheduled an interview with President-Director Jeanne Clarke Wood, to ask "if Tina now has a teddy bear": As Les sat with Mrs. Clarke in her palatial mansion, she began to bristle after a few questions:

MRS. CLARKE: I'm sure she has a Teddy bear now. We've used that ad for several years.

KINSOLVING: If Tina now has a Teddy bear, why have you been advertising for years that she "has never had a Teddy bear"?

MRS. CLARKE: Maybe she *doesn't* have a Teddy bear.

KINSOLVING: Mrs. Clarke, you have just told me—and I quote: "I'm sure she has a Teddy bear now."

MRS. CLARKE: We must consider what will make people help these children. I think this is an attitude of mind. I don't think our contributors mind . . . if we changed these ads every time the child was helped, the costs would be astronomical!

KINSOLVING: Is truth in advertising an obligation only when it's inexpensive?

Seeing that "Mrs. Clarke showed no sign of willingness to spend any such modest amounts of money in the cause of honest advertising," Les cited other former false advertising examples in his ensuing exposé: "In 1969, *Redbook* magazine published a CCF ad with the headline: "LITTLE MARGARET IS DYING OF MALNUTRITION." This ad kept running for nine more issues into 1972—so that Little

Gadfly

Margaret's Amazing Malnutrition was one of the most elongated death scenes since *Camille*."

By the spring of 1982, frightening reports had surfaced in the gay community of a new pneumonia that was killing its young men—first coined as GRID (Gay-Related Immune Deficiency) and later AIDS (Acquired Immune Deficiency Syndrome), due to a discovery that the virus had originated as early as 1959 in Africa. Les was growing concerned, enough to pose an urgent question at the White House:

KINSOLVING: Larry, does the president have any reaction to the announcement—the Centers for Disease Control in Atlanta, that AIDS is now an epidemic with over 600 cases?

SPEAKES: What's AIDS?

KINSOLVING: Over a third of the [the victims] have died. It's known as "gay plague." (laughter) No, it is. I mean it's a pretty serious thing that one in every three people that get this have died. And I wondered if the president is aware of it?

SPEAKES: I don't have it. Do you? (laughter)

KINSOLVING: No, I don't.

SPEAKES: You didn't answer my question.

KINSOLVING: Well, I just wondered, does the president—

SPEAKES: How do you know? (laughter)

KINSOLVING: In other words, the White House looks on this as a great joke?

SPEAKES: No, I don't know anything about it, Lester.

KINSOLVING: Does the president, does anybody in the White House know about this epidemic, Larry?

SPEAKES: I don't think so. I don't think there's been any—

KINSOLVING: Nobody knows?

SPEAKES: There has been no personal experience here, Lester.

KINSOLVING: No, I mean, I thought you were keeping—

SPEAKES: I checked thoroughly with [Reagan's personal physician] Dr. Ruge this morning, and he's had no—(laughter)—no patients suffering from AIDS whatever it is.

Michael Bronski, author of *The Truth About Reagan and AIDS*, stated the following:

Although AIDS was first reported in the medical and popular press in 1981, it was only in October of 1987 that President Reagan publicly spoke about the epidemic. By the end of that year 59,572 AIDS cases had been reported and 27,909 of those women and men had died. How could this happen, they ask? Didn't he see that this was an ever-expanding epidemic? How could he not say anything? Do anything?

Former press secretary Ron Nessen once remarked, "Lester, by his mannerisms, can be an irritant, but in my experience he often asked important questions on important issues long before other people realized they were important," such as his question to President Ford on when he believed life begins, which is now a major issue in today's abortion debate.

Science writer Jon Cohen, whose book *Shots in the Dark: The Wayward Search for an AIDS Vaccine* featured the exchange between Larry and Lester at the White House press briefing, also took the Reagan Administration to task:

Gadfly

Lester Kinsolving was right—he was exactly right to raise the issue, and the White House's behavior was appalling. It was shockingly crass, and really let the mask fall down and show how little both Reagan and his staff cared about this. . . . I think [Kinsolving] was rightfully proud of it. He was ahead of the pack. And I think his dogged questions are exactly what somebody had to do.

Although it was evident that Les had the instinct of a journalistic visionary, his concern about AIDS also harbored a deep-seated resentment against certain aspects of the gay community, undoubtedly sparked by actor Will Geer's aggressive attempt to seduce him when he was a young man. Later on, he rebutted one protestor's letter, which stated, "comments of a highly derogatory nature were aimed at members of the Lesbian and Gay community. These statements were made during remarks about the choice of San Francisco as the site for the next Democratic National Convention."

I am at a loss to understand why your unidentified listener feels that either of [my] statements is "highly derogatory," unless, possibly, he resents my inclusion of Leather Boys, S&Ms and NAM/BLA [North American Man/Boy Love Association] along with the Lesbian and Gay community.

If so, his (or her) quarrel is not with me, but with the organizers of such events as New York's annual Gay Pride Parade, which among others, featured the elderly men of NAM/BLA parading in their bathing suits—accompanied by little boys, similarly attired.

If your listener was offended by the term "sex deviates," his quarrel is with page 227 of Webster's New Collegiate Dictionary, 1960, in which the noun "deviate" is defined as: "an individual who differs considerably from the average."

Although terror was sweeping through gay communities nation-wide, some comic relief was provided by Les and Henry Catto, as published in the *San Francisco Chronicle* on August 8, 1982:

MURDER IN THE PENTAGON?

Lester Kinsolving, an Episcopal minister turned reporter, rel-ishes his role as a self-appointed gadfly who comes on like a cluster bomb at the daily White House and Pentagon news briefings. The Pentagon's Henry Catto is one of the few gov-ernment spokesmen who have demonstrated a cool ability to defuse Kinsolving under fire.

The other day Kinsolving pounced on Catto in mid-briefing over the question of whether American ships should be used to evacuate the Palestine Liberation Organization's armed forces from Beirut.

KINSOLVING: If you were Secretary of Defense, Henry, and the State Department suggested that you allow armed PLO people to come aboard the ships over which you had supervision, you'd resign rather than allow that, wouldn't you, Henry?

CATTO: Lester, I am reminded of another Henry, in this case Henry II, who at a point of exasperation with Thomas à Becket said, "Who will free me of this troublesome priest?"

KINSOLVING: He was murdered in the North Transept, and Henry went and scourged himself every year for the rest of his life, remember that?

CATTO: By George, it might be worth it, Lester.

Frustrated with the meager wage Mike Gilbert was offering at *Washington Guide*, as well as an unforeseeable follow-up of a national (and profitable) franchise of the magazine, Les was actively seeking additional gigs anywhere he could. By January 1983, Bob Cobbins, a radio producer and sales manager with whom he had worked in the past, approached Les to broadcast for his new station, WJOK, "the country's first 24-hour, all-comedy radio station," in Gaithersburg, Maryland. The station not only aired comedy shows and stand-up comedians, but also featured the lighter side of breaking news and political commentary. According to the *Balitimore Sun*, "Mr. Cobbins first got the idea for all-comedy radio in 1965 when he learned that a dial-a-joke phone number in New York was getting 40,000 calls a day. Ever since [then], he's been collecting funny albums and tapes."

Teaming up with another *Washington Guide* contributor, Shelly Tromberg, Lester broadcast a daily afternoon "give-and-take political and point-counterpoint social commentary" called "News Items."

TROMBERG: News Item!

KINSOLVING: HARVARD BIOLOGIST SUGGESTS THAT SOVIET "YELLOW RAIN" MAY REALLY BE THE BOWEL MOVEMENT OF BEES!

TROMBERG: I didn't know that bees were big enough to have bowels.

KINSOLVING: They do indeed. And Dr. Matthew Meselson of Harvard contends that what the U.S. Government says is Soviet chemical warfare in Afghanistan, Laos and Cambodia is almost certainly pollen-filled bee feces, from the giant Asian honeybee, the *Apis Dorsata.*

TROMBERG: Are these the same as publisher Rupert Murdoch's classic reports of South American killer bees?

KINSOLVING: No. Those are the *Apis Mellifera Adansoni.* These are apparently *K.G. Bees!*

TROMBERG: What does our State Department say about Dr. Memelson's Bee Feces Theory?

KINSOLVING: They cite eyewitness reports of planes dropping yellow clouds. And they point out that one sample weighed 300 milligrams, which is more than a bee can excrete.

TROMBERG: Even the giant *Apis Dorsata*?

KINSOLVING: To suggest that even the giant *Apis Dorsata* can excrete 300 milligrams is almost as phantasmagoric as the Heinrich Hammerschlogen theory.

TROMBERG: The Hammerschlogen Theory?

KINSOLVING: Col. Heinrich Hammerschlogen was an ornithologist who was assigned to the Kaiser's Propaganda Office in World War I, and won the Iron Cross for his response to charges that the German Army used poison gas on defenseless Russian troops on the Eastern Front.

TROMBERG: What was the Hammerschlogen response?

KINSOLVING: Col. Hammerschlogen advanced the theory that it wasn't gas the Germans were using. It was the flatulence of battlefield buzzards!

TROMBERG: I don't believe it!

KINSOLVING: You're perfectly right!

Besides "News Item," Les broadcast Capital Commentary, with such headlines as "The Latest Scandal at Lorton Prison—Bullets in Virginia Homeowners' Backyards," "National Public Radio's President Mankiewicz Finally Follows Our Advice and Quits," and

Gadfly

"A Way Out of Washington's Municipal Financial Mess: Buy Marion Barry Bonds!" He also included his Daily Media Report at 5:30 P.M., immediately following ABC Sports News:

THE LATEST ATROCITY FROM THE PAGES OF THE WASHING-
TON BOAST-BOAST-BOAST-BOAST

On Sunday May 29th, *Washington Post* columnist Haynes Johnson wrote that today's journalists appear to be viewed with "increasing suspicion, distrust and outright dislike" by citizens everywhere, "because they see in the press common attitudes that are "arrogant, uncaring, snide and smug," and therefore "we in the press have a real problem."

Within 24 hours, the *Post*'s TV critic, Tom Shales, had perfectly illustrated—in *Post* print—what Johnson rightfully calls a real problem. For on Memorial Day, Mr. Shales described The Battle Hymn of the Republic as a "dreadful, militaristic atrocity" and a "terrible, oversung song" that is "hideous and hoary" and ought to be "buried in a forgotten room in the Smithsonian," because it "makes the national anthem look like Beethoven's Ninth."

(Perhaps Mr. Shales meant to write *sound* like—or was he comparing the appearance of sheet music?)

By striking contrast, critic Shales found nothing "dreadful," or "atrocious," or "terrible," or "hideous" in the Democrat telethon's featuring of Hanoi Jane Fonda, on the Memorial Day weekend when the nation is supposed to be remembering, among others, those Americans who died at the hands of Miss Fonda's friends in North Vietnam.

For the vast majority of Americans, the Battle Hymn of the Republic is cherished as an anthem of lyrics and music that [is] so moving as to be one of the classics of American patriotism (a term we use with some trepidation in anything addressed to those sophisticates at the *Washington Post.*).

Although WJOK received ample press coverage and appeared to be a bright new choice for channel surfing, it suffered an early demise by August, due to a poor radio signal which didn't reach the more populated areas of Metropolitan Washington. Along with this disappointment came the sad news that Lester's mother, Edith Kinsolving, had passed at the age of eighty-five. Lester wrote a tribute to his beloved mom, which included the infamous story of how Edith handled a pest during her early days at West Point Military Academy:

One clergy wife, who helped pioneer a breakdown of the dreadful ecclesiastical chattel system, began her marriage as the wife of an Army chaplain. Her husband's commanding officer, a major general, was a pompous martinet who derived a particular pleasure from his sadistic needling of the wives of his junior officers.

One summer Sunday morning, after an outdoor worship service, the general, accompanied by his claque of staff officers (who could always be depended upon to laugh at all his attempts at such humor) approached the young chaplain's wife. He snickered, and then asked her: "Madam, since when is it appropriate for the chaplain's wife to attend divine services without stockings?" At this, all the staff officers chortled—as if on cue.

This chaplain's wife was a native of Washington, D.C., where generals come by the dozen. So she waited until the chortling faded. Then she smiled sweetly and looked the general straight in the eye as she replied: "General: since when is it appropriate for the commanding officer to spend his time during divine services inspecting the chaplain's wife's legs?"

The astounded general simply bowed, and fled—accompanied by his (no longer chortling) staff. That afternoon, she received 27 phone calls from other officers' wives—calls of gratitude and thanksgiving.

Gadfly

Edith's memorial service was held August 31, 1983, at St. Andrew of Scotland in Alexandria, VA, where Lester preached a homily at the Requiem Eucharist:

Five years after [my father] died, in 1964, one Christmas Eve after the midnight service, I thought that everyone else had gone to bed. I went into the living room to get something I had forgotten, when I saw her sitting in a corner, looking out of the window and sobbing, quietly, as do so many of the bereaved at Christmas time.

I went to her, and put my arm around her. Then she said to me: "Oh, I miss him so terribly! So terribly!"

And this is why I believe with all my heart, that through the infinite goodness of God, sometime between one and three on this past Sunday morning, when she crossed over, heaven's arches rang with the absolutely glorious joy of their being together again, at last. And that is what I believe is implicit in the affirmation that God will wipe away all tears from our eyes.

. . . Let us pray from one of their favorite hymns:

"O then what raptured greeting, on Canaan's happy shore,
What knitting severed friendships up, where partings are
    no more.
Then eyes with joy shall sparkle, that brimmed with tears
    of late,
Orphans no longer fatherless, nor widows desolate."

A few days later, Les received a gracious letter from the Senior Warden at St. Andrew's, Donald Baldwin:

I don't think I have ever attended a more moving, loving memorial service than the one we had at the church last evening.

Surely your mother as she looked down from her resting place must have felt the love that was expressed for her memory by her two sons, her family, and the wider family of friends in the church.

. . . I remember her so warmly when she came to church. During the coffee hour, after a brief period of time, she'd go over to Lester and pull on his sleeve and command: "Lester, you've talked long enough. It's time to go. Now." She did, indeed, have a mind of her own.

Another letter came, which proved to be a rather touching surprise:

Dear Les:
    I read with sorrow of the recent death of your mother. There is really nothing an outsider can say to ease your pain. However, I want you to know my thoughts and prayers are with you in your time of grief.

                                            Yours truly,
                                            Ron Nessen

As Christmastime was fast approaching in the nation's capital, Les was mentioned in *Washington Inquirer*'s gossip column *The Eye*, the conservative antiphon to *The Ear*:

Les Kinsolving, the White House press corps' bad boy, loves nothing better than exposing, shall we say the inconsistencies, of his fellow pressies. At the White House daily press briefing last week, Les took note of the ardent concern shown by the pressies for the poor and hungry in their stories about Ed Meese.

Addressing Larry Speakes, Les said, "I think it would be of great human interest, in view of the great attention to the feeding of the hungry by the press corps here and in view of the fact that on the first two rows (of seats assigned to the pressies) the total income is more than $1 million, could we find out what the people on these two front rows are doing to help the hungry?" Only one of the pressies declared his charitable contributions. Bruce Drake of *The New York Daily News* said that he intended to donate three dozen bagels. Les pressed on, asserting that most of the reporters made more money than Mr. Reagan. Would anyone tell seriously what he or she was doing to help the poor? The silence was deafening. "I can see a column here," observed spokesman Speakes, perhaps not entirely displeased to see his tormentors put on an embarrassing spot.

By the spring of 1984, Tom Kinsolving was fed up with *Washington Guide* publisher Mike Gilbert, calling him a "sadistic and power mad egomaniac who degraded Dad and turned us into delivery boys." In addition, Gilbert devised a way to have the fledgling magazine appear to have more writers than it actually did, by adding a new name, Philip Thomas, under the Senior Editors credit. In fact, this was Tom's middle and first name and not an actual person. "I was so infuriated with Gilbert's exploitation I began calling him 'Fuckhead.'" Tom finally quit, only to have his name and pseudonym still appear in the credits.

Les, still being paid his meager monthly wage of $500, finally realized that "Fuckhead" was not forthcoming in his promise of a national franchise and decided to bow out as well at the end of the year. "He refused to pay my final salary, so I threatened him with small claims court . . . when he received a summons, my paycheck was delivered through the mail. After that, I never saw or heard from Gilbert again."

One *Washington Guide* reader, Mike Kearney, was a Coast Guard officer in charge of quelling mutinies. He had become an avid fan of Lester's columns in the magazine, and made a call to his home office in May. Kearney was friends with Dominic Quinn, a program director for WWDB/96.5 FM in Philadelphia. He informed Les that there was a weekend post available—for a talk-show host.

"What I Should've Been Doing All Along"

S HORTLY AFTER THE phone call from Kearney, Les met with him and Dominic Quinn, and brought samples of his former KCBS talk-show program from the late 1960s. Impressed by Lester's fire-eating style, Quinn proposed that he fill the Saturday slot from 8–11 P.M., and that he could start in two weeks. For Lester, the offer was like a resuscitation, since his days with *Washington Guide* were numbered. In addition, his syndicated column was carried in only a few papers.

For the next two weeks, Lester organized his format for the *The Les Kinsolving Show*. He would broadcast two commentaries (entitled "Special Report") for the first hour, one for the second and another for the third. In case calls were lacking, he had two commentaries in reserve. Like his days at KCBS, Les would ring a loud bell every time he had a first-time caller. As the show gained popularity, he had press cards printed up for his fans, where they could fill in their names above the following: "[ ] is a credible, though unaccredited member of the Lurking for Les Press: An auxiliary of valiant volunteers whose reporting helps provide The Rest of the Story."

Gadfly

He composed a captivating opener, guaranteed to pull in anyone turning the dial:

From the Susquehanna River, to Sandy Hook on the Atlantic . . .
From the Poconos, down through Delaware . . .
From Cape May to Kunkletown!
From the suburbs of Baltimore to Brooklyn—and the New York Battery—and covering the Mighty Market of Philadelphia–New Jersey like a great glove . . .

This is *The Les Kinsolving Show,* featuring your humble and obedient servant of the same name. We are known, ladies and gentlemen, to our detractors as *The Outrage Hours*, or, something to offend everybody—to our friends, however, we are known as some-sweet-reason-and-relief from all those hard-left trendies who infest so much of the Big Media—and who won't tell you the rest of the story!

Ladies and Gentlemen, you are tuned to **Uninhibited Radio!** On WWDB *The* Talk Station!

If you're a first-time caller, please say so when you go on the air, and we'll ring the welcome bell! It's an open line—anything that's on your mind, and on mine—in our three-minute commentaries. And this free-wheeling mixture of yours and mine is what makes this show! It's the reason why they call it Uninhibited Radio—the pulse of all the people—where active Americans can do dozens of things, while they listen—instead of sitting paralyzed in front of a tube of the vast wasteland!

With the aid of the Lurking for Les Press Corps, we report the news that the Big Media misses, or censors. We're the people's media, where, each day and night, we allow forty times as much public expression than the newspapers, news magazines or TV!

"What I Should've Been Doing All Along"

At the show's close, Les would bid good-bye to his listeners with the following valediction:

> My manager, Mike Kearney, and assistant manager Jim Crowley, two absolutely invaluable associates and friends; and our producer, the ever watchful, ever resourceful Rich Teplitsky, signal me that the Time of Departure is at hand.

> . . . For those whose calls we did NOT get to, but really TRIED to get to—try again, next Saturday night, 8 to 11, on WWDB THE Talk Station . . .

> This has been *The Les Kinsolving Show*, on *Uninhibited Radio*, where we love mail, especially when it has information, which the other media have either missed or ignored.

> Until next Saturday night, this is Les Kinsolving saying: HUMILIS, HUMILIBUS, INFLECTENS ARROGANTIBUS, which means:

> *Humble to the Humble, Inflexible to the Arrogant!*

Since it was coined *"The* Talk Station in Philadelphia," WWDB had several other talk-show personalities, including Bernie Herman, Yvonne Kay, Dr. Jim Corea, Stan Majors, Susan Bray, and Irv Homer. "I got along with all of them very well," Les recalls, "although I got into big political arguments with Irv—we disagreed on everything!" When invited to attend a fitness expo and sign autographs in the WWDB booth, Les brought along daughter Kathleen, who was asked by fellow liberal Susan Bray, "How did you turn out normal?"

As always, Les fearlessly expressed his opinions, even in the present-day climate of political correctness. He didn't flinch when he took certain black leaders to task, as evidenced in the following exchange one Saturday evening on WWDB:

Gadfly

CALLER: How do feel about Rev. Jesse Jackson?

KINSOLVING: I think he's a horse's ass!

CALLER: Oh yeah? Well, what about Minister Louis Farrakhan?

KINSOLVING: He's a horse's ass as well!

CALLER: Hmmm . . . you're good, man . . . you're good!!

Shortly after, Les received a memo from Program Manager Stan Majors:

> LES: Not because of what YOU say . . . but because of the reaction from some callers to your comments . . . let me remind you of our sticky situation with the "black-white" issue here (WWDB).
>
> If you can . . . judge whether your caller has something to offer or if they just want to vent their prejudices on the air . . . if so get rid of them.

Although Lester was generally considered to be a conservative talk-show host, he still remained liberal on abortion and the death penalty. One listener sent him two newspaper clippings of horrific crimes, one involving a father who murdered his family, and another of a man who had decapitated his former lover. A hand-written note was also enclosed:

> Rev,
> How can you not be for absolute death penalty after reading cases like this?
> Love your show, anyway

An irate listener, Elsie Koury of Philadelphia, also expressed her views:

Mr. Lester Kinsolving

I sure agree with the gentleman that said you are anti Catholic. You are the worse anti Catholic that I ever heard, since you were hired by W.W.D.B.

Not one week has gone by that you haven't put out your hate against the Catholic Church or anything that has a Catholic name. I think W.W.D.B. hired you to put out your hate to boost your haters of Catholics. I notice you have nothing to say of the Israeli spies or Black killers you are afraid of them as they are your boss you are a coward.

Richard Aregood, Editor of the Editorial Page at *Philadelphia Daily News,* scrawled off a gripe as well:

Dear Sir,

May you some day get the attention you so desperately crave.

Amicably enough,

R.

Since this listener was a fellow journalist, Lester shot off a response:

1) Apparently we got YOUR attention!
2) When you go home tonight, ask your nice wife to take a safety pin and deflate your obviously swollen head. ALL media people crave attention, R., that's the name of the game. How desperately some crave it is quite apparent in the stuff you write.

Ever cordially,

L.

He also rebutted Robert C. Siegel, Director of News and Information Programming at National Public Radio (NPR), after he received Siegel's letter of thanks "for the transcript of your radio commentary which is some of the dumbest crap I have ever read":

Gadfly

Among all the encomiums or maledictions ever received by *The Les Kinsolving Show*, few if any have exceeded the poignancy of your written notification that the transcript of our commentary is: *some of the dumbest crap I have ever read.* This vivid terminology of yours fills me with curiosity. What other "dumb crap" is it that comprises your regular reading?

. . . I would be most obliged if by way of clarification as to the precise nature of your excoriation you would be good enough to explain whether your use of the word "crap" refers to A) the familiar dice game, or B) some sort of fecal reference to the cause for which the late Sir Thomas Crapper provided the world with his invaluable invention?

And whichever of these two was your intent, would you be kind enough to tell me if you know of any crap which is NOT dumb? Is it possible that you know of some sort of crap which could be described as eloquent?

Along with the usual hate mail came an equal chunk of fan mail, including one from Paul M. DuPont in Hatboro, Pennsylvania:

Rev. Les:

First I will tell you as I write this, I am also recording my wife's contractions, now about seven minutes apart! I must remain calm. I finished work last night and was tired when I got home, but had good reason to stay up until 11:00. You were on! It was one of your best shows!

Les featured this letter in his commentary, "Something Else You Can Be Doing While Listening to Radio—Rather Than Being Immobilized by TV":

Most Americans want to be doing something—rather than just sitting there, succumbing, like a slob, to that national paralysis of inactivity and often hypnosis, as the Boob Tube brings them the latest sitcom stupidity from the Vast Wasteland.

He then listed fifteen different activities "you can do while listening to radio," from driving to sculpting to necking, and affirmed that Paul DuPont's letter "adds another category to the vast number of things that people can DO, while listening to *The Les Kinsolving Show* . . . " Since Dupont sent an announcement of daughter Stephanie Diana's arrival, Les celebrated joyously:

WWDB is touched beyond measure to learn that out there in Hatboro, our signal was stimulating the impending arrival of this Bundle From Heaven. . . . How many other radio stations or talk-show hosts on earth have been so gloriously privileged as to be an electronic midwife?

Back at the White House, Les had been noticing that many women on the staff (as well as the country) were adopting Nancy's choice color of red for their own wardrobes, which made Lester wonder whether if *he* wore red, perhaps he could catch President Reagan's eye a bit more, especially since the 1981 lottery for press briefings had been abandoned. Les decided to purchase a bright red jacket which he would wear at the next presidential press conference. In addition, he was able to grab a seat in one of the first three rows.

"I had this black overcoat on, and as soon as Reagan recognized Sam Donaldson at ABC, I took it off, and displayed this flaming red jacket. Reagan immediately noticed, and interrupted Donaldson, saying, 'Wait a minute, Sam, I have to call on this red jacket because I know that Les is going to have to give it back the next morning.' Since I'd had the jacket monogrammed with my radio station's call letters in gold, I responded with, 'No, Mr. President, this jacket belongs to WWDB in Philadelphia!' When I returned to host my show at the station, all of the salesmen were raving about the free promotion, since they received lots of phone calls after the televised press conference."

Gadfly

Henry and Bobbie Shaffner of Bala Cynwyd, PA, "respectfully submitted" Les a rave as well, in the form of a touching but catchy poem:

A PALPABLE HIT

Never let it be said
That wearing RED
Would ever go to Lester's head.
But, after all, it was he, who got
the Presidential Nod,

And he, who got DB in Philly a
National plug;

So, Les, go ahead and crow a bit,

Your wearin' o' the RED

Was one big TV HIT!

Lester's question for President Reagan was noted in the Annapolis *Capital*:

WHO WAS THAT MAN IN RED?

Kinsolving, who lives in Virginia and hosts a radio talk-show in Philadelphia, then asked why the State Department was opposing efforts in Congress to erect a memorial on federal property to a Yugoslavian general credited with saving the lives of more than 500 American fliers in World War II.

"I will have to tell you, Lester, that is the first time I've heard about it, and so you've given me a question to ask when I leave here tonight, to find out about that," the president said. Kinsolving replied, "I salute you."

Kinsolving said when a fellow reporter saw the jacket, he said, "You're shameless."

Sam Donaldson, who was good-natured about being upstaged that evening, once stated to Les, "Sometimes you press too hard, and sometimes you press the envelope. But you often ask questions we're dying to ask!' At one press briefing, he defended Lester among the groans and snickers of the press corps and declared, "These are perfectly legitimate questions!" Grateful for such support from ABC's spokesman, Les shouted, "THANKS, SAM!!" as the television cameras rolled for the next C-SPAN broadcast.

In September 1984, Les was welcomed back to the Washington, D.C., radio scene, as reported in *The Ear:*

And that wicked Les Kinsolving is already cackling up his cuff and planning his Media Watch Awards, over the new WNTR chatter-show station. (You'll find it where WGAY used to be.) Keep your ears peeled, 'round 3:20 in the afternoons, for Les' Ben Bradlee Humility Award, his Idi Amin–Louis Farrakhan Race Relations Prize, the Jody Powell Truth-in-Government (Usually) Award and the Larry Speakes–Uncle Remus Button for Ingenious Government Evasion.

Although not a talk-show format, Les's commentaries would be aired weekday mornings and afternoons, and were also picked up by WHK in Cleveland, Ohio. However, by September 19, *The Ear* also reported:

Lester Kinsolving, former Priest of Panax, freshly hauled aboard the new WNTR yak-fest to do Morning Commentary and Media Criticism, has been canned, after mountains of wrathful mail and furious phone calls. You'll have to tune in to WWDB in Philly or Gary D's show in Cleveland to catch him. Cries Gary D, "Washington Radio's run by Spineless Wimps."

Gadfly

Although the firing was all rumor, and Lester would remain on WNTR for another two years, he still appreciated a letter of condolence, dated September 27:

Dear Les:

You were shafted; what's the matter with WNTR?
Will keep Maddox in mind as a "Crossfire" Guest. Maybe we can put you two together. I will take it up with Sol Levine (who also is strong on separation of Church & State).

Best regards,
Patrick J. Buchanan

Mrs. Ivy "Scottie" Berge also sent a congenial note to WWDB, after Lester made his broadcast "Scotland the Brave" on the eve of St. Andrew's Day:

Dear Rev. Kinsolving:

I was delighted and touched by your talk last Saturday night about my native land Bonnie Scotland. I was born in Glasgow, and during World War II I drove a double decked trolley car, in the blackout, with the bombs dropping all around me.

After working all day, I would sit in the Air Raid shelter, shivering with cold and fear, listening to the ack ack guns firing at the German planes, right above us. There is no doubt, that young Duncan MacIntyre was a hero. And he greatly deserved the highest honor of the land, the Victoria Medal of Honor.

Your singing Scotland the Brave, was superb, and I sang it, along with you—and I must say we sounded very good. I often listen to you on W.W.D.B., and enjoy your show, but thought you were outstanding last Saturday night. I wish you Good Health & Good Luck and God Bless You.

Les continued to thrive on WWDB, and broadcast the following at the end of the year:

"A Christmas Greeting"

Somewhere, some place in the nation, there may be another station with a lineup of such characters on the air, and an audience of equal delight, or in some cases, of such perverse fury. But if there are, somewhere, such stations as even mildly approximate the Uninhibited Radio of THE Talk Station, there surely are not many.

My mailbox has been filled this week with Christmas cards and other expressions of great kindness, concern, interest—or rage, to be sure—from people who I have never seen. I so very much wish that I had the air time to acknowledge all of these. But I'm sure you can understand why this can't be a Letters to Les Show. Every once in a while, however, there comes such a classic through the mail as veritably cries out for broadcasting—and sadly, this one is unsigned:

> Mr. Lester deselvo
> Thank you for being on the air. On Sat or whenever—we turn you on the radio and we leave our home, we know *your voice* will keep any burglar away. Thank you we are safe

I have suggested to WWDB's management that a possible money-maker might be the WWDB–Les Kinsolving Burglar Alarm Cassette—accompanied by a glossy photograph, in case they are also troubled by rodents or varmints.

By January 1985, Les broadcast on "Two Reagan News Conference Catastrophes," which included the following:

The Great and Impressively Reelected Communicator repeatedly demonstrated to an international TV audience that he was so terribly anxious to avoid the question of one reporter, that he resorted to calling on another—who had not even raised his hand to ask for recognition. And, to the horror of Mr. Reagan's handlers, the fellow wasn't even paying visual attention.

Gadfly

(The President had just previously pointed his finger in my direction without specifying who he had called on for a question):

KINSOLVING: Mr. President!

PRESIDENT REAGAN: No, not you, her!

(after the lady reporter finished and the Presidential finger pointed in my direction again):

KINSOLVING: Mr. President!

PRESIDENT REAGAN: No, not you, him!

"Him" was Barry Seaman of *Time* magazine, who was sitting directly in front of me. The world watched, stunned, as Seaman said nothing, and didn't appear even to have looked up at the President. From behind, Seaman appeared to have fallen asleep. So, in order to try to rescue Mr. Reagan from this acute and unprecedented embarrassment—an eternity of Prime Time seconds with no audio except gasps—I leaned forward and murmured in his ear:

KINSOLVING: Wake up! The President wants you.

(Seaman jumped up from his reverie and managed to conjure up a question. The following Monday, he furiously denounced my effort at Good Samaritanship.)

The following morning, during Speakes' news briefing, the transcript reveals that one reporter contended that a Speakes aide named Kim Hoggard "went running back and told Ronald Reagan 'Don't call on Lester.'"

MR. SPEAKES: No, I—

QUESTION: Because if you look at that video tape, Mr. Reagan spent three quarters of his time on the right quadrant . . .

MR. SPEAKES: Right. He avoided Lester.

QUESTION: He avoided the left one [section] like the plague, finally realized he had to call on the *Time* guy because you told him to; called on the *Time* guy, who didn't have his hand up and wasn't looking— (laughter)—Lester jumped in. I mean it was very risky, as you know.

MR. SPEAKES: We always point out to the President where certain people are sitting that he may or may not want to call on. (*Confession Time! The Reagan News Conferences are rigged.*)

QUESTION: But let the record show that Lester was persistent and got in a question and he [Reagan] answered it: "Would you ride alone and unarmed on a New York subway?" And the President said: "Security regulations prohibited" . . . so Lester won in the end.

As Lester happily bantered with his loyal listeners on other such topics as "Anti-Nuke Encampment of Fire-Walking, Moon-Howling, Goddess-Worshipping, Vegetarian Lesbian Witches of Upstate N.Y.," "Will the People's Republic of Berkeley Build a Berlin Wall?" and "Philadelphia Inquirer Columnist Defends Jane Fonda," one listener new to WWDB's Saturday night line-up tuned in. He was Bob Bruno, Program Director of WOR News Talk Radio 710. Bob was looking for new talent, since Dr. Judith Kuriansky, noted sex therapist, was leaving her nightly show to launch a career on TV. WOR was not only New York City's top-rated AM station, but the most widely listened to talk-radio station in America. Bruno liked what he heard on Uninhibited Radio, and put a call in to Lester.

On Sunday, October 6, 1985, the *New York Daily News* ran the following feature in their City Lights: Radio section:

Gadfly

"HE'S WOR's 'SMOKING GUN'"

[Les Kinsolving] is WOR Radio's newest full-time personality, with a nightly 7–10 P.M. talk-show that began last month. He's an older, soft-spoken man who doesn't rant or rave, say like Bob Grant once did. But don't let that fool you; he's full of vim and thunder.

. . . "I don't plan on giving up my residence in Washington," he says. "If I did they would confiscate my White House credentials—which would make some people very happy. So I decided to stay with a delightful professor at Princeton, and my wife will commute three times a week."

. . . While it isn't unusual for Kinsolving and his callers to engage in heated debate, he draws the line at profanity. "Once a listener called me a filthy, stinking fascist four times in a row. I said, "You're a horse's ass." That's about the strongest verbiage I've ever used." Occasionally, his subjects are, well, earthy. "I once did a show on AIDS that was *very* graphic. But you don't have to use four-letter words to get your point across."

. . . "We're here to inform and entertain and to allow people to get their say. There are those who say I enjoy controversy. I prefer to call it 'uninhibited radio.' I raise issues that the rest of the media seems to ignore. People formulate very strong and emotional opinions about issues, and they want to be heard."

At WOR, Les would use his scripted opener and closing from WWDB, with some revisions and one addition—he now included West Point marching music, something he hoped would "lift the spirits" of anyone tuning in. On Monday, September 16, the first night of broadcast, Lester made a special introduction before he went to the opener:

Ladies and Gentlemen, this is Les Kinsolving. Tonight's a home-coming for me. I was born only blocks away from WOR at Tenth Ave. and 59th, at the old Sloane's Hospital. Five years later, when I lived in Garden City, Long Island, I was an avid listener to WOR, so I think you can understand why I feel so honored. My first home was just up the Hudson River, at a beautiful place called West Point, where the first music I can ever remember sounded very much like this . . . (CUT TO MUSIC, CONTINUE DURING OPENER):

From the venerable, yet vitally virile WOR, premiere pioneer and pace-setter of American RADIO—that senior electronics medium where active Americans can do DOZENS of things while they listen—instead of SITTING, PARALYZED in front of the tube of the VAST WASTELAND. . . .

From the heart of New York, the mightiest market on earth, to listeners in forty states and Canada: This is THE LES KIN-SOLVING SHOW, featuring your humble and obedient servant of the same name!

Since he was now in "the big time," Les was handled by an astutely professional crew which he introduced during one broadcast: twenty-four-year-old producer Alexander "The Great" Banker: "brilliant, ingenious, imaginative and extraordinarily talented," engineer Bob "Fingers" Ioreo, who was "the fastest thing I have ever seen working the board . . . when I look in [his] direction, I see an absolute Grand Canyon of teeth in a huge grin, under a moustache and flashing eyes." He was also assisted by part-time secretary Judie Fabian, who handled "an onslaught of mail with dispatch. Aside from hours and hours and hours of volunteered overtime, she has hovered like a mother hen in diligent search for ways to help."

Les was especially grateful for the inestimable patience of Chief Engineer Paul Stuart:

Gadfly

When I first arrived, Paul spent an absolutely fruitless hour trying to teach me how to operate The Board—that great huge thing with what I estimate is 1,275 working, sliding, pushing and blinking parts—that lies in front of me and makes the panel of a B-1 Bomber simple by contrast. Paul must have concluded that technically speaking, I am the dumbest talent in the history of American radio. But this good and kindly man never said this—although I now confess it, as "The Great Unmechanic."

After his first grueling week, Les received a memo from Bob Bruno who stated that there were "several critical areas which require immediate attention, such as: 'Rehearse proper hand cues and back timing techniques . . . be personally involved with the structure, content and execution of each program . . . you're still having trouble transitioning in and out of phone calls . . . listen for recurring mistakes and develop solutions to correct them . . . control listener calls. Take charge of the conversation. Know when and how to gracefully terminate calls. You needn't be over solicitous or abrupt . . . just clean.'" If Bob's high-standard demands seemed intimidating, he softened the blow by (1) complimenting Les as "an eloquent extemporaneous conversationalist," and (2) suggested that he "relax and have fun."

Although Les continued to target liberals with such broadcasts as, "How Mayor Koch Is Cracking Down on the AIDS-Incubating Bars and Bathhouses: An Election Eve Epic in the Art of Political Flip-Flop," and "Should America's Taxpayers Have to Pay for Two Left-Wing Networks, to Which Few of Them Listen or Watch?" He also took conservatives to task, as in "Why Ronald Reagan Doesn't Go to Church," broadcast on November 8, 1985:

Prior to his being elected President, Ronald Reagan was a fairly regular church attendant, at the Bellaire Presbyterian Church near Los Angeles. The President's explanations of why he hardly ever goes to church are fairly well known—since House Speaker Tip O'Neill, his leading critic, has needled him about it.

Mr. Reagan contends that he doesn't want to inconvenience any congregation by his presence, obliging them to walk through a metal detector. Repeatedly at the White House I have asked spokesman Larry Speakes what congregation in all Metropolitan Washington would not willingly—eagerly—walk through one of those metal detectors—twice if necessary—in order that the President and Mrs. Reagan be able to worship with them.

Speakes always brushes off this question, because there is no answer, other than the fact that almost every congregation would willingly undergo this experience for our President. In 1984 (an election year) the Great Communicator added an explosive twist to the Great Explanation. He explained that he didn't want any church to undergo any risk of being bombed because he attended.

This awful contemplation seemed to mollify the questioners until, during the last week of the campaign he visited a Long Island synagogue, in the great (electoral) State of New York. I asked Speakes, "Since when are synagogues safer from bombers than churches?" But Larry once more evaded the question.

The Reagan commentary, along with "The Rise of Black Conservatives" aired the evening after the *New York Post*'s story, "Fire Rips Times Square Skyscraper," appeared on page five:

A two-alarm fire on the 34th floor of a Times Square skyscraper forced the evacuation of the building last night and disrupted a live call-in show on WOR Radio. The fire broke out at 7:30 P.M., in a garment showroom at 1450 Broadway, at 41st Street.

Controversial WOR radio talk-show host Les Kinsolving was on the air live with a show about the rise of black conservatism when the studios next door at 1440 Broadway were also ordered evacuated. "We were just going into a commercial break and things were getting very exciting," said Kinsolving. "I looked up and there was a big cop. They told us to leave. I said, 'But we're on the air.' He said, 'If you don't get out, you'll be *in* the air.'" Kinsolving joked: "I think its proof positive we have the hottest show in town."

Grateful for such a gallant rescue, the *Post* further reported, "When the all-clear was issued, Kinsolving returned to the air, and he brought with him new guests—the cops who ordered him to evacuate."

WOR listeners were both delighted and outraged by the flamboyant new host, and sent off their letters to Les: "Welcome, welcome, welcome!! I'm totally delighted with your show. WOR has finally done something right for a change." . . . "When you first substituted for Dr. Judy, you seemed to be stable. However, after listening to your own show, we decided that you are a flake. Although some information can be gained, basically you have a neurological disorder." . . . "Congratulations—you have the *best* talk-show in all radio." . . . "Lee Kinsolving #2 Ghoul of Radio: When you look into the mirror you see an ugly, ugly face. But an ugly face doesn't mean one has to be so ugly & wild & cuckoo as you do on the once most enjoyable radio station in NY." . . . "You're terrific! We need more of *you*." . . . "We think you are one of those characters in our unquiet society that contributes to our decadence." . . . "Congratulations on your life saving inspiring uniquely courageous and vitally needed radio program." . . . "I see that Bob Grant is not the only raving, maniacal, imbecilic cretinous homophobic mutant on radio. From under what rock do the radio stations find your creeps?"

Fellow talk-show host Roy Fox of WMCA also fumed when he heard Lester's commentaries, especially those dealing with race relations. In his November 18th broadcast, "Affirmative Action: Replacing Jim Crow With Crow Jim," Les disclosed how New York was practicing "reverse racism" in their plan "to use racial quotas to pick at least 1,000 police sergeants":

The City of New York spent one half a million dollars of the taxpayers' money to develop a test, which Assessment Designs, Inc. of Florida developed in consultation with experts in New York's Police and Personnel Departments. But this test had what proved to be a fatal flaw: it was not formulated to guarantee that minority group candidates would pass.

. . . The City says it must resort to this patent racism and unconstitutional discrimination because it does not believe it can win the lawsuits filed by minority groups. . . . 968 white officers, 44 Hispanic officers, and 23 black officers manifested enough of such knowledge to pass. . . . Too bad, officers! If only your skin pigments more closely resembled the desired racial quotas. . . .

In an effort to enforce the FCC's Fairness Doctrine policy, WMCA sent, by certified mail, a recording of Roy Fox's comments he made about Lester on his show which aired January 20th (Martin Luther King's birthday). They also invited Les to respond, which Les did on WOR, after he listened to the enclosed cassette of Fox's program:

I would be inclined to agree that it could indeed be construed as a personal attack when Mr. Fox described me as a "racist, with a poor soul, who putrefies the airwaves over at WOR with his hate glands."

. . . First, after he called me a "racist putrefier of WOR's air waves," he went directly from me to the President of the United States, whom he described as "a good ole boy" who is a "stupid hypocrite" and a "loser." (And on the envelope of WMCA's letter, I saw: "WMCA Good Guy Radio.")

. . . Finally, your Mr. Fox has shown such rapt interest in *The Les Kinsolving Show* that he has quoted at length, and almost verbatim, from one of my commentaries. Who could ask for anything more? I trust Mr. Fox will keep listening.

Ten days later, on February 3rd, Les would be replaced with Sally Jesse Raphael, as stated in a memo from WOR General Manager Lee Simonson:

I am very pleased to announce that WOR Radio is about to become the New York affiliate of the *NBC Talknet*. This means that we will be adding to our line-up two extremely popular personalities: Sally Jesse Raphael and Bruce Williams. Because of their local roots, these are people whose names have constantly popped up in our listener research as being very formidable with the New York talk audiences.

Sally's personal advice program will run from 7 P.M. to 9 P.M. weeknights. . . . Les Kinsolving, who has done an excellent job in the 7 P.M. to 10 P.M. slot, will remain with the station at a date and time to be announced.

. . . Happy New Year to all of you!

Although Les would remain at WOR on Sunday evenings from 11 to 1 A.M., the station management still received letters of protest:

The decision to cancel Kinsolving is a great loss for your listeners and represents a cave-in to the journalistic establishment. . . . Kinsolving was a fresh informative controversial stimulating voice. Shades of the Soviet Union: when only one point of view can be heard on our airways. I would bet your tenure at WOR will be shortened by your poor judgment.

—Joanna Rose

Before Les Kinsolving arrived on the scene, I switched from WOR and that strictly from Dullsville shrink right after the

Daily News. . . . The stimulating and challenging Les Kinsolving program was a bad habit that caused me to neglect other
things—but a bad habit with a positive side too. I'll miss it!
　　　　　　　　　　　　　　　　　　　　—Allen L. Bartlett

Both fans sent copies of their letters to Les, with personal notes: "Please
advise when we can read your newspaper column. You are a stimulating
controversial character. We need people in journalism who are not dull,
flat, and dishonest." . . . "Thanks for a bit of stimulation and fresh air.
I don't always think you right—but you do make one think! Thanks!"
One listener who didn't protest to management sent off a swift note to
Les: "Your replacement on WOR is pure unadulterated pap."

　　Although Lester was deeply disappointed in the cutback, he was
somewhat relieved, since his commute from Princeton to Manhattan
took two hours every day, and his car, parked outside of WOR near
Times Square, had been broken into more than once. After a grind-
ing Monday through Friday schedule, he would then travel down
to Philadelphia every Saturday to broadcast at WWDB. With more
flexibility during the week, Les would also be able to attend the
White House press briefings again and settle back in at home in Virginia, thus saving Sylvia the commute up to New York every week.
It would also be a blessing to his eldest daughter Laura, since her
beloved dog Brandon was now very sick.

　　In 1975, as Laura was traveling cross-country with brother Tom,
she came upon a couple giving away puppies. The pups were an adorable mix of Black Labrador and Dalmatian, which Laura couldn't possibly resist. She chose the one with the spotted chest and white tip on
the end of his tail, and decided to name him Brandon, in honor of one
of her favorite actors, Marlon Brando. Laura brought him to California, where Lester, who was crestfallen after the Peoples Temple squad
squelched his new exposés, fell in love with the new puppy.

　　Ten years later, Laura married and moved to Massachusetts, leaving
Brandon with her parents, since her husband's apartment in Amherst
didn't allow large dogs. Les and Sylvia were more than happy to look
after him, as Brandon was now a member of the Kinsolving family.

Gadfly

Les had nicknamed him "Black Dog," after the pirate in *Treasure Island*. He loved Brandon very deeply, and was anguished when they discovered he had developed an enlarged esophagus, and couldn't keep his food down.

After several months of the affliction where he was fed a liquid diet of nutrients, Brandon still lost a frightening amount of weight, and required more visits to the specialist who first diagnosed him. Laura traveled down from her Amherst home to be with him, when Brandon contracted pneumonia for the second time. After a few days, she made the compassionate yet agonizing decision to end Brandon's life. Les held Laura in his arms when she came home, and could only assuage his own grief by honoring Brandon over the airwaves, in his tribute, "Does My Dog Have a Soul?" which aired January 27, 1986:

> I have known dogs who definitely have souls. They are different from any human being, yet certainly not outside the love of God who created them. If some of the theologians opt to smirk at this belief, I can recall that one of history's most widely beloved saints had no such low esteem for animals—with whom he is usually pictured, or sculpted, there in Assisi.

> . . . More than a quarter of a century has passed since that occasion when I took my five-year-old daughter Laura to a Walt Disney movie called *Perri*. It was about a family of squirrels. I've never forgotten the scene when one of that family was caught and killed by a predator and how my daughter wept—it made me weep, too. Her love of animals has grown through the years. That love brought into our home the most unforgettable dog I have every known. . . . He was three-quarters Labrador and one-quarter Dalmatian—which I can now affirm is the most devastating amalgamation since nitroglycerine. He took one look at me, and I was hooked.

> Those in that blessed company known as owners of Labradors will attest that in all zoology there is nothing that can quite match

or exceed the absolute tidal waves of affection emanating from Labrador Retrievers. . . . Brandon had a bark that could be heard in the next county. That was the greatest sort of reassurance when we learned from the FBI that Rev. Jim Jones of Jonestown had put me as number two on his hit list—and that he had organized death squads. Anyone unknown to Brandon who put a foot on our property was confronted by that tremendous bark.

Then, eighteen months ago, Brandon, who was ten years old, and growing into old age for a big dog, began losing his voice; his bark and all of the rest of his expressive noises and irresistible expressions which made him part of our family were threatened. . . . No longer was he inclined to look at me and cock his head to the side—something in the manner in which our President so often overwhelms reporters at his news conferences.

. . . He was in constant hunger, and often could not walk—an almost terrifying listlessness . . . his eyes, which once flashed with energy, became painful to look at for those of us who loved him. Yesterday morning, my daughter Laura, who first brought Brandon into our lives, made the almost unbearable decision to "let him go," as she put it so poignantly.

. . . While she is happily married and a psychiatric nurse, I saw her weep when she returned yesterday morning without him, just as I remember her weeping in that theatre twenty-seven years ago. For my daughter, and for all those who have suffered bereavement in losing such a beloved friend—an animal whose returned affection is complete, without guile or without reservation—there is St. Basil's great affirmation:

For thou hast promised to save both man and beast.

On that, and on St. Francis, and on so much in the Bible, including Jesus and His assurance that even a sparrow is not forgotten before God, do I commend this beloved friend, Brandon, to the Everlasting Arms. . . .

After Les delivered his broadcast, calls poured in from tearful listeners who offered their deepest gratitude for such a heartfelt tribute. Driving back to Amherst, Laura cried too, as she listened to her father over the radio.

"Does My Dog Have a Soul?" was also published in the *Tribune-Review*, the *AV* (American Anti-Vivisection Society's magazine), and the *Christian Challenge*. It received more mail, requests for copies, and repeated broadcasts than anything Les had ever aired. One *Christian Challenge* reader, Walter H. Boyd, sent Lester the following letter:

I'm writing this to thank you for your beautiful article . . . It was just a year ago yesterday that my 13½ year-old beloved cat died so your piece hit home. . . . That cat (Miss Muffin) was the greatest companion for me. She was always loving and attentive.

. . . I have often thought about the theological questions you raised and I do believe strongly in the possibility that such dear creatures have souls. My own mother (fundamentalist though she was) almost believed that her dogs had gone to heaven.

. . . At least those animals whom we have loved so deeply and whose deaths can cause us to suffer so painfully are never lost to us completely in this life. By the way, I have another cat who is about a year old. She helped me through the pain of the loss of Miss Muffin. . . .

That May, Lester was notified that the Delta Society, an organization dedicated to "the interactions of people, animals and the environment," honored him with the 1986 Delta Society Media Commendation Award, for "Does My Dog Have a Soul?" since "the judges felt your presentation excelled in illuminating the relationship between people and their companion animals, and the meaning in those persons' lives." Besides receiving a monetary gift of $250, the Delta Society presented Les with a commendation plaque. Les placed it on the wall at home where it still hangs, underneath a framed photo of a happy, healthy and forever-loved Brandon.

Returning to his old stomping ground at the White House, Lester bounded back into the fray at President Reagan's press conference on February 11, which was promptly reported by Eleanor Randolph in the *Washington Post*'s "The Non-News Conference," on February 13, 1986:

> With some of the nation's best journalists sitting in front of the president and asking him questions, why did so few answers qualify as news?
>
> Some journalists said the allotted half-hour was devoured by Reagan's opening statement (in this case on how his budget cut only "unessential items"), by the president's suggestions that he could not comment on a variety of matters, and by questions from "nonestablishment journalists," as one establishment journalist put it.
>
> For example, one question went to Evelyn Y. Davis, best known for her appearances at various stockholder meetings where she has, on occasion, loudly needled corporate officials about policies she finds objectionable.
>
> . . . From there, Reagan had apparently planned to let *Baltimore Sun* White House reporter Robert R. Timberg have a question, but Timberg was preempted by Lester Kinsolving. . . . "Lester just took it, he just took it," said an irritated Timberg. "He clearly has no compunction to ride roughshod over his colleagues."
>
> Kinsolving, who was wearing a red sports jacket, bellowed about the "injustice" of Reagan giving an exclusive interview to the *Washington Post* this week when the president has complained

about Herblock's cartoons showing Secretary of Defense Caspar Weinberger with a toilet seat around his neck.

Defending his right to give exclusive interviews, Reagan laughed and compared the cost of a $600 toilet cover with the one on commercial airlines—a comparison that brought laughter from reporters.

Some reporters suspect that Reagan uses such questions to get the mainstream journalists off the track. "It may be that he deliberately tries to get a question that is not in the normal flow of news," said [Lesley] Stahl.

Lester could barely wait to broadcast his side of the story, in "*Post*-Toasted and Sun-Beamed—at the White House":

This honor of a *Post*-toasting is compounded by a similar malediction from the *Baltimore Sun*. For Miss Randolph quotes the *Sun*'s reporter, Mr. Robert Timberg, in an allegation that I somehow "took it"—"it" being the possibility that he might have been recognized for a question.

. . . I tried, unsuccessfully, to explain to an enraged Timberg: President Reagan looked directly at me, in which direction he pointed and said: "You." Had he named Mr. Timberg, or any other correspondent, I would never have proceeded to ask my question. For when Mr. Reagan looked our way and called on reporters for NBC and Reuters, I surely did not "preempt" either of those who the President had clearly recognized.

. . . Miss Randolph [accused] me of "bellowing"—with no such notation of the stentorian voices of either Chris Wallace of NBC, or Sam Donaldson of ABC. In point of fact, Miss Randolph, assuredly, has never heard me bellow; unless, by some chance, she heard me drilling truck drivers at Fort Ord, or if she covered any of the football teams I have coached. I simply threw my baritone into overdrive. This was necessitated because I was so far back, and because, as has happened in the past to a number of us, some of these ladies and gentlemen make a practice of interrupting any reporter with whom they do not agree, and who is insufficiently identified with the prestige press. Media reporter Randolph also quotes me as using the word "injustice"—which the transcript will reveal I never used.

On February 25, Les received a letter of thanks from Pat Buchanan at the White House:

Dear Les:
    Appreciate the copy of that piece you wrote on Eleanor Randolph's *Washington Post* column. You were awfully hard on them, Les, and I'm sure you're plagued with guilt.
All the best.

Patrick J. Buchanan
Assistant to the President

Although the "prestige press" was often lofty and disdainful of the "nonestablishment journalists," they could be playful at times, especially Sam Donaldson. In June, the *Washington Inquirer*'s the *Eye* reported the following from the White House:

Les Kinsolving pulled out all the stops last week during a White House briefing. Les queried **White House spokesman Ed Djerejian** about accounts that **Liberian Gen. Samuel Doe's** troops killed, dismembered and ate a rebel general.

"Now, could you explain why we're sending $50 million in aid to Liberia?" asked **Les**. "If we're concerned about human rights, why are we sending $50 million a year to this cannibal?" **Sam Donaldson** saw the opportunity and wagged: "For ketchup!"

White Houser Ed Djerejian summed up the riposte, saying: "Well, that's food for thought."

Another bit of banter was also reported in the *Washington Times* on December 16: "In response to Lester Kinsolving's suggestion that the president has the right to question reporters at news conferences, Sam Donaldson said if that occurs, then 'I get to be president for a day.'"

By December, the *Eye* proffered the juiciest newsflash of 1986 from the press corps:

When outgoing White House pressie Larry Speakes began the December 10 daily briefing, he couldn't help noting that media maestro Les Kinsolving had sidled in, toting a tape recorder the size of a small suitcase. "Lester, you look like an organ grinder," chirped Larry.

To which Les promptly shot back: "Would you like to climb on my shoulder, Larry?"

Les's rapidfire comeback earned him the distinction of asking the first question, which was as follows: "Larry, would it be entirely wrong for us to compare Pat Buchanan's relationship with the president now with that of Sir Francis Drake to Queen Elizabeth, when she rebuked him publicly but rewarded him privately for giving the Spaniards hell?"

Before Larry could deny this comparison, there was laughter, and Bill Plante of CBS shouted: "Sir Francis Drake was (bleeping) her!"

Warning to Maryland: "Hide the Women and Children!"

1987 PROVED TO be a landmark year for Les. In January, he received a call from Harry Shriver, president and general manager of WFBR AM 1300, a radio station located in downtown Baltimore, Maryland. Shriver was looking for new, controversial talent, since WFBR's format was changing from a mixture of talk and music to all talk. Les would fit in perfectly with a gaggle of Maryland radio veterans, including Joe Lombardo, Alan Christian, Frank Luber, Ken Maylath, Karen Francis, Stan Charles, and Tom Marr.

Broadcasting Monday through Friday from 7 to 10 P.M., Les was slated for the evening time slot in order to "add listeners." According to *Baltimore Business Journal*: "WFBR needed a strong show at night during the baseball season especially, and that resulted in the Les Kinsolving Show, which went on the air in February."

Two days after his first broadcast on February 2, the *Baltimore Evening Sun* ran a feature story, "Lester Kinsolving: Opinionated commentator is quick with a barb:"

Gadfly

Barely a third of the way into his radio talk-show debut and already the host is giving the business to an incredulous physician and microbiologist on the other end of the phone line. The AIDS virus, he says with an I-know-better-than-you-do tone of voice, can be contracted just by sitting in a chair that has been occupied by a carrier of the disease.

. . . He's tagged popular sex counselor Dr. Ruth as "Dr. Crotch" and advised that her bottom be spanked; suggested that "if everyone in this country who made an ass of himself were to be deported, Jesse Jackson would be the first to go"; called for the strict isolation of all AIDS victims; referred cheekily to retired U.S. Sen. Charles "Mac." Mathias as "Charlie Charming"; dismissed another city radio talk program as "a cure for insomnia"; denounced gay activists as the "militant sodomy lobby"; and attempted to enlist his listeners as card-carrying members of his private clip-snipping press corps.

Welcome to "uninhibited radio." The airwave soap box occupied by the sometimes quirky, always feisty journalist, columnist and Anglican parish minister Lester Kinsolving . . . "Hide the women and children!" jokes Robert Bruno, programming director at New York City's WOR station. . . .

"People love Les or they hate him. But they never ignore him. . . . He has quite a loyal following in New York. I describe his appeal as that of a man who every night is going to drive his car 60 miles an hour into a wall. People line up to watch something like that." . . . Although Bruno describes Kinsolving as a "serious professional" and a "consummate gentleman," there are times when his passions rule his reason.

"That passion sometimes builds to a fever pitch," Bruno reveals. "Sometimes he does cross the line of good taste. . . . You have to frequently remind him of the parameters you want him to operate in . . . "

Besides his opening onslaught on the AIDS crisis, one of the more eccentric topics Lester introduced to his new Baltimore audience was "Should the U.S. Post Office Provide Partners for Perverts?":

The identity of those who purchase post office boxes is a closely guarded secret of the U.S. Postal Service—unless the box holder deals with the public in business. So it is that one of my radio listeners has no idea who was the previous owner of a post office box in the Philadelphia suburb of Havertown, Pennsylvania. This is unfortunate. For he is receiving mail addressed to this post office box, which is apparently intended for the previous renter, whose identity is unknown. One such letter was addressed: "Dear Prospective Member—under the letterhead: NATIONAL ASSOCIATION OF SLAVES. . . . "Thank you for responding to our advertisement!" opened this letter—which was signed: "Sincerely, The Mouse."

. . . What seems to be a question in need of some Congressional legislation is whether or not the United States mail should be used to provide partners for perverts. . . . Does President Reagan believe the U.S. Postal Service should be used to promote the National Association of Slaves?

One former Episcopal High School chum sent Lester a note, three days after the first broadcast in Baltimore:

Dear Lester:
    I almost wrecked my car when I heard your voice on WFBR. I don't believe you have changed one iota since our youthful days at EHS. If you are in town soon enough someday before your show, maybe we could get together for lunch, coffee or

just a chat to remember the good old days of strolling around the demerit track. . . .

As always, Monk

By mid-March, Laura Charles of the *Baltimore Sun* included a blurb on Les in her "Eyes Only" column:

SOME LIKE IT HOT: If you happen to see WFBR-AM talk-show host Les Kinsolving leaving the radio station after his provocative nightly jabfest with police protection, don't be alarmed. Kinsolving, who has a way of stirring things up wherever he goes, has been the object of several death threats since taking over the show five weeks ago.

Word quickly spread, and the *Washington Times* added more news from another *Sun* writer:

Columnist Sylvia Badger chastised the town for this unwholesome welcome: "No one has to agree with Kinsolving, but certainly Baltimore audiences can tolerate someone with whom they disagree."

The commentary which instigated the death threats was "Blacks Who Owned Black Slaves in the United States—and Blacks Who Own Black Slaves in Africa Today":

Rarely, if ever, is it mentioned during Black History Month. And rarely, if ever, is it ever mentioned by the fortunately dwindling number of what pioneer civil rights worker Bayard Rustin warned in predicting the advent of numbers of what he called "protest prostitutes" and "racial racketeers."

Their stock in trade is their skin. If anyone still dares to sing the civil rights anthem "We Shall Overcome" with its lyric "Black and White together"—they furiously object. Instead, they insist on singing that patently racist pigment song called "Black National Anthem" or "The Black Pledge of Allegiance."

As fanatic racists, they have largely turned the civil rights movement into a racial spoils system of civil wrongs, drum majored
by that Prime Minister of Hate Merchants, Louis Farrakhan,
Chicago's version of Idi Amin. . . . These race hustlers blame
ALL whites for American slavery. The fact that the ancestry of a
solid majority of America's whites did not arrive in this country
until 300,000 whites had given their lives to wipe out slavery
is of no concern to these pigment protestors.

. . . One of this nation's most distinguished black historians
has discovered and reported that in North Carolina alone, there
were 721 slaves owned by 232 black slave owners. . . . I was
able to reach Dr. [John Hope] Franklin by phone this week. I
asked him if North Carolina was any kind of rarity in having
black slaves owned by blacks. "No," he replied, "I would estimate that there were surely more in Louisiana, South Carolina,
Virginia, and Maryland.

"They were absolutely furious when I broadcast that one," Les
recalls. "But I had a very courteous, nice-looking female police officer who escorted me to the car for a few weeks afterward. She took
one look at my producer Scott Hollenbeck, and showed up every
night after that!"

By the end of March the threats subsided, and Les was not deterred
from broadcasting other controversies such as "Black Bigotry Breaks
Out in New York's Courts," and "The Incredible Black Caucus Budget Backed by Hoyer," which aired in April and May. By the spring
of 1987, President Reagan vetoed legislation that attempted to
make the FCC's Fairness Doctrine into law. According to wikipedia.
org, the Fairness Doctrine "required the holders of broadcast licenses
both to present controversial issues of public importance and to do
so in a manner that was [in the Commission's view] honest, equitable
and balanced."

Two years earlier, *Broadcasting* magazine included an item in their
Washington Watch column on "AIDS and fairness":

Gadfly

FCC Mass Media has rejected complaint by Philadelphia Lesbian and Gay Task Force alleging that Aug. 10 broadcast of *Les Kinsolving Program* on WWDB (FM) Philadelphia was in violation of fairness doctrine and personal attack rule. Task force alleged that station ran afoul of FCC rules because the program's moderator and guest called for health officials and police officers to quarantine victims of acquired immune deficiency syndrome (AIDS) and to equip them with electronic locators. Station, however, noted that personal attack rule applied only when persons or groups are specifically mentioned, not the case here, it said. Station also said it had scheduled contrasting viewpoints on other programming. Bureau agreed with station's analysis on personal attack rule. On fairness grounds, bureau said it couldn't conclude that "licensee has failed to afford a reasonable opportunity for contrasting views."

With the dissolution of the Fairness Doctrine by the FCC in August 1987, the way was paved for partisan politics on AM talk radio, led by Rush Limbaugh, when he began broadcasting nationally from his flagship station of New York's WABC in 1988. No longer was there a stipulation for station managers to air both sides. As Les stated in his March 31st commentary, "Pulse of the Nation: Talk Radio," before the August abolition,

> There are still some radio talk-show hosts who are under strict orders to conceal whatever opinions they may have, and to confine themselves to functioning as a sort of castrated traffic cop for random opinions. There are others whose only discernible opinion is that it is indeed a joy to be able to stroke celebrities, who can be used in lieu of any research or convictions of their own. There are, fortunately, other kinds of radio talk-show hosts, who are of an entirely different sort, like those at WFBR in Baltimore.

After WFBR made the switch to all talk, a large ad ran in Baltimore's *City Paper:*

Warning to Maryland: "Hide the Women and Children!"

WFBR AM 1300
"You have made T.V. irrelevant!"
—District Judge Tom Curly, Annapolis

"I made the switch in March, from progressive rock music stations. I'm hooked. I've never learned this much in my four years at college!"
—Ed Anderson, Baltimore

"WBAL TALK-SHOW HOSTS WON'T DEBATE WFBR RIVALS"
—*Baltimore Sun*
(Discretion is the better part of valor)

"Crazed ilk" . . . "turgid, hysterical prose"
—*City Paper*
(Even indiscretion is appreciated when it is this attentive)

The ad also featured photos and time slots of their top-rated, regular line-up:

LOMBARDO
5:30–9:00 A.M.

CHRISTIAN
9:00–1:00 A.M.

MARR
1:00–5:00 P.M.

KINSOLVING
7:00–10 P.M.

Between commentaries that enraged many listeners, Les provided ample comic relief, such as "Mayor Barry Berated by Breedolater: The Case for Compulsory Sterilization":

Gadfly

"Why don't you stop having all those babies?" asked Washington D.C.'s Mayor Marion Barry—in one of the most sensible things he has ever said. The object of his question is a woman named Jacqueline Williams, who has contributed 14 children to the city's welfare rolls.

This is costing the taxpayers $1,300 a month. And Mrs. Williams has announced: "If I can, I'll have 14 more." The taxpayers who have to pay for this blood-boiling breedolatry are not just Washingtonians. For the taxpayers nationwide are taxed to provide a nearly one half of a billion-dollar Federal subsidy to the District of Columbia.

. . . In answer to Mayor Barry's question . . . this creature asked: "As mayor, you tell me which one of my kids I should have killed." To his credit, Mayor Barry did not lower himself to the level of this absurd rhetoric—by saying anything on the order of "None of *them*, Madam. *You!*"

. . . "I don't want to mess up my body with birth control" declares this assembly-line breeder, who also announced: "It's none of your business." Quite to the contrary, Madam, it *is* our business, until you use either birth control or self-control—and all of us have to pay for what you produce.

. . . Is there anyone in the D.C. City Council or Congress with enough good sense and courage to introduce legislation to tie the tubes of this angry nitwit who wants to saddle everybody else with 14 more of her babies?

And "How to Handle Uninvited Telephone Solicitors":

Last year, Paul Marshall of Babylon, Long Island wrote a letter to the *New York Times* which describes what has become an insufferable national annoyance and invasion of privacy. . . . In addition to Mr. Marshall's excellent letter, let me add the lamentable fact that there are even machine-operated recorded sales pitches, to which it does no good to respond. And if you slam down the phone, it doesn't even register, because these machines have neither ear drums, nor hearts.

What I find particularly insufferable is that syrupy voice that says, "Is this Mr. Kinsolving?" Which immediately informs me that the caller is nobody I know. Then, in apparently following step two in what must be a widely distributed telephone sales manual this alien voice asks: "How ARE you?"

This is no doubt designed to be an ice-breaker, in order to warm me up for the presentation of the pitch. Instead, it is an inane and enraging violation of privacy in which people are usually interrupted by some unknown telephone huckster. If I have time I ask, "*Why* do you want to know how I am? Are you really interested in anything other than trying to sell me something I have not asked for, on the phone?"

This usually evokes confusion—when I can restrain my rage long enough to sound scholarly and generally inquisitive. While this telephone solicitor is trying to figure out how to handle THIS kind of unexpected reaction, I follow up with: "How, on the other hand, are YOU? And WHO are you?— Since you have come, totally uninvited, into my life?"

Often they will hang up, or call a superior, or, rarely, begin their life's story—which doesn't last very long, because time for them is money: YOUR time makes them THEIR money. . . .

Since Les was broadcasting full-time and closer to home, he would resign from WOR in February, and WWDB in July of 1987. Among letters from listeners who expressed their sadness at his departure, Les received another from one of his biggest fans in the Philadelphia area:

• • •

Gadfly

Les,

. . . I do so envy those who are able to hear you in the Baltimore area! I really miss your show! . . . I have several of our phone conversations on tape and do have a recording of "things you can do while listening to the radio." This was the story you did about us over two years ago as I listened while timing my wife's contractions!

Never to be forgotten and with highest respect, I hope to hear you again someday,

Paul M. DuPont

As was the case for Lester's New York and Philadelphia audiences, Baltimore was delighted to hear the latest brouhaha from the White House press corps:

For a while there, in the White House Press Room last Friday morning, it looked as if there might even have been fisticuffs, between the chief correspondents for two of Big Media's Biggest Networks.

First they tried out-shouting each other, just after President Reagan's four-minute appearance, when it had been announced that he would take no questions. Then, after ABC's Sam Donaldson tried to out-shout the similarly stentorian bellowing of NBC's Chris Wallace, the cacophony became so incomprehensible that Mr. Reagan asked NBC's Andrea Mitchell if she could possibly translate all of this noise. When the noise resumed, the President left—and the fireworks commenced.

For Wallace, the son of Mike Wallace of "60 Minutes," tried to move on Sam's accustomed (but hardly entitled, authorized, or leased) space to do a standup—in front of the White House sign just behind spokesman Marlin Fitzwater's podium.

After the melee, Donaldson announced, "I moved him." But the *Washington Post* reports that Wallace mocked Donaldson, by bellowing: "You're just mad because he wouldn't answer your question! You just hear footsteps behind you!"—a searing reference to Donaldson's reference to a small army of young reporters who lust after his job.

Since Les's radio show ran until till 10 P.M. every weekday night, he would stay over in Baltimore on a somewhat regular basis, and dine at the John Eager Howard Room in the Belvedere Hotel. After a few months, a letter was sent to Harry Shriver from Maître d' Roland Goodwin:

Dear Mr. Shriver:
. . . In recent months it has been my pleasure to act as host to many new customers who say they were referred to us by your station. Some typical remarks are:
"We've heard all about your restaurant from Les Kinsolving on WFBR Radio so we're really looking forward to dining here!"
"We like to listen to Les Kinsolving, and he always talks about how much he likes to eat down at your place."
"So if your restaurant is good enough for Les, it sounds like our kind of place and we'd like to make reservations!"
It was important to me to simply say "thank you" to Les and let you know that the seed he plants does bear fruit.

Although the death threats subsided, and the fans were aplenty, Lester still contended with seething detractors, especially since he had teamed up with Tom Marr, as both colleague and crony. In his letter to the *Evening Sun*, Mike O'Brien bristled about these Terrible Two:

If you listen to either of these two men, and listen is all you can do if you disagree with their views, it is clear that they have their view of this situation, and that is fine. However, I am tired of anyone who disagrees as being labeled a communist or a terrorist.

Gadfly

. . . I detest all that communism stands for, but I am a Democrat with liberal tendencies and therefore, according to Marr and Kinsolving, I am by definition un-American and a commie sympathizer.

. . . I thought this country stood for freedom of speech, the freedom to disagree with another party's ideas. However, the airwaves emanating from WFBR want you to believe that only their views make a loyal American.

Newly elected Maryland Senator, Democrat Barbara Mikluski, reacted with typical gusto when she received another invitation to appear on the Kinsolving and Marr shows:

Public officials are public servants! They should not object to even the most robust questioning. During the campaign, I repeatedly promised that I would FIGHT for Maryland! And I am sure as hell not afraid to mix it up with these two male chauvinist pigs!

On New Year's Day, 1988, another WFBR ad was run in the *City Paper*:

Are
YOU
Listening?

- The *ABC Network* was—because they featured *Alan Christian's* exclusive story on 20/20 last Friday.
- Governor William Schaefer was—because he telephoned *Tom Marr* to straighten Tom out, and in the course of that undertaking, the Governor of Maryland also mimicked *Les Kinsolving's* laugh as well as "Uninhibited Radio."
- The *American Radio Networks* were—because on Monday, January 4th 1988, they will make WFBR the

flagship of the first network to originate from Baltimore, when they begin broadcasting The Les Kinsolving Show nationwide via satellite.

That evening, Les made a special broadcast on this exciting new development:

It is together that we will, in just 46 hours, on Monday night, go up 24,000 miles to satellite. I say together because it is YOUR show too. . . . No one will ever fail to know that this show originates in Baltimore, that city which gave this nation its national anthem, in Maryland, that distinctive colony that gave this nation its first President John Hanson, as well as the land on which they built our first nation's capital, named for the NINTH President of the United States.

This familiar reminder of Maryland's unique and distinctive contributions to the United States will be included in my revised opener each night. This will be done because I don't want anybody anywhere to fail to recognize where this network show is coming from; and how very glad I am that Baltimore, which has been so very good to this show, is its home.

Later that month, Les would also introduce Baltimore and the rest of the nation to his wife Sylvia, where she would be christened with a new nickname.

Thirty miles into suburban Washington's Virginia countryside there is one of those planned communities like Columbia, Maryland, called Reston. Reston already has two newspapers, one of them called The Connection. . . . In its January 20th edition, there is the question: "IF YOU COULD NOMINATE ANYONE FOR PRESIDENT, WHO IS NOT CURRENTLY RUNNING, WHO WOULD IT BE?"

• • •

The one male who was interviewed replied: "Lee Ioccoca." One of the females replied: "Tom Brokaw, because he's on top of what's happening in the world, and up to date on current issues." A third interviewee replied in favor of her mother. And the fourth, whose picture reveals a stunning brunette, replied: "Well, I was sorry that Pat Schroeder dropped out. I wish she had stayed in. I'd like to see a woman be nominated. I think we should have a woman as President."

. . . This beautiful photograph, above this blood-curdling idea, is identified as that of SYLVIA K-O-N-S-O-L-V-I-N-G. . . . I shall have to give satisfaction, and sadistic glee, to my ideological and political adversaries, by admitting that this hair-raising desire for Schroeder as President of the United States came from my very own spouse, The Berkeley Democrat.

As I have mentioned, I prayed for patience—and God sent me a wife!

The Berkeley Democrat would now make a monthly appearance on *The Les Kinsolving Show*, and would fend off any right-winger's call with grace and aptitude. Soon after, an anonymous card was sent to Lester, along with a special gift:

You have rescued me from the banality of primetime TV and the frustration of the limited access to unbiased news anchors. I am now informed, amused, and occasionally—I must admit— overwhelmed by your rhetoric. Thank you and God Bless.
A new—but faithful—listener

The gift was a framed bit of lovely needlepoint, with the message,

"I prayed for patience, and God sent me a Berkeley Democrat!"

Warning to Maryland: "Hide the Women and Children!"

Although Les was known in Baltimore as a mainline conservative with such headlines as "A Proposed National A.I.D.S. Memorial: Why Not a National Syphilis Monument?", "The Case of Tawana Brawley Strongly Resembles Swiss Cheese," and "A White Student Union at Philadelphia's Temple University—and the Liberal *Philadelphia Inquirer* Goes Bananas," he would inform a local reporter that "Generally, I'm more conservative. But I'm liberal on a few subjects. I don't adhere to party lines—I call them as I see them." He proved this with a scorching commentary on fundamentalist evangelism, "Brother Jimmy Isn't Swaggering Now":

Christianity has survived three centuries of Roman persecution; four centuries of Barbarian invasions; the Black Plague; The Holy Inquisition; The Crusades; and a former theological seminary student named Joseph Stalin.

Therefore, there is a good chance that Christianity may also survive those Four Horses' Asses of the Apocalypse: Jimmy Swaggart . . . Pat Robertson; Pat's former associate Jim Bakker, and Oral Roberts.

Let's begin with Oily Oral, the Oklahoma God-Will-Get-Me-If-You-Don't-Shell-Out Sensation. . . . The poor, gullible and devout suckers shelled out, as Oral the ecclesiastical snake oil salesman told them to do. Eight million dollars they contributed, for medical scholarships at Oral Roberts University Medical School. But the *Ft. Worth Star Telegram* reports that Brother Oral, having raised the money for this purpose, has cancelled the scholarships!

. . . PTL's Jim Bakker, the second of the Four Horses' Assmen, was exposed and thunderously denounced by the Rev. Jimmy Swaggart . . . for adultery. And now, lo and behold! . . . This Hell Fire and Damnation Hypocrite hounded his fellow clergy while paying whores to provide him what sounds like *Hustler* live—while he was crusading against porn!

. . . What is equally disgusting is the conduct relating to this scandal by Jimmy Swaggart's friend, who he endorsed for the Presidency, the formerly Reverend Pat ("You're a Bigot if You Call Me a TV Evangelist") Robertson.

This absolutely vile knave has suggested that the George Bush campaign was somehow responsible for leaking the news of Swaggart's Porn Folly "two weeks before the most important primary in the nation." . . . Next, we suppose Robertson will announce that he knows that there were Bush people who did this—"Because God told me so!"

Poor God. As the philosopher once observed: "Christianity must be divine, to have lasted so long, despite such villainy and nonsense."

One of the most enjoyable musicals Les had seen on Broadway during the 1980s was *Barnum*, which celebrated the life of circus giant P.T. Barnum. A song from the show which Les especially loved was "There's a Sucker Born Every Minute," which he would sing on the air after exposing various patsies, such as the ones who turned over huge sums of money to Oral Roberts:

There is a sucker born every minute
Each time the second hand sweeps to the top
Like dandelions up they pop,
Their ears so big, their eyes so wide,
And though I feed 'em bonafide baloney
With no truth in it,
Why you can bet I'll find some rube to buy my corn,
Cause there's a sure-as-shooting sucker born a minute,
And I'm referring to the minute you were born!

Since Lester was now broadcasting nationally via satellite, he caught the attention of *The Morton Downey Show*, a highly successful television

gabfest with ratings that had skyrocketed since its October 1987 premiere. It fashioned itself after *The Joe Pyne Show* of the late 1960s, in
which host Pyne would smoke cigarettes, insult his guests, and sometimes attempt to throw them off the set. Morton Downey capitalized
on this tabloid format, and, thus, created a national phenomenon.

On June 8, 1988, Les appeared as a guest on Downey's show, along
with three other radio personalities: the legendary Bob Grant from
WABC in New York, Tom Leykus of KFI, and WNEW retired host,
Alan Burke. As Les recalled, "We were lured onto this show by an
absolutely beguiling and wonderfully enthusiastic producer named
Andy Regal. [He] explained that the program would be 'a focus on
radio talk-show hosts from across the country.'"

After agreeing to appear, Les signed a release shortly before the
show aired. It was then that he noticed the show's title, "Radical
Radio Personalities." After making an inquiry to senior producer
Peter Goldsmith about the title, Goldsmith reassured the four guests
gathered in the Green Room that "this REALLY meant, 'Great
American Broadcasters—Whom People Love to Hate.'" Before they
"were lured inside Emperor Downey's Coliseum," Les and the other
three radio hosts were rushed into makeup, and then were required
to walk through a metal detector: "It's the first time I've ever seen
one of these at any TV studio—but then, there's only one *Morton
Downey Show*."

As the cameras rolled on the hollering audience members, Mort
the Mouth walked on the set with cigarette in hand, and, after yelling "ZIP IT!!," announced to the nation, "These are the RUDEST
TALK-SHOW HOSTS IN AMERICA—THE BARBARIANS OF
BROADCASTING!" After the audience shrieked its approval, the
guests were prompted by Downey to engage in a brief match of
"Insult Ping Pong":

LEYKUS: I have heard Kinsolving's show, and I think he's perfectly
terrible.

Gadfly

KINSOLVING: Since you listened to *my* show, I commend you for your appreciation of culture—sadly, I have never heard *your* show, nor in fact, I've never heard of *you.*

DOWNEY: Bob, do *you* know Kinsolving?

GRANT: (wearing a pained expression and looking off into the distance) I'm not familiar with him.

DOWNEY: Les, what do you think of Grant and Leykus?

KINSOLVING: I regard Mr. Grant as a professional anger-artist, a melodrama actor who hams it up, and Leykus as Hairless Joe, the Phoenix Whorehound.

LEYKUS: (now tangling with a feminist in the audience) Women who stay home and take care of their husbands are prostitutes!

DOWNEY: (walking toward Kinsolving) Do you know you look like a fat Walter Mondale?

KINSOLVING: There's more of me to love—and this remark comes from the Man With Ten Thousand Teeth!

At this point in the broadcast, Downey grabbed Lester's yellow legal notepad, on which he'd written three pages of notes, and ran off with it:

I thought I might release Morton's grasp on my notes with a diversionary strategy. So, I reached for a cup of ice water and poured it on Mr. Downey's head. He seemed surprised by this instant Baptism. . . . I had just retrieved my notepad—when it happened. "It" felt as if I had been embraced by an enraged mother grizzly bear, whose cubs I had attempted to steal, shoot, or eat.

Warning to Maryland: "Hide the Women and Children!"

The *New York Post* described the incident, in "Downey guest in scuffle with Slammer":

> What Kinsolving didn't count on was Downey's aide de camp: "Then this guy hit me from the rear. He was 265 pounds, 6-4½. His name is David Geigel. He works as their security guard. . . . Geigel, a professional wrestler known as the Secaucus Slammer, grabbed Kinsolving from behind by the elbows. . . .

> To escape, Kinsolving kicked twice with his foot: "That knocked him loose. But we fell and he landed on top of me." . . . Four people came out to separate Geigel and Kinsolving, who "never got a look at this giant squid. He was just doing his job, but he was a little overzealous." Kinsolving says he won't sue, but that he won't be back "unless they provide me with bodyguards."

Five months later, Les was invited to return for a special show, "Mort Downey's All Stars," "in which I was to share star billing with a murderer, a bounty hunter, a transvestite, a telephone sex addict, and the ACLU—and at no fee." In his commentary "Yet Another Morton Downey Show Alumnus Will *Not* Return—and Why," Les posed the question to the producers who had contacted him four times during that week to appear on the show: "Does Downey work for nothing?" Shortly after, "they hung up." Les added a bit of prophecy to the future of the Trash TV genre: "The Downey people are still able to get guests to volunteer for this kind of masochistic national appearance—gratis. But they may run out of such unpaid punching bags."

In July, Harry Shriver sent a memo to all employees at WFBR, with great news: "WFBR scored a major increase in the Spring Arbitron. Our 12+ share was up almost 30 percent to a 3.9, putting us back in the Top 10 stations in Baltimore. . . . The 'TALKRADIO 13' format is finally coming into its own. . . . It takes everybody on the team to make the big play . . . and I appreciate your cooperation."

By August 1988, the *Evening Sun*'s top story on the 24th read, "WFBR FIRES ON-AIR STAFF," since the radio station's new owner, "JAG Broadcasting Co., the corporation that also owns 'easy listening station WLIF-FM' would replace the talk-show format with golden oldies of the '50s and '60s, starting at noon on September 16." As JAG's treasurer Daniel Bowles stated to the *Washington Post*, "We are not unhappy with the ratings, but even with that [3.9], it is not making a profit. Talk is not cheap to put on. . . . The majority of the advertising dollars are going to FM stations. . . . The talk format has never been profitable to us." Ironically, talk radio would prove to be a ratings giant by the early 1990s, starting with the national popularity of Rush Limbaugh.

One maddened listener addressed a letter of joy to both Les and Tom Marr:

Dear "Fat Cats" (Literally Speaking):

Thank Goodness Clean and Unpolluted Air will travel over the air waves again soon! Thank goodness daily and nightly race baiting will publicly cease and desist, however briefly. Thank goodness racial slurs, racial denigration, sarcasm . . . gross misrepresentation of facts, gross exaggerations of facts about subgroups in our society, exaggerated scare tactics about the private, sexual habits of certain people . . . will cease, however briefly!

. . . I am unconvinced that you two are Queens not *Fully Out of the Closet!* Never mind the fact that you two are married to females—there are more married queens than single ones; there are more with *deep* voices than *light* voices. It is well established that males who criticize homosexuals most often, most loudly are either jealous of them or *seek them out under the cover of darkness!* Are you really gay, Les? Tom?

. . . Let me point out to your dense mind, Les, that neither political organization (democratic or republican) is free of homosexuals.

Both you and Tom should know this. . . . Right in your station are other homosexuals, I have no doubt. There is no occupation in which homosexuals are not in membership. . . .

Thank goodness, both of you will soon be gone!!!!

On September 7, Les made a special announcement on his show that "Baltimore's *City Paper* has, in its edition just off the presses, a cover story on Your Humble and Obedient Servant. . . . The headline (—and what did I ever do to deserve such magnanimous kindness) is A WAY WITH WORDS: A CONVERSATION WITH LES KINSOLVING."

Interviewed by *City Paper*'s Clinton Macsherry, the front cover featured a silhouette of Lester's profile, his mouth agape as he howled with laughter. Les answered Macsherry's "penetrating" questions, on such topics as movies:

CP: Who are your favorite movie directors? Do you have any?

LK: Well, I like the movies, but I don't really identify with the directors that closely. I can tell a movie, in my view, when I think it's badly directed.

CP: What was the last movie you saw?

LK: I'm trying to think. Oh, yes. *Cocktail*, which I thought stunk.

CP: Uh huh. What'd you see before that?

LK: I saw *Bull Durham*, which was very amusing. However, it left me the question: how did these baseball players ever find time, I mean how do they ever have strength to play baseball if they're fornicating all night?

Politics:

Gadfly

CP: Aren't the papers just as hard on liberal candidates as they are on conservatives?

LK: No.

CP: The whole thing with Gary Hart, what did you call him, "Hartpence"?

LK: "Hotpants."

CP: Wasn't that a case where the press pretty much destroyed someone's political career?

LK: No, he did, because he's a damn fool. He's an absolute, unmitigated damn fool. I mean, did you see the picture with that bimbo sitting on his lap?

CP: In the *National Enquirer,* yeah.

LK: I mean, here is a candidate for president of the United States who has a wife and children at home, and he goes out and plays with this bimbo and takes her off on this thing called *Monkey Business*, and then *poses*.

And journalism:

CP: Reportage and editorial comment are two different things, of course.

LK: Oh, are they? Where did you learn that, dear friend? What journalism school taught you that fable?

CP: The school of hard knocks.

LK: Oh, does it?

CP: Of course.

LK: Well, now, let me tell you. Have you ever heard *Time* magazine referred as a 176-page editorial? Where do you find the editorials in *Time* other than in their [news stories]? It's very subtle.

In closing, Macsherry inquired about Lester's future plans and his opinion on the WFBR's format change:

CP: Can you give any indication what your plans are?

LK: Well, there's the Atlantic Coast Radio, which was incorporated several months ago. That's Alan Christian's firm that is in the process of buying stations right now.

CP: Do you have any yet?

LK: Not yet, but soon.

CP: Presumably [WFBR is] going to a golden oldies format. What does the changeover say about the talk-show?

LK: . . . I believe in free enterprise, but I think there's a great future in talk. Particularly the type that we do, because we really work hard. . . . It's similar to the [old] days. . . . The thing is [people] would listen to half an hour of commentary every night, sometimes three and four on the same station. And the problem was you couldn't talk to them [e.g., Edward R. Murrow, Walter Winchell, Lowell Thomas].

On Lester's final WFBR broadcast, on September 15, 1988, he announced that "Alan Christian, President and Chief Executive Officer of the recently incorporated Atlantic Coast Radio, announced today that he is in the final stages of negotiation for purchase of a Maryland radio station." He also described ACR as having "nearly 1,000 investors and capital exceeding $50 million . . . negotiations are under way for the purchase of additional radio stations, on which to syndicate the Christian and Kinsolving Shows, via satellite, as well as the acquisition of at least one television station, and the financing of a major Hollywood film production."

Besides this exciting announcement, Les bid a fond (if not temporary) farewell to his listeners, both pro and con:

> How can I ever begin to give any adequate expression of the deep gratitude that I feel, for the hundreds and hundreds of letters, cards, and phone calls, from so many of the wonderfully loyal listeners, who have so honored Uninhibited Radio by being a part of it?

> . . . Of course, there are some listeners, like Tom or Forrest, who rejoice that we have to leave the air—even for a little while. But these kinds of critics go with the territory. . . . As Baltimore's Great Sage, Mr. H.L. Mencken, used to write on the bottom of his negative fan mail, which he mailed back: DEAR SIR (OR MADAM): YOU *MAY* BE RIGHT. CORDIALLY YOURS.

> . . . Last night the Governor of Maryland called me to say farewell; and today, on *The Tom Marr Show*, both the Mayor of Baltimore and the President of the City Council, who I embraced, as she deluged me with confetti. So, I shall look forward with immense pleasure to coming back to Baltimore—and, dear listeners, to the absolutely immense pleasure of your company. This is Les Kinsolving.

Later that month, the *Evening Sun* ran the news story, "WITH-AM sold for $1.7 million," which reported that "former WFBR-AM 1300 radio talk-show personality Alan Christian has purchased WITH-AM 1230 for $1.74 million." Along with WITH, "four other radio stations in Maryland are affiliated with the Maryland State Network, which is owned by Atlantic Coast Radio . . . WAMD in Aberdeen, WANN in Annapolis, WCEI in Easton and WMET

in Gaithersburg." The transition of format change would be completed by early November, when Les would be on the air in Maryland once again.

Christian had approached Les to join his ranks, as both broadcaster
and vice-president of Maryland State Network. Les heartily accepted,
since Nick Mangione, owner of WCBM-AM 680, had made offers
only to Tom Marr and Joe Lombardo. Les would miss Tom, since
they'd become close friends, but was grateful not to work at the same
station with Joe anymore, since "he hated my guts."

Although Les the Night Owl was informed that he would broadcast during the horrifyingly early morning hours of 6 to 10 A.M., he
nonetheless rose (at the crack of dawn) to the occasion, and promoted
his upcoming show to drive-time listeners:

> If you want penetrating, in-depth, hard-hitting analysis of the
> news, as an alternative to the Big Media herd—where you can
> sound off and talk back to the whole state, then you belong
> with Uninhibited Radio, mornings Monday through Friday, on
> MSN, The Maryland State Network.
>
> Mornings are for *Stimulus, Information and Exhilaration—not
> Hypnosis!*

In October, Lester began his first broadcast on WMET with the
following intro:

> As I was saying, before I was so RUDELY interrupted. . . . As
> the inimitable Douglas MacArthur said forty-six years ago, "I
> leave—but I shall return!"

> . . . This is due primarily to the undying loyalty, support, and
> generosity of our listeners—surely the most extraordinary in the
> history of American broadcasting. It is also due to the business
> genius of my colleague and dear friend, Alan Christian, surely
> one of the most unforgettable people I have ever known.

> . . . This is Uninhibited Radio, and this is Les Kinsolving!

Gadfly

And just to prove that *The Les Kinsolving Show* was still uninhibited, one commentary that would surely awaken any sleepy morning listener was, *"Washington Post* Reports a New Presidential Campaign Issue: Bestiality—Does Dukakis Tolerate Bestiaphobia?"

Since Lester was now broadcasting for four hours daily, rather than nightly, he made a special manual "for screeners, board ops, and producers of *The Les Kinsolving Show*," which included the following requirements for each extended morning show to run smoothly and sufficiently:

- The caller should be excluded or panic-buttoned *ONLY IF* the caller is very apparently:
  A) Drunk.
  B) So totally crazed as to be incoherent.
  C) Speaks with such broken English as to be incomprehensible.
  D) A victim of coprolalia (a neurosis in which the person cannot resist using obscene words).
  E) Either obviously libelous (and, if in any doubt, allow *me* to decide) or threatening violence.
- Talk radio is a format which I believe is by far the most exciting of all.

  It demands of its people (hosts, board ops, and screeners) *absolute attention at all times* that we are on the air. I recall one screener/board op in Philadelphia that four of us who were hosts all caught reading magazines. She was also rude to callers. She is now in another line of endeavor, to which she was sent, promptly.
- As a talk-show host, I have rather strong opinions.
  Some of these opinions may curl your hair, or cause peptic ulcers in your lower intestine. I do not ever ask, or expect, you to agree with me on every issue—or even on *any.* . . . If you want to disagree, either with my commentary or with anything else I do as a broadcaster, you are welcome to do so, by asking for a meeting with me *after the show is over.*

- If you have any problem of your own that you think I might help with, try me—and as both a priest and a journalist of the old school, I will guarantee you confidence.

Along with giving directions on the usual musical selections ("Kinsolving Opener: West Point; Kinsolving Closer: West Point, and Song of the Navy"), Les listed the titles and running times of several additional numbers:

THE SUCKER SONG 1:59
BRITISH GRENADIERS 1:50
"ROACHES" 0:10
INTERNATIONALE 1:17
THE SHAME SONG 3:36
"MI NOMBRE EST DUKAKIS" 0:40
SARBANES CAMPAIGN SONG 2:13

By the year's close, Les delighted in sharing with his new audience the exhilarating experience he had one evening at 1600 Pennsylvania Avenue:

I've never seen the White House more beautiful than last night at the President's annual Christmas reception for the press. There were six giant trees in the East Room, all glistening white, four of them bordering the great portraits of George and Martha Washington which Dolley Madison saved from the old White House which was burned by British troops during the War of 1812.

Almost everyone buries hatchets and professional jealousies and resentments—although, to be sure, there were a few of the Big Media Biggies who looked at me as if I were a cockroach on the Christmas Turkey. But, I try to take this philosophically in that I count no day wasted in which I can annoy these pompous elitists who take themselves terribly seriously.

Gadfly

The food was very good, served by a corps of the most regal and gracious waiters in the land.

. . . What should I say to the President in what is probably the last time I'll ever have a chance? You have about ten seconds—unless he detains you for more talk—before those wonderfully attractive Army, Navy, Marine, Air Force or Coast Guard White House aides, or the Secret Service guide you away with marvelous professional grace.

So I said, "Mr. President I will miss being able to ask you questions at news conferences—and this is my wife who likes you a great deal—but who always votes for Democrats!"

. . . I didn't dare look back at the Berkeley Democrat, who gulped, and grinned and said "Merry Christmas Mr. President!" And who did not murder me in my bed last night—because I threatened to do this for eight years and, once I did it, she found she had to laugh.

And so did Nancy.

Trouble in Paradise

O N NEW YEAR'S Day, 1989, Lester greeted his listeners as "Dear Friends," and gave them an update on the Kinsolving Family:

... We rejoice to have [Tom and wife Lourdes] back [in] the U.S. after two years in Noriega-land, where Tom taught at night at the extension of Florida State University, and worked for the U.S. Army's Southern Command as a public relations officer.

Our oldest, Laura, has a good job as a psychiatric nurse-counselor at the intake section of a hospital near the Daryl Elliott-Laura Kinsolving home in Winchester, Massachusetts. . . .

Kathleen continues [as] a stalwart for animal rights, and has evoked national attention for her street theater and rap compositions and presentations. (In Philadelphia, on WWDB, one caller asked Les: "Are you related to Kathleen Kinsolving?")

Sylvia has expanded her piano teaching, manifold. She continues singing in two choirs, with occasional solos, as well as an official of our local election precinct. (Les arrives, and, before voting, always announces: "I am here to cancel my wife's vote!") Sylvia has also been a frequent guest on Uninhibited Radio, where she is known as "The B.D." (The Berkeley Democrat).

Les has to get up before dawn to do morning drive. But he has learned that therein is a whole new world. So is the TV project, the pilot for a weekly series called "Outrage!" . . . Hence, with expanding radio audiences and possible TV, 1989 looks to be exciting.

Just days after this cheerful celebration of the new year, Les got down to business, and zeroed in on such characters as Idi Amin, former Ugandan dictator:

Idi Amin, all 300 syphilitic pounds of him, tried last week to enter Zaire on a false passport. This crazed cannibal who murdered an estimated one quarter of a million Ugandans during his eight-year reign of terror was also the monster who held a plane-load of civilians hostage at the airport in Entebbe. Amin, before he was deposed by Ugandan rebels aided by Tanzanians, was elected and publicly applauded by the Organization of African Unity.

This was at a time when he made periodic visits to a Kampala cold storage vault where he had preserved, on the end of spears, the heads of the most prominent of his victims. He visited this macabre setting in order to lecture the heads.

And Howard Stern, "of the Lavatory Wall School of Broadcasting": a full-page ad in the Washington Weekend section of the *Washington Times* announces with pride that radio station WJFK is now featuring—and this is a quote: "HOWARD STERN ALL MORNING" followed by "THE BEST OF ROCK AND ROLL ALL DAY."

Imagine having Howard all morning followed by more noise—(*possibly* less scatological—but *not* assuredly)—MORE RHYTHMIC NOISE ALL DAY!

Les also took the President to task, in "The Last Two Months of Ronald Reagan's Presidency: A Disaster."

Ronald Reagan, eclipsed by the understandably greater public interest in the president-elect, has done a number of horrendous things. He failed to pardon Colonel Oliver North [and he] also failed to repudiate his daughter, Big Mo, when she announced that Colonel North ought to be shot.

President Reagan also pulled the rug from under forty of his fellow Republicans in the House. They are co-sponsoring a bill to stop that disgraceful procedure of automatic pay raises without a vote. Mr. Reagan now has endorsed American history's most massive Congressional pay raise, when he could have said: "I will favor a pay hike for Congress only *after* they balance the budget."

. . . Look at the enormous Congressional fringe benefits and wonder why on earth Reagan, the alleged apostle of thrift, supported this huge, voteless pay grab. . . . In addition to his snuggling up to what he once admitted was the Evil Empire, Mr. Reagan failed miserably to clean out that Augean Stable called the State Department.

. . . Former White House Chief of Staff Donald Regan . . . said he hoped the president-elect "has learned from Reagan's shortcomings—his baffling reluctance to give orders, or even guidance, to his close subordinates, and the tendency to permit some of his advisors to manage the presidency for effect, rather than for results."

On February 7, the *Washington Post*'s "On the Dial" included the heading, "Maryland Talk Network Grows."

The four-month-old Maryland State Network Inc. has paid $1.74 million for 1,000-watt WITH-AM (1230) in Baltimore and converted its format from nostalgia a week ago. The first caller to *The Les Kinsolving Show* told the often cantankerous host that his show stank. The second caller was Maryland Gov. William Donald Schaefer, who welcomed Kinsolving and fellow talkers.

The network . . . has been broadcasting from the Broadcast Institute of Maryland, a former mortuary in Baltimore. According to Kinsolving, the studio used to be an embalming room. When asked about that yesterday, network program director Dale Andrews said, "I wish Lester would keep his mouth shut about that."

By February 22, Les sent a gracious invitation to Governor Schaefer, since Maryland State Network was now moving out of the mortuary and back into WFBR's former headquarters in downtown Baltimore.

We would be most honored if you and Mrs. Hilda Mae Snoops could be with us on Saturday afternoon April 1, 1989, at the dedication of our new corporate offices, broadcasting studios and art gallery. The ceremony outside will be brief and will involve Mrs. Snoops breaking a breakaway bottle on our new front door sign at the building 13 East 20th St. . . . Following this, we would appreciate your cutting the traditional ribbon and leading us all up the stairs and into the facilities. . . .

From a news standpoint, this may be the first time in American broadcast history that a radio personality who was fired (on September 16th, 1988) will return to reoccupy the same premises. . . .

You have been a boon to economic development and employment in Maryland. And we will always remember your signal kindness in telephoning us on the first morning we began to broadcast on our Baltimore Affiliate. . . .

Two days earlier, Governor Schaefer held a press conference, where one reporter brought up the issue of speeding, since the Maryland speed limit was 55 mph:

JENSEN: A couple of times [your] speedometer crept up to around 65 or 70. I recall your taking a pledge about the speed limit before. . . .

GOVERNOR: You know, there was a man by the name of Les Kinsolving who most of the time was following me in my car. . . . I was so harassed by people pulling up beside me and pointing to the speedometer. . . . Our policemen, and they're superb guys, really are fine men, and every once in a while they get a little ambitious and they take me at 56 miles an hour. I am not going to increase the speed limit. . . . The statistics do show in those states where they did raise the speed limits, accidents went up 19 percent versus 12 percent or something like that. . . .

Inspired to assist in Maryland's enforcement of the law, Les sent a letter to Judge Scott Davis of the District Court of Maryland on March 10:

Dear Judge Davis:

As you may have noted from media reports, the Governor of Maryland's bus, while traveling on Route 13 near Salisbury last month, was clocked by observant reporters as speeding—at a rate of 65 to 70 miles per hour.

Since no one was willing to issue a citation to Governor Schaefer (who was obviously in charge of, and therefore responsible for, the unlawful conduct of his vehicle), I am enclosing a check for $45.

This is a contribution from me and from News Director Jeff Blumm of our affiliate, WANN Annapolis/Baltimore. We hope, in the last-century tradition of whipping boys, to touch our Governor's conscience, so that he will either help change this unrealistic 55-mile-an-hour speed limit (which nearly all

Gadfly

Marylanders violate) or else that he will observe the law, instead of repeatedly violating it.

We are both very fond of Maryland's wonderfully entertaining and diligent Governor. But he is, after all, mortal.

Les not only sent a copy of his letter to Governor Schaefer, but also to Attorney General Joe Curran. This may have prompted the embattled governor's stunt during the MSN dedication ceremony, as reported by the *Washington Post* on April 4:

There was some foolishness in Baltimore as Maryland Gov. William Donald Schaefer helped dedicate the Maryland State Network's new studios on Saturday. Schaefer kicked off the ceremony by bopping the network's irascible talk host Les Kinsolving on the head with a breakaway champagne bottle. . . .

Les told The Rest of the Story of the dedication in his broadcast, "Schaefer Dedicates Headquarters for Two Maryland Corporations; Also Dedicates Talk-show Host's Head; The News That Baltimore Big Media Refused to Report to You."

A Baltimore Police cruiser, with lights flashing and siren screaming, was to arrive and discharge me, in blazing blazer, wearing red plastic handcuffs, with a huge lapel button: "SPEED LIMIT 65."

Escorted by assistants Tina Morris and Lisa Knoll, Les climbed the stairs in handcuffs, where Governor Schaefer, "with eyes flashing and nostrils flaring," waited for him.

"KNEEL!" I remember hearing, in the midst of all this crowded hilarity. So I knelt. And I was, as you might say, "knighted" . . . after a fashion. Alan Christian handed the Governor one of two special stage prop breakaway bottles, this one marked with a special

label: "SCHAEFER'S 86.7 PROOF, PINCH-MEDIA, OLD MARY-
LAND FIREWATER . . . BY APPOINTMENT TO HIS EXCELLENCY
THE GOVERNOR. . . ."

Thrilled to receive such a prestigious honor by the governor of
Maryland, Les was also deeply touched by an anonymous fan's poem,
which was sent shortly after he was anointed into "knighthood":

"A TRIBUTE TO LES"

You are our conscience, our heart, our voice.
For those of us, who do not by choice,
Speak our opinion on paper, or air.
You give us hope, when we despair.

You give your opinions and your personal views.
We're grateful for a different start to the news.

We're stronger and wiser because of you.
So please know, you're among the chosen few,
Who are honest and present another side to the news.

Stay with us Les, leave us never.

But, under advice from his lawyer, Les would resign from Maryland
State Network, after stories ran in the *Baltimore Sun* and the *Washington
Post* in early November: "Talk Show Hosts Ordered to Halt Securities
Sale," and "Radio Host Accused of Violating Md. Securities Law."

Outspoken radio talk-show host Lester Kinsolving and three
other people have been accused of violating Maryland securities laws in a complex broadcast investment deal that involves
a Panamanian bank suspected by U.S. authorities of launder-
ing drug money.

Gadfly

. . . In documents filed in the Circuit Court for Baltimore City yesterday, state securities commissioner Ellyn L. Brown said the group had broken the law by selling securities without registering with state authorities and failing to make adequate disclosures about the deal.

[Kinsolving] told listeners that his legal counsel had advised him not to comment on the charges of securities law violations. But he told one caller that "the suggestion that I would ever get involved with drug money is an absolute lie." He accused the *Baltimore Sun*, which reported the allegations yesterday, of "desperation to smear."

A smear was evident, just by the photographs of Alan Christian and Les in the *Sun*'s report. While Alan's was fairly benign, Lester's resembled a rabid bedlamite, complete with arched eyebrows, bulging eyes, and bobbing tongue. They ran the same unsavory photograph a week later, in their follow-up story, "Kinsolving Broadcasts Resignation: Talk Show Host Cites 'My Respect for Law'":

Les Kinsolving—the voice of "uninhibited radio," the self-described milker of sacred cows—resigned on the air yesterday, attempting to put some distance between himself and the troubles of his employer, Atlantic Coast Radio Inc.

. . . Mr. Kinsolving's on-the-air resignation provided the first comment by anyone associated with the company since its difficulties arose. He said he wanted to "underline" that he was not part of the disputed sale of securities or in any other aspect of the company's management.

. . . "I was never in on any of the financing or fund-raising," he said. He said he had never seen any of the company's records—not so much as a checkbook, he said. He said he did not try to sell investments in the company on the air. . . . He said he knew the company was in serious trouble by August, the last month in which he got a paycheck. There was considerable budget-cutting at the station, he said.

After Lester's announcement that evening, "regular call-in fans" lit up the callboard:

CHET THE JET: Your program and its listeners are like a church!

KINSOLVING: You know, I am a clergyman.

SUSIE: How dare you quit! I've got a lot of sadness in my life without this.

KINSOLVING: There's a lot I simply can't explain. I would never do this unless I honestly felt I had to do it.

RICHARD: Like they say in the song, you might've been a headache but you never were a bore.

RUTH: You're like a breath of fresh air in this corrupted state we live in. I am absolutely devastated. When you get back on the air, a reunion should be held at the Belvedere Hotel, where we can all sort of meet again.

KINSOLVING: It would be a great joy.

MARY: I am so terrified if they can quell your voice. What is happening to our freedoms?

The *Sun* concluded its report with, "Then, in a specially prepared farewell message, he recalled the words of his father: 'Do out your duty only where honor lights the path. Then there can be no real failure.' The message was followed by the strains of 'Auld Lang Syne,' played by a marching band."

While many fans of Lester rallied to his cause and hoped for a speedy return, two other listeners made their opinions known by mail:

Gadfly

Retching Rev,

The artical in the "Sunpapers" revealing the scam operation of you and fellow rogue A.C. was very enlightening. You and A.C. should be shipped out of town on the poo poo choo choo, the pair of you would blend in very nicely. Happy days at the "country club."

Friend, L. Feinroth

Kinsolving: You were rude and unfair to me. "What thou sowest thou reapest."

Larry Ottenstein

By November 30, the *Sun* and the *Post* again ran subsequent stories, in "Judge Dismisses Charges Against Talk Show Host," and "Judge Withdraws Charges Against Kinsolving."

A Maryland judge withdrew charges of securities law violations against radio talk-show host Lester Kinsolving after prosecutors asked that the case against him be dropped.

... Circuit Court Judge Joseph H.H. Kaplan formally dismissed the charges Wednesday evening. He also removed Kinsolving from a freeze on assets applied last month and an injunction intended to halt the company's securities sales activities.

"I feel enormously relieved," Kinsolving said yesterday. Charges were filed against Alan Christian, identified by prosecutors as president of the company, and two other people who prosecutors say were officers. All three appeared in court yesterday morning for a hearing before Kaplan.

It would be a long, tough five months of unemployment for Lester, but his confidence was renewed when he made an appearance at Cross Street Market in February 1990, for "Washington's Birthday Special," as promoted in the *Baltimore Enterprise*, which also carried Lester's column, "Uninhibited Opinions." A large ad adorned with President Washington and President Lincoln read:

South Baltimore Business Association Presents:
How Would You Like to Get Nose to Nose With
Les Kinsolving, Formerly of WITH & WFBR
You've Heard Him, Read Him—
Now Come and Meet Him
This Saturday, Feb. 17th
From 12 Noon Til 2:30 P.M.

Accompanied by the Berkeley Democrat, a photo bore the following caption: "Mr. Kinsolving, noted radio talk-show host and syndicated columnist, spent several hours meeting the people of South Baltimore. He was overwhelmed by the reception and the many readers of his column in the Enterprise, who told him "get back on the radio soon, we miss you."

Two months later, Les was approached by Washington, D.C.'s station, WPGC-AM Business Radio 1580, where he would return to broadcasting commentary during morning and afternoon drive time. Not to be outdone by their Baltimore counterpart's 1988 interview of Les, the *Washington City Paper* provided a great promotional, in "Lester's Last Mission":

"Do you know the origin of gadfly?" demands Lester Kinsolving, thrusting his beefy head and torso across the dining table. "It's divine. The gadfly first appeared at the behest of Hera, queen of the [Greek] gods, whose husband was Zeus—who was as oversexed as a number of people I could name—and who was in the habit of coming down to Earth to seduce. He seduced one particularly delectable young maiden, and when he suddenly found out Hera was getting wind of this, he turned [the maiden] into a cow.

"Hera sent a gadfly to punish the cow and drove the cow all the way out of Greece, across the Hellespont, and finally down into Egypt, where the cow was finally alleviated. Yes, Bradlee called me a gadfly journalist . . . and I'm very honored."

. . . Now, in what might prove to be his last performance in Washington, Kinsolving has signed on as a commentator with all-business news WPGC-AM (1580), a daytime-only radio station with ratings so low the general manager admits he has nothing to lose by letting this quixotic Episcopal priest use it to tilt at personal political windmills.

"We're the underdog and we're looking to get noticed," explains general manager Ben Hill. "We get a lot of requests for copies [of Kinsolving's] commentaries. Whether they want them for their lawyers so they can sue me, I don't know."

. . . Last year, after an ill-fated run as a radio talk host with the Baltimore-based Maryland State Network, Kinsolving found himself out of work for the first time since coming to Washington. He was on the streets for five months before he landed the WPGC gig, which he says he enjoys immensely.

But at the same time, Kinsolving makes it clear he wants to get back into talk radio, and to do that, he will almost certainly have to leave Washington, something he seems prepared to do. Kinsolving refuses to judge what, if anything, he has accomplished during his 17 years as a gadfly Washington journalist. "That," he says thoughtfully, "is for God to decide."

Reporter Randall Bloomquist's words were quite prophetic, for, after six months of commentary for WPGC, a grateful Lester was welcomed back to Maryland talk radio in October 1990. His fans cheered and rejoiced at his long-awaited return, where he would find a permanent home at WCBM, with dear and trusted friend Tom Marr. He has been happily broadcasting there ever since.

"Mississippi's Ready!"

S INCE HIS DAYS as a youth, Lester continued to cultivate his deep love of history, and was now an expert on the Civil War, after reading nearly 100 books on the subject. The "most moving"—in fact, the only historical novel "that ever made me weep"—was *The Killer Angels,* a story of the Battle of Gettysburg which won the Pulitzer Prize for Fiction in 1975. Shortly after he began over at WWDB in 1984, Les read that the book would soon be turned into a film. Completely thrilled, he got in touch with its author, Michael Shaara. After listening to Les's many praises, Shaara put him in touch with director Ronald F. Maxwell, who was preparing to shoot *The Killer Angels* during the summer of 1984.

For his feature story, "New Movie on Gettysburg: In Search of an Ancestor," Les interviewed Ron Maxwell in New York:

> Maxwell treats this production as if it is almost sacramental, as he should. For this will be the first time in history that Pickett's charge will be filmed, among other combat scenes. I knew he was a producer-director who is qualified to create this epochal

remembrance when I happened to mention that my father's middle name was Barksdale, and that Jonathan Barksdale of Charlottesville was my great-great-great-grandfather—and Gen. Barksdale's uncle. . . . Maxwell promptly walked into a closet and returned with an eight-by-ten photograph of Gen. Barksdale. "You look like him," he noted—and then we discussed the possibility of my saying one line, shrieking the Rebel Yell, and charging into the smoke of a hundred Union guns.

For Les, the opportunity to play his ancestor, who fought and died so bravely in this battle, was thrilling beyond belief. "It is also a single honor, even for one minute, to portray an exceptionally colorful and courageous cousin." Besides this, Les agreed to help behind the scenes, as discussed in one of Maxwell's memos:

> I have retained Lester Kinsolving as special consultant. He will among other things be coordinating procurement of extras and procurement of horses, as well as engaging in promotion and research for the film. Any courtesies and assistance rendered him will be very much appreciated.

Although filming was scheduled to begin shortly after the interview, financing fell through, a typical predicament when embarking on a Hollywood movie project. In spite of the situation, Les scouted locations and soldiers by attending Civil War reenactments from West Point to North Carolina. Eight years later, financing came through from Ted Turner, and *The Killer Angels* would open in theatres in November 1993, but with a new title: *Gettysburg.*

Les was overjoyed to hear that the battle scenes would be filmed right at Gettysburg, only seventy-five miles from his home in Virginia. Having never been on a major movie set before, he felt a bit intimidated by the seasoned performers and professional crew who surrounded him. However, it wasn't long before he was respected and welcomed by the overall congeniality of everyone involved. On his first day of shooting, Lester watched as General Robert E. Lee, played by Martin Sheen, rode his horse Traveler down a hill with hundreds of troops. "It was exhilarating, to say the least," Les recalls, "to see history come alive like this."

Since Les was slated to act in a scene opposite Martin Sheen, they engaged in conversation at times. Although he and Sheen didn't agree on many political issues, Les found the revered actor to be warm, friendly, and always willing to participate in a lively discussion during a short filming break. Tom Berenger, who played Lieutenant-General James Longstreet, was also very talkative, but only off the set. During filming he kept to himself, as he felt it necessary to focus solely on his role. To his utter delight, Les found a fellow needler in Richard Jordan, who played Brigadier-General Lewis A. Armistead. They would argue incessantly, but always cordially. Lester's son Tom, who was assisting the crew and filling in as an extra, stood by during one of their friendly bickerings, which eventually left Jordan speechless. He then exclaimed to Tom, "Your father just doesn't STOP!!"

For the Confederate scenes, filming would take about a month during the summer of 1992, starting at 6 A.M. and finishing around 8 P.M. every night. The making of a movie is generally a grueling experience, so producers make certain that cast and crew are happy and well fed. "The food was excellent," Les remembers, "they served us from this huge trailer after we'd stand in a long line. The caterers did a magnificent job and were always happy to accommodate."

During one lunch, Lester found himself in the company of Ken Burns, director-writer-producer of the multi-award-winning 1990 documentary *The Civil War*. Ken had agreed to play a Confederate officer that day, and when word got around, he was soon encircled by awe-inspired extras. They flocked around his table, graciously thanking him for his inestimable contribution to history. "Ken couldn't have been more kind; he smiled and thanked everyone, and was a joy to have lunch with."

Since Les had engaged in recruiting extras for the film, he was familiar with Civil War reenactments and those who participated in them. Near the set, 1,000 volunteer re-enactors had camped out, since they were completely devoted to the cause. "Occasionally you'd find a real fanatic—they were so into it that they blotted out every-thing else, and just lived in the fantasy that the Civil War was still going on!" During one break in shooting Pickett's charge, Les was assigned to be a Confederate color sergeant, along with his role as General Barksdale. As he and three other extras were sitting down, a Confederate "officer" marched over and yelled, "ON YOUR FEET!!" Les looked at him and stated, "On the set you can give orders, but now you can't!" The infuriated "officer" ran off to the assistant direc-tor in charge of extras, and brought him over to reprimand the "insubordinates." When the assistant director corrected the "officer," he shut his mouth, and "slunk away. . . . Every re-enactor I dealt with was fine, except for the trouble I had with this one guy, who just went too far."

One soldier not among the "fanatics" was a popular personality, and very much liked on the set. It was strange that he didn't show up for shooting one day, as he was completely dedicated to playing his small part in the film. They soon discovered that, the night before, he had died in his sleep from a heart attack. Later that day, they held a special memorial service for him on the set. "Everyone was moved by the ser-vice, but very saddened by this tragedy. . . . He was a dear man."

Besides Sheen, Berenger, and Jordan, Les very much enjoyed the company of Stephen Lang, who portrayed Major-General George E. Pickett. He also admired the actor's willingness to submerge himself into his role, as well as his diligence in conducting intensive research on Pickett. While Les was waiting to be fitted for his color sergeant costume one morning, Lang came up to say hello, and the two had a jovial talk. When Les mentioned a somewhat obscure fact about Gen-eral Pickett, Lang peered into his eyes very seriously. He then told Lester, "I didn't know that!" Les was stunned: "I couldn't believe it!"

The filming of Pickett's Charge would take approximately six days on the Gettysburg battleground, in the sweltering August heat. Les proudly carried the Confederate flag as part of Garnett's Brigade of Virginians, among thousands of other extras. As he marched onto the field, the band began playing "Dixie" and Johnny Rebs every-where screamed the Rebel Yell. Sylvia, the Berkeley Democrat, was on hand to watch the filming, and later told a reporter, "With the 5,000 re-enactors charging and the cannons exploding, it was the most spectacular thing I've ever seen."

What Sylvia wasn't prepared for was her husband's dizzying enthusiasm, which led to a broken rib, along with being kicked in the head by "two damn Yankees, who later fled out of sight." As Les the color sergeant and 300 others ran over a stone wall, he was confronted by the Union soldiers, who tried to grab his flag. He was unwilling to surrender the colors and ended up being pummeled, after the Yankees broke the flagpole in two. As Lester lay there in pain from the broken rib, two first-aid people appeared and hoisted him up on a stretcher and into an ambulance. They had also taken over eighty-five extras away who were suffering from heat prostration and exhaustion. At the hospital, Les was "'strapped up" so he could return to filming. "I've never been so moved. I made it for the next take. . . . If I'd broken an arm, I would've told the doctor to give me a temporary cast [so I could] continue on in Pickett's Charge— that was how terribly meaningful the film was to me."

For General Barksdale's scene, Les appeared with General Lee, General Longstreet, and other Confederate officers, at a large table where they were actively drawing up plans for their battle campaign. As Les stood stoically among the two master thespians, director Ron Maxwell yelled "CUT!" and moved on to setting up the next shot. Lester hadn't seen a line written for him anywhere in the script, so he assumed any possibility of dialogue was futile at this point. It didn't matter; he was so deeply grateful to be given the chance to portray his distant but silent cousin from Mississippi. It was right then that Ron said, "Les, Martin is going to approach you and say, "General Barksdale, is Mississippi ready?" and you respond with, "Mississippi's ready!" The thrill was incomprehensible—and not only that, it was a golden opportunity to join the Screen Actors Guild, and receive a SAG card. When Ron yelled "ACTION!" and Martin Sheen gave him his cue, Les recollected the momentous occasion by rejoicing, "And Mississippi had never been SO READY!!"

Besides broadcasting on the making of *Gettysburg* every night on

WCBM, Les also went on a promotional tour for the film, He would lecture around the East Coast and South, including the Sons of the American Revolution in Maryland, the riverboat *Mississippi Queen*, and downtown Jackson, Mississippi, where he stood in 96 degree heat in his heavy wool costume. As reported in Jackson's *Clarion-Ledger*: "Kinsolving's flushed, if eager, appearance made one wonder if perhaps his similarly uniformed ancestor had not perished of a nineteenth-century heat wave. But no; it was Yankee bullets that did Barksdale in . . . on the famous field of battle in southern Pennsylvania."

The *Washington Times* plugged the tour as well, as part of their "Inside the Beltway" section:

LESTER'S CHARGE

Where won't Lester Kinsolving turn up next? Tomorrow he'll be at Atrium, the farmhouse where Gen. George Meade watched Pickett's charge at Gettysburg, playing the parts of Confederate Gens. George Pickett and Lewis Armistead in a radio re-enactment of "Thirty Minutes That Changed the World."

Mitch Tullai, chairman of the history department and head football coach at St. Paul's School in Baltimore, will play Gen. Meade and President Lincoln. The three-hour program on WCBM radio in Baltimore will conclude with a reenactment of the Battle of Bunker Hill and a recitation of the Declaration.

Even though it was over four hours long, *Gettysburg* received rave reviews nationwide, from notable film critic Leonard Maltin ("Magnificent awe-inspiring re-creation of the Civil War's most famous battle") to ABC Radio Network ("4 Stars: A towering achievement! *Gettysburg* explodes on the screen in all its horror and heroism"). After playing theaters across the country in the fall of 1993, it aired on Ted Turner's TNT the subsequent year, and attracted, at that time, the biggest TV audience in cable history.

Although Les was ecstatic about the film's great success, he was crushed to hear that his fellow needler, Richard Jordan, had died in August 1993, three months before *Gettysburg*'s premiere that fall. The role of General Armistead would be Richard's last, although he had begun filming *The Fugitive* before he became ill with a brain tumor. Ironically, Armistead would die too, on the Gettysburg battlefield. Just before he commanded his troops to march forward, including the brigade for which Lester held the Confederate flag so high, Armistead recited the final words of Jesus, in a quiet prayer: "Into Thy hands, I commend my spirit."

In 1996, *Gods and Generals* was published, written by Shaara's son Jeff, after Michael died of a heart attack in 1988. Jeff would then write a third novel in the Civil War trilogy, *The Last Full Measure*, in 1998. Because of the popularity of *Gettysburg*, Ted Turner would finance the making of *Gods and Generals* as a prequel, where all actors returned to their major and supporting roles, except for General Lee, who would be played by Robert Duvall, and Stephen Lang, who would play Lieutenant-General Thomas Jonathan "Stonewall" Jackson. Tom Berenger's General Longstreet was a much smaller part and belonged this time to actor Bruce Boxleitner.

Unlike *Gettysburg*, the film would focus on four major Confederate victories in battle: Manassas, Fredericksburg, Chancellorsville, and Antietam (which never made the final cut). As General Barksdale, Les would have a key scene in the Battle of Fredericksburg, as Commander of Barksdale's Brigade, in the Army of Northern Virginia. The battle, waged during December 1862, would be filmed 139 years later in December 2001. Trent Lott, the senator from Mississippi who suggested the phrase "Once a Week, But Never Weakly" in 1978 for *Washington Weekly*, was supposed to play alongside Les, as a Confederate captain and aide-de-camp. The deal fell through, however, and, after a suggestion from Les, Senator Lott was replaced with Les's son Tom, who had worked previously on *Gettysburg*. After they fitted Tom with a handsome uniform, cap, overcoat, and gloves, Les proudly told his daughters, "You should see your brother, he looks just like Clark Gable!"

The original scene called for Les to run up a hill and into a house, where he would then plunge facedown into a basement. This stunt sounded alarming for a seventy-four-year-old man to perform, but Les assured his family that the crew would provide some sort of mattress for him to fall on. To everyone's relief, the scene was changed to one where Les and Tom would stand at a look-out point, behind a wall of defense. Unlike the fourteen-hour days of filming the Gettysburg battle, this scene would be completed in four hours.

Second Unit Director William Wages gave Les ample suggestions on just how to bring the binoculars up to his face as the cameraman slowly zoomed into Barksdale and his captain. After a follow-up point-of-view shot in which Barksdale saw the Yankees approaching quickly, Les then dramatically threw down his binoculars, picked up his sword, and in the greatest roar he could muster, bellowed, "PICK YOUR TARGETS, BOYS—FIRE!!!" The guns sounded off, and the Yankees were defeated. "We had fun," Les happily recalls, "Wages seemed amused by me, and he gave very good directions which were easy to follow. I yelled the line as best I could, and it seemed to please him."

Besides reprising his role, Les was happy to provide his services as clergyman, and performed a wedding for a re-enactor, who planned to have the marriage ceremony on the Battlefield of Antietam. Les was deeply touched that during the middle of the wedding, many members of the cast and crew came and sat down. "Everyone was very pleasant, and it was a great joy to work with Stephen Lang again, and to meet the actress who played Jackson's wife, Kali Rocha. She was very sweet." He also got along very well with Robert Duvall, who, when Les interviewed him, discovered they were both related to Robert E. Lee, thus making them distant cousins.

Unlike *Gettysburg's* success, *Gods and Generals* opened to mixed reviews in February 2003, and did not fare well at the box office. It was criticized by many for being sympathetic to the South, in the tradition of *Gone with the Wind*, and because the characters appeared stilted and far too formal. "That was ridiculous," Les stated bitterly, "that's the way the people acted in those days!" Undeterred by the unfair treatment of these cinematic quibblers, Les presented his tenth annual "Leaders at Gettysburg" on July 3rd at Farnsworth House Inn located near the battlefield, and promoted the event on a flyer which included a photo of Les leaning on a cannon in full Confederate regalia:

> WCBM will broadcast to six states: Cast of ten, music and sound effects . . . Sons of Confederate Veterans with Sons of Union Veterans; Cast members of the movies *Gettysburg* and *Gods & Generals* . . . Relatives of Generals Trimble and Barksdale.

Les also included info for the fourth of July, where he would participate in four different parades:

> Look for WCBM's most colorful White House correspondent and evening host as he greets people throughout Maryland in four community parades in Dundalk, Towson, Catonsville and Annapolis.

Looking back, Les will forever be "deeply honored" for being a part of these two films on the Civil War, an event in American history which he felt so impassioned about, ever since he wrote his essay "The Hero of the Oak Tree Guards" at Episcopal High School, which he dedicated to General Barksdale. "It was an enormously moving experience . . . somewhat like celebrating communion as a priest." It truly was "a higher calling."

In the summer of 2003, *Gods and Generals* was released on home video, where it immediately shot to the #1 selling DVD in America. To this day, it continues, along with *Gettysburg*, as a perennial DVD favorite.

"I'll Never Retire"

A S THE TWENTY-FIRST century approached, seventy-two-year-
old Les found himself riding on a new wave of success. Having completed ten marvelous years at WCBM, he was offered the
position of White House Correspondent for Talk Radio Network
in 2000 and WorldNetDaily.com in 2002. He was also voted one
of the top 100 talk-show hosts by *Talkers* magazine, where Editor
Michael Harrison stated, "Les' daring demeanor makes him dangerous to his foes and unpredictable to his audience, and that is
what great radio is about. He is absolutely fearless. The Grand
Inquisitor of political talk radio, [Les is] its favorite troublemaker
and preeminent provocateur."

"I'll never retire," Les asserted on many occasions. "I'd rather
die . . . at the microphone, making that my final broadcast to my
beloved Baltimore audience." Although Lester's political commentaries kept WCBM's ratings high on the chart, he felt a duty to
return to his role as worker-priest, in a special broadcast on September 11, 2002, the first anniversary of the worst terrorist attack
in American history:

"Where Was God on September 11th, 2001?"

Neither the *New York Times* nor the *Washington Post* are religious newspapers. But the *Times*, in reviewing this week's Public Broadcasting production, called *Faith and Doubt at Ground Zero*, opened its review with a question that its religion writer Peter Steinfels repeats: "Where was God on September 11?"

He repeats this question no less than *eight times*, . . . and he contends: "for those who want to believe that God is a living reality in their daily existence, ignoring this question would display an almost blasphemous indifference. . . . Where was God on Sept. 11? It is an inevitable, a necessary and a valuable question. . . . Not a few voices have answered that God was right in the midst of the horror, especially in the heroism and self-sacrifice."

So, on this day of remembrance of the mass murder of nearly three thousand of our fellow Americans—two of whom, a young couple, faced with being burned alive or jumping, held hands together as they went down—which brought so many of us to tears.

Years before this mass murder, there was a parish priest in New York who concluded a Sunday service on Memorial Day. He had finished greeting the congregation outdoors, and had gone to his office—when there was a knock on the door. He said "Come in" and there entered a man about fifty years old, who stood silent and facing him saying nothing—but with eyes that were both piercing and lined with tears.

"What can I do for you, my friend?" asked the priest. And after silence this man finally answered: "You can tell me where was God when my son died in Korea?" And this priest

Gadfly

replied with a near-silence, with compassion and defense of his Christian faith: "Sir: God was in the same place he was when his own son died."

. . . I hope so very much that those of you in this wonderful audience to whom I am so privileged to broadcast, who are atheists or agnostics, will give me—out of the tradition of tolerating free speech—a fair chance, in listening—for what may help the faithful who are hurting, as well as the doubters—and even present to the deniers some measure of reasoned and reasonable conclusions.

. . . Why in this world, in this vale of soul-making that I believe it is—why is there so much good, and love, and beauty and courage and good humor—along with the suffering? . . . There is no full and satisfying religious or philosophical answer to the problem of pain—of why a good and all-powerful God allows suffering.

. . . But time and again through history, my religion has taught millions of people how to behave in the presence of pain—with a courage and an unconquerable faith that for millions has turned death into life, sickness into health, and sorrow into joy. . . .

Les then concluded with a description of another attack on American soil, and how the brave people of Baltimore fought the British in 1812:

When, after this terrible bombing of Fort McHenry, a Maryland lawyer who was held on a British prison ship, saw, at dawn, the raising of the same Star-Spangled Banner that has been raised by millions of people all over the United States today, he wrote this:

O thus be it ever when free men shall stand
Between their loved homes, and the war's desolation
Vast with victory and peace, may the heavy-rescued land

Praise the power that hath made, and preserved us a nation!
Then conquer we must, when our cause it is just;
And this be our motto, "In God is our Trust"
And the Star-Spangled Banner in triumph shall wave
O'er the land of the free, and the home of the brave!

On November 18, 2003, Les would remember another American mass murder, on the twenty-fifth anniversary of the Jonestown Massacre in Guyana:

News of American history's worst mass killing of American citizens, besides 9/11, first reached me twenty-five years ago, in a radio news report. Not long after news of this horror, I received a phone call from the FBI informing me of their discovery that I was number two on the "hit list" of the Disciples of Christ Christian Church's pastor of the Peoples Temple, the Rev. Jim Jones.

This ordained monster, who caused the slaughter of his mostly mesmerized disciples in Guyana, could so easily have been stopped before they were killed. Their death is an eternal moral indictment of both the *San Francisco Examiner* and the *San Francisco Chronicle*, as well as the dozens of other metropolitan dailies and other media to whom I pleaded to send their own reporter to investigate, if they had any doubts about the evidence I mailed them.

. . . Of these dozens to whom I pleaded, not one of them followed up. And only one of them apologized as the Guyana death toll came in. He was, at that time, Jack Anderson's assistant. Today, he is Fox News Anchorman Brit Hume.

In my office, I have a framed citation, a tribute to one of the bravest women I have ever known, named Brenda Ganatos, who, with fifteen other residents of Ukiah, California, were, at the risk of their lives, my sources while the Peoples Temple was located in that Northern California town.

. . . I also have a framed copy of Methodist District Superintendent John V. Moore of Berkeley's letter of April 21st, 1975, in which he writes: "I have known the Rev. Jim Jones and the work of the Peoples Temple for a number of years. I have been impressed with the quality of community life of the Church and of their service to the communities in which they reside."

I have another letter from this endorser of Jim Jones, dated Aug. 2, 1975—seventy-two days later—in which Moore threatens to sue me. He has never done so, I suspect, because he knows I would countersue with abundant evidence.

I wish I could be present at the twenty-fifth annual memorial service for those more than 900 victims of Jim Jones. I hope that your allowing my daughter, Kathleen, to relate my message, and that it will help the media and others to avoid any defense of Jones and his supporters—and avoid ever again the media cover-up which allowed this mass murder.

Although Les regretted not being able to read his remembrance at the memorial held at Evergreen Cemetery in Oakland, California, that year, he would make a trip to the West Coast on a family vacation in December 2004, to visit his eldest daughter Laura, now working at Atascadero State Hospital, and Kathleen, who had presented Les and Sylvia with their grandson, Spencer, the previous April in Santa Rosa, California. After he agreed to return home without the Berkeley Democrat, who wanted to visit with Spencer for one more week, Les flew back after New Year's Day, 2005, and prepared for his return to the Baltimore airwaves.

On Monday, January 3rd, just hours before his nightly WCBM broadcast at home, Les felt a sharp pain in his chest and found it terribly difficult to breathe. He quickly realized it was a heart attack and immediately called 911, since no one was there to come to his aid. He stumbled downstairs and lay near the front door, in preparation for the medic alert team who would soon arrive, and rush him to the nearest hospital.

After receiving an anticoagulant at a local emergency room, Les was moved to the Heart Center at Fairfax Hospital, a state-of-the-art facility in Northern Virginia. Sylvia flew home early and stayed by his side, before he was informed by the on-staff heart specialist that he would have to undergo a triple bypass operation as soon as possible. Les agreed to the procedure, and as they wheeled him into the operating room, he recited a prayer, as General Armistead had done in *Gettysburg* before marching into battle: "Into Thy hands, I commend my spirit."

Cards, letters, and flowers poured in from everywhere, including a large fruit basket from fellow talk-show host and Fox News commentator Sean Hannity, and heartfelt e-mail responses from Hannity's Fox co-host, Alan Colmes, to daughter Kathleen, who was keeping Alan updated on the hour. Talk-show host Brian Maloney posted this January 11th message on his website, "The Radio Equalizer":

The oddest irony for me on Monday was that as the Rathergate report was being released to public and heads were rolling at CBS, the person who was responsible for propelling my CBS story into national coverage last September was undergoing triple bypass surgery after having a heart attack.

Legendary White House correspondent and radio talk-show host Les Kinsolving is who I'm talking about. They don't make reporters like this anymore, a man who takes nothing at face value, always questioning, always stirring the pot.

Have you ever heard him host a talk-show? No need for callers—Les has too much to say of importance. Not only did he make sure my story got the coverage it deserved, he had plenty of great personal advice for dealing with the situation. His *WorldNetDaily* column on the story was the most accurate of anything written about the affair.

Kinsolving has always had the ability to see the angle that others overlooked, underplayed, or missed entirely. That's why we must have him back as soon as possible. Our thoughts and prayers are with you, Les.

To everyone's tremendous relief, the operation was a success. However, since Lester was nearing seventy-eight years of age, his recovery from the whole ordeal would be slow and plodding, and he wouldn't be able go back on the air for a few months. Les was grateful to return home, since, after using the remote control to operate the television above his hospital bed once or twice, he "didn't realize how much garbage there was on TV . . . thank God for the mute button!"

After a few weeks of resting and ingesting the battery of pills per the doctor's instructions, Lester was feeling stronger and began to skim the papers in an effort to catch up. He also did a bit of writing and noticed, in spite of the terrific physical blows he'd suffered, the boundless zeal to work still thrived. Les missed his audience terribly, and couldn't wait to sit in front of the microphone once again. However, by mid-February, a letter arrived from California, which took Les by surprise, to say the very least:

February 11, 2005

Dear Les,

I have wanted for a long time to write a letter of apology to you, and reading (on the Free Republic weblog) of the sad event of your recent heart attack, am prompted to do so now.

You were right about Jim Jones and Peoples Temple. I was totally wrong. If I had not been ideologically blinded by a utopian worldview, I should have been open to the truth you were trying to tell.

You were willing to confront [and] take on the Machiavellian Jones when other critics were too faint-hearted to do so. You were able to see beneath the surface of the glitter. You deserve an award for both insight and courage.

From my heart I apologize for my mistreatment of you,

including organizing the picketing, filing the lawsuit, and castigating your motives.

I have asked God to forgive me for my wrongdoing in being part of Peoples Temple. He has mercifully given me a second chance. But the natural consequences of my wrongdoing, especially the death of John Victor and those Temple members who joined because they trusted me—cannot be erased.

I am still a prosecutor but understand, far more than ever before, the reality of original sin. In conclusion, I pray God's blessing on you for a speedy and total recovery. I also pray you can forgive me.

Sincerely,
Timothy

The letterhead above the date included a full name: Timothy Oliver Stoen.

Two days later, Les sent his response:

Dear Tim,

I was deeply moved and grateful for your Feb. 11 letter of apology, with your kind words about me regarding my opposition to Jim Jones, and to you, as his one-time leader three decades ago.

I will value your letter in much the same fashion that I cherish another letter—from Brenda Ganatos and 14 others in the Ukiah area. They risked their lives to provide me evidence for the eight stories I wrote—four of which were censored by my employer, the *San Francisco Examiner*.

I note with particular interest that your Feb. 11th letter to me, as a working journalist, has no stipulation at all of requested confidentiality which, as both a priest and a journalist, I would have respected.

Since there was no such proviso, I believe your good letter should go to the only medium in this nation which has honestly reported all details of what was second only to 9/11 in the slaughter of innocent American people in Jonestown, where I understand you lost part of your family.

The only U.S. medium I recall as having constantly told the entire truth about the Peoples Temple has been the *Santa Rosa Press Democrat*, to whom I am sending a copy of your letter.

. . . I believe your letter may well help expose one of the most disgraceful and inexcusable mass-media cover-ups in American history.

Sincerely,
Les Kinsolving

On March 5, 2005, the *Press Democrat* ran the story, "After 30 Years, Jim Jones Aide Seeks Forgiveness," which included two photos of Stoen and Kinsolving side by side, the contents of Stoen's letter of apology, and a large image of Jim Jones in a leisure suit, which took up the majority of the front page:

After a near silence of almost 30 years, a former top aide to cult leader Jim Jones has asked for forgiveness for his role in events that led to deaths of more than 900 people in a mass murder-suicide.

Tim Stoen, Jones' former chief legal adviser and now a Humboldt County deputy district attorney, sought redemption in the form of a handwritten apology to the first reporter who publicly exposed bizarre behavior at the Peoples Temple's Mendocino County headquarters in the early 1970s.

. . . Stoen, whose Peoples Temple connections still haunt him three decades later, acknowledged writing the two-page letter but said he was reluctant to expand on its contents. "It seems everything I say about that time is read one way or the other. I wasn't looking for any attention. I was doing what I thought was right," he said.

. . . Kinsolving said he decided to publicly release what he described as Stoen's heart-felt letter, largely because he has forgiven Stoen. . . . "Heavens, I'm a Christian. We have no choice but to forgive," he said.

News of the apology spread, after the *Press Democrat* story was immediately picked up by the Associated Press. It ran up and down the West Coast, across the country and around the globe, where it was featured on the *Australian Christian Channel*. Since the beleaguered *San Francisco Examiner* had been sold by the Hearst Corporation in 2000, the only other prominent Bay Area media outlet chose not to run Stoen's apology to Kinsolving: the *San Francisco Chronicle*. As Les has stated over the years, "The cover-up still continues."

In his 2005 book, *Taking Heat*, Ari Fleischer, former press secretary to President George W. Bush, included a chapter entitled "Lester," where he described how he came to know the infamous White House Gadfly, and his experiences with him during the press briefings:

I first heard of Baltimore's Lester Kinsolving during the 1980s, when I did communications and political work for Republican congressional candidates and causes. Before talk radio was big, Lester was known in conservative circles as an important radio talk-show host.

. . . I met Lester late in 2000, at our transition headquarters in downtown Washington, after the Supreme Court ruled that George W. Bush had won the election. "Help me," Lester said, collaring me after one transition briefing. The Clinton White House had pulled his press credential, he explained, and wouldn't let him in the daily briefing anymore. He had to wait for an hour or two at the front gate each day, waiting to be cleared in. If he could have his credential restored, he wouldn't have to wait.

Gadfly

Although Ari's predecessors Marlin Fitzwater and Mike McCurry had made fairly light-hearted and congenial comments about Lester, such as "Les is an extra-hard worker who's become an almost legend in D.C. circles," and "We would rather hear from him than not hear him, even if it's only for grand theater of it all!" Former President Clinton's third press secretary, Joe Lockhart, continually locked horns with the Irreverent Reverend: "Listen Lester: You find it easy to cross the line. I'm going to let you make your statements, but I don't have to respond to them!" Lockhart became so fed up that he banished Les from the press briefings, and made him wait outside for clearance.

Ari further stated:

I must have given someone instructions to give him back his pass, because Lester . . . became a fixture at my briefings. I also didn't think it was my place to pick and choose which reporters were allowed into the White House. That's a slippery slope for any press secretary to walk. Lester didn't have an assigned seat like reporters from mainstream organizations, but he made his presence known.

. . . In the summer of 2002, Les raised an interesting topic: "There has been nationwide media coverage of a McKees Rocks, Pennsylvania councilwoman who has charged that racial profiling has been done by Dolpho, the borough's one police dog, for whom she has demanded the death penalty. And my question is, while I know of no law allowing the President to commute the capital punishment of a dog, as the owner of two beloved dogs, the President surely hopes that McKees Rocks will not allow this execution on such an absurd charge, doesn't he, Ari?"

"I think you just validated the point I was making to Terry [another reporter] that the President is not involved in every issue across America with everybody who does or says anything," I said.

"But he doesn't want that dog put to death, does he, Ari?"

"Lester, " I said, "I think you need to bark up a different tree."

One final experience Ari shared involved a brouhaha between Les and *Corporate Crime Reporter*'s Russell Mokhiber:

At one briefing shortly before the war in Iraq began, Les and another reporter almost came to blows. . . . Russell asked me one day about opposition to the war from various church leaders who, he said, were "uneasy about the moral justification for war on Iraq."

I told him that the President was a deeply religious man himself and that he respected the views of others and would act as he saw fit as Commander in Chief to protect the country. "One question on that," Russell followed up. "You just said the President is a deeply religious man. Jesus Christ was an absolute pacifist. How does the President square his militarism with Jesus' pacifism?"

Before I could even answer, Lester the minister rose from his seat like a rocket ship, exclaiming with his deep radio voice, "No he wasn't—How about the—at the temple with a whip, where he beat the hell out of those money changers? Does that sound like he's an absolute pacifist, Ari?"

Horrified that two reporters were fighting with each other at the televised briefing, Steve Holland, the senior wire reporter in the press corps, exercised his authority to call an end to the proceedings by shouting an instant "Thank you." As I walked off the podium, Russell and Lester were still yelling at each other about whether Jesus was a pacifist.

Tony Snow, Lester's "first fellow talk-radio host" to later serve as President Bush's third press secretary, began in May of 2006, after Ari Fleischer's replacement Scott McClellan resigned. The charitable comments he

Gadfly

made to Les, such as "I think you're one of the most colorful reporters I've ever worked with. I'm always eager to find out what you're going to ask!" would eventually be replaced with exasperation, such as in the case of Les coming to Helen Thomas's defense in February 2007:

KINSOLVING: Last night CNN featured the president of the White House Correspondents Association saying of Helen Thomas: "We love her, and we'll take care of her." But CNN also reported that in order to accommodate one more network in row one, Helen, our senior-to-all colleague, is to be relegated to row two when we move back into the White House press room. And my question: Assuming that CNN is accurate, how can you allow this dean of our corps, senior veteran and undeniably colorful character, to be backseated as has been done to her at presidential press conferences?

(Laughter.)

And what does this say about Bush-Snow treatment of senior citizens, who wonder how you and the president can allow a network such ageist favoritism over a veteran?

SNOW: Okay, good. Well, let me—this is about—

THOMAS: I would never think of his questions in a million years.

SNOW: This is about a thousand-part question, so let me parse it, Les.

KINSOLVING: Okay.

SNOW: Number one, of course we love Helen. Number two, the White House does not make decisions about where people sit, so you can address that to the Correspondents' Association. And number three, regardless of the seating arrangement, you'll still be looking at the back of her head.

(Laughter, cross talk.)

KINSOLVING: Why do you allow this? Why do you and the president allow this discrimination against a senior citizen, who is our senior reporter?

THOMAS: I don't need a defender. Thank you very much. *(Laughter.)*

In July, Tony delivered an angry rebuke:

KINSOLVING: The AP reports that Sydney, Australia's lord mayor, Clover Moore, is leading a campaign urging all residents to pack an emergency survival kit in preparation for any terrorist attack or other disaster in Australia's largest city. And my question—does the White House believe that this is a campaign U.S. cities should be launching, or not?

SNOW: That would be something that I would not be privy to comment on. And, Les, let me just—before we get back into a situation where it will be more difficult to get called on, let me just point out that you need to ask questions that bear on the president's responsibilities. I saw the piece you wrote the other day, that has been thoroughly twisting out of context the answer I gave you when I told you that the president, in fact, was—

KINSOLVING: That's what—

SNOW: I don't care. What you did—

KINSOLVING: They wrote it out there.

SNOW: You know what, I don't care, OK, because the fact is, if somebody is going to take questions about things that do not fall under the president's purview—and I answered that question—and it gets twisted, that is a disservice to this White House and to the craft of journalism. So if I were you, I'd pick up the phone and tell them to start cleaning up or writing corrections.

After Lester received Tony's reprimand, *WorldNetDaily*'s editor-in-chief Joseph Farah wrote the following commentary, "Enough of the Snow Jobs":

> We have seen Snow repeatedly allow reporters from the Old Media in the first two rows of the briefing room to ask five to 10 questions—while reporters from other media, like WND, have either been repeatedly denied the right to ask any questions, or limited to two, and in those, rushed by him, or given responses of both brevity and hostility.

> Since Snow has been so repeatedly unfair to WND and Kinsolving, we shall begin covering him differently—unless and until we hear from him that he will be fair.

> Every time there is a news briefing at the White House, we will publish one question from WND, one from our White House correspondent, Les Kinsolving, and *one selected from among our 8 million readers.*

> If Snow answers any of these three questions, we will be happy to so report.

> What we suspect, however, is that rarely will such questions be either answered, or asked, in the presently Tony Snow-censored White House news briefings—which Kinsolving will no longer attend.

Using an old line of Richard Nixon's, Farah promised that Tony Snow "wouldn't have Les Kinsolving to kick around anymore."

Shortly after, Lester called off his boycott after he received a phone call from Tony, who apologized and stated, "in terms of deepest affection," that he hoped he would return to the press briefings. "Of course," Les admitted later, "I could not resist." As one of Snow's aides would affirm to *WorldNetDaily,* "Tony is very fond of Les and holds him in high personal regard."

On September 12, 2007, Tony Snow would hold his final press conference, since he had been grappling with colon cancer for two years, which had now spread to his liver. Shortly before the briefing ended, Les made a special plea for the reporters not seated in the first few rows, and who hadn't been called on after they'd been raising their hands throughout the briefing:

KINSOLVING: Tony, wait a minute. Come back—no, wait a minute. Tony, this is the last—

SNOW: Is this a meltdown, Les? (*Laughter*). Is this—

KINSOLVING: Really, Tony, none of us in the back have had a chance. You've been in the front. This is your last briefing. You want to go out well.

SNOW: Les, please, be as rude as you want. Go ahead. (*Laughter*).

Connie Lawn, a reporter for IRN-USA Radio and White House press correspondent since 1968, also implored Tony:

LAWN: Les is right, actually. There are a lot of us who would like to ask questions.

SNOW: OK, you know what? We will—this will be an open-ended commitment. (*Laughter*).

LAWN: Thank you very much.

Not only was Connie Lawn able to ask her questions, but four other reporters in the back rows did as well.

Gadfly

On July 12, 2008, Tony Snow passed away, and Les and Sylvia attended a moving memorial service at the National Shrine in Washington, D.C.. Les had read Tony's obituary, written by Bloomberg's Holly Rosenkrantz and Roger Runningen, which mentioned Tony Snow's final press briefing: "That day as Snow ended the briefing, Lester Kinsolving . . . known for offbeat and confrontational questions, objected, saying he hadn't yet asked a question. He demanded that Snow stay on. 'Is this a meltdown, Les?' Snow asked as the pressroom erupted in laughter. 'Les, please be as rude as you want. Go ahead.'"

Les then took the two reporters on, in "How Bloomberg mutilated an obituary—with a smear": "It clearly reveals how much these Bloomberg writers resorted to out-of-context reporting for their absolutely incredible use of an obituary as an opportunity to smear. . . . What Bloomberg *refused* to report is what Paul Harvey so often mentions as "the rest of the story."

Dana Perino, who would be the fourth and final press secretary under President Bush, grappled with Les when he asked a question on AIDS, as a follow-up to World AIDS Day, which took place on December 1st, 2008. Perino's handling of the matter conjured up memories of Larry Speakes's evasion in 1981:

KINSOLVING: Two domestic questions. The Media Research Center—with the Centers for Disease Control's statistics that HIV/AIDS in the U.S. is still a great deal higher among men who have sex with men—

PERINO: Let's move on to the next question. I'm not even going to dignify—

KINSOLVING: No—

PERINO: I'm not, Les, unless you want to just move on altogether. What's your next question?

KINSOLVING: All right. In major cities like Washington, Chicago, and San Francisco, there are reports that gay bathhouses facilitate—

PERINO: Okay, Keith, go ahead. Les, it's inappropriate—

KINSOLVING: Inappropriate?

PERINO: Just stop it, stop it.

If Lester had been allowed to ask his questions, Ms. Perino might've answered the following:

1. The Media Research Center—with the Centers for Disease Control's statistics that HIV/AIDS in the U.S. is still a great deal higher among men who have sex with men. Then should any AIDS officials be claiming that all Americans are equally at risk?

2. In major cities like Washington, Chicago, and San Francisco, there are reports that gay bathhouses, which facilitate promiscuous sex that fuels the AIDS epidemics are being allowed to reopen. What is the White House reaction to that recent report?

RHRealityCheck.org, a website on "Information and Analysis for Reproductive Health," made the following comments after Lester's censure:

Considering the news splayed all over the mainstream media last week that HIV/AIDS rates in the United States are either rising or remaining steady, it's important—no, crucial—that our federal government address the story. President Bush sincerely believes that his administration's handling of HIV/AIDS in the United States has been stellar—he considers it his greatest public health success. But why did Perino jump all over Kinsolving when he tried to bring up the issue?

Gadfly

. . . Still, Perino cut him off so unequivocally, as if inquiring about the latest CDC statistics on HIV/AIDS in this country was unsuitable discussion for the press room. It's obviously not, and Perino displayed poor judgment in the way she shut him down.

During the summer of 2009, an eighty-one-year-old Les enjoyed needling President Barack Obama's press secretary Robert Gibbs, who continually battled with him on the controversial issue of the President's birth certificate. On July 13, Les asked the following questions at the White House:

KINSOLVING: While you and the president were overseas on July the 7th, there was on the Internet a copy of a letter on White House letterhead dated January the 24th, 2009, with the signature "Barack Obama," which stated, "The place of my birth was Honolulu's Kapi'olani Medical Center." And my question is, can you verify this letter? Or if not, would you tell us which Hawaiian hospital he was born in, since Kapi'olani, which used to publicize this, now refuses to confirm?

GIBBS: Goodness gracious. I'm going to be, like, in year four describing where it is the president was born. I don't have the letter at my fingertips, obviously, and I don't know the name of the exact hospital.

KINSOLVING: . . . The image posted on various websites is not a birth certificate or a certificate of live birth, but a different "Certification of Live Birth" document.

GIBBS: I know. Just a document from the state of Hawaii denoting the fact that the president was indeed born in the state of Hawaii. You know, Lester, I—I want to stay on this a second, Lester. I want to stay on this for a second, because you're a smart man, right?

REPORTER: (unidentified) Hypothetical.

(Laughter)

GIBBS: All right, all right, settle down in here. Only I get to make jokes like that! Lester, let's finish this one. Do all of your listeners throughout the country the service to which any journalist owes those listeners, and that is the pursuit of the noble truth. . . . Lester, the next time you ask me a question I'm going to ask you what reporting *you've* done to demonstrate to your listeners the truth, the certificate, the state, so that they can look to you for that momentous search for the truth, and you can wipe away all the dark clouds and provide them with the knowing clarity that comes with that certainty.

After the briefing that day, Les drove home and checked his e-mails, which usually total in the hundreds on a daily basis. Countless numbers of them included the following: "I just watched you at the White House briefing. It is extremely sad that you were the only one who had the courage to ask pertinent questions" . . . "Robert Gibbs is side-stepping your questions on this issue, I appreciate your continued questioning" . . . "I realize it takes real fortitude to ask what's needed to be asked knowing you will get mocked. But if people like you don't ask we'll never get the truth" . . . "I just wanted to thank you for standing strong in the White House Press Corp. It must be really hard to have them all laughing at you, but you are the one doing your job. It won't be long until they are all the ones with egg on their face. Keep standing strong. . . ." "These dear people," Les said, as he shared the many e-mails with the Berkeley Democrat. "I'm so deeply grateful to them."

"My Producer Signals Me that the Time of Departure Is at Hand . . ."

NOT MANY CAN say they've lived a life like Les Kinsolving's. It has been an incredibly rich and colorful adventure, full of drama, passion, laughter, and tragedy. There have been terrible struggles, and tremendous triumphs. Lester's ability to survive as a maverick in the conventional world he has rebelled against is somewhat of a miracle; he has done it his way, and he has succeeded. As Les stated to Chip Brown during his interview for the *Post* in 1981, "I realize what I am makes me a kind of leper, but journalism is my ministry. I'm going to ask the questions I think are important and anybody who doesn't like it can take a long walk off a short pier."

Analyzing the complex character of Les is not an easy enterprise. As WOR's Bob Bruno so eloquently stated once, "The man can't be tucked away neatly into a pigeon hole of convenient description." Perhaps Spencer Rice, his close friend at seminary and beyond, said it best: "Lester is a living contradiction. He's loyal; he has a sense of honor and respect for the family and the church's traditions; he wants to do for other people, and on the other hand there is his thrashing at life with a rapier, a slashing out at people like they were mannequins. Perhaps the most thoughtful thing his detractors can say is that he has made a living marketing the foibles of others."

For those who support and work alongside him, Les has been relegated to the level of near-worship; as a talk-show host, *The Enterprise*'s Bryan R. Moorhouse said it plainly: "Four hours on the air with Les Kinsolving is an educational lesson in conversational control. A talk-show host is constantly assaulted by efforts to compromise him. Kinsolving is a master of avoiding the squeeze and reversing the pressure." And *WorldNetDaily*'s Joseph Farah is honest and yet admiring: "I'll admit it. Kinsolving is a character. He sometimes asks tough questions. He sometimes asks perplexing questions. He occasionally asks ridiculous questions. But he's not just "a character." He *has* character. He is a living institution—the kind of man who should be honored with dinners and testimonials."

Gadfly. Ecclesiastical Curmudgeon. Smart-Ass and Irreverent Reverend. The Mad Monk. A Gorilla in a Priest's Suit. Les has adopted these appellations because he has completely devoted to his life to the Kinsolving Motto, which is the last thing his listeners hear every weekday night on WCBM: "Humble to the humble, inflexible to the arrogant!"

If there is one dramatic character Les could identify mostly with, it would be Cyrano, from Edmond Rostand's play, *Cyrano de Bergerac*. Cyrano, "a free spirit who dared to fight City Hall," once responded to a friend who suggested he "gain preferment by compromise with the Cardinal":

"What would you have me do?
Shall I go leaping into ladies' laps and licking fingers?
No thank you!
Tickle the horns of mammon with my left hand; While my
    right, too proud to know its partner's job, takes in the fee?
No thank you!
Scratch the back of any swine who roots up gold for me?

Shall I crawl upward, like a creeping vine about a tall tree
Because I have not strength to stand alone?
No thank you! And again I say, No thank you!
I stand not high, it may be—but alone
I watch some other people making friends—as dogs make
    friends!
I mark the manner of these canine courtesies and think
My friends, though few, are of a cleaner breed

Here comes—thank God! Another enemy!"

"You May Love Him! You May Hate Him! But You'll Never Want to Miss Him!" These words, from National Newspaper Syndicate's 1971 promotional of Les as he became the nation's most celebrated religion columnist, still ring true today. Those who have detested Les so intensely would have to admit that they cried when they listened to his tribute,"Does My Dog Have a Soul?" or that they admired his courage for standing up to the Peoples Temple cult leader Jim Jones.

"And now, my producer signals me that the time of departure is at hand . . . " It is 11 P.M., and the West Point marching music is playing. As it fades out, Les thanks his producer on WCBM for another "glorious" show, where he has laughed, argued, and bantered with over a dozen callers in two hours. He walks to the living room from his home office upstairs, and winds down for a few hours, before retiring in the early hours of the morning. Les smiles as he thinks back on one of the letters he received from a colleague after the 1957 *Time* article appeared, when they covered the very first Kinsolving controversy, "The Damnable Doctrine of Damnation" sermon: "I had no idea that you went to bed at 4 am and got up at 11 am—my, what a horrible man you must be. Honest, Les—I haven't been able to stop laughing all morning!"

After reading one or two chapters of another fascinating history book, Les is ready to sleep. Feeling satisfied that he has done his duty for another day, he turns out the light next to his bed, which is adorned with a portrait of Jesus who humbly and lovingly looks up to his Father. Lester thinks of "Pop," whom he loves so deeply, and of the time when he was ordained into the Episcopal church, so many years ago, which he once shared with his audience in a special broadcast:

"Immediately after the processional hymn, there is the sermon. At the close of the sermon, the person to be ordained, along with the priest who presents him, stands up alone, in that front pew. Here, they stand and face the pulpit, to receive what is known as the charge to the ordinand. It is a deeply moving moment—especially when the preacher looking down at you is your father.

"My father was able to get through this without his voice wavering. But his eyes glistened as he told me:

"Do out your duty, only where honor lights the path
And there can be no real failure,
Whether you reach to grasp
The golden keys of success
Or whether disasters
Buffet and beat you down
Somehow those who do more, with less
Touch eternal things
And live the life indeed
And know that is known
By Christ himself
And that, my son, *is what really matters.*"

. . . and this is Les Kinsolving.

Bibliography

Arthur B. Kinsolving, *Texas George: The Life of George Herbert Kinsolving* (Milwaukee: Morehouse Publishing Co., 1932).

Kathleen Kinsolving, *Madman in Our Midst* (2002).

Kathleen Kinsolving and Tom Kinsolving, *Madman in Our Midst: Jim Jones and the Caliofrnia Cover-Up* (http://www.freedomofmind.com, 1998).

Lucie Lee Kinsolving, *A Pioneer Childhood 1901-1913 and Family Letters* (1985).

Index

NOTE: The acronym LK stands for Lester Kinsolving; EC stands for Episcopal Church

Index

Index

Index

Index

Index